W9-AXC-579

CHINA'S ECONOMY

CHINA'S ECONOMY

A Basic Guide

CHRISTOPHER HOWE

Basic Books, Inc., Publishers
New York

Contents

Maps

Figures

Tables

Preface

As recently as ten years ago the Chinese economy was a subject of very limited interest. Remote in every way, seemingly irrelevant, its study engaged only a handful of specialists. Today, demand for economic information about China is considerable. Several developments explain this transformation. One is that China's industry has now achieved a size and (on a limited scale) a sophistication that make it a significant force in world politics. In 1949 industry employed one four-hundredth of the population and consisted of 15,000 miles of railway, six million cotton spindles, an annual output of one million tons of steel, and an assortment of other plant. In relation to China's possession of a quarter of the world's population, this industry was microscopic. Twenty-seven years on, China is the world's third largest producer of coal, cotton textiles and radio receivers; the fifth producer of steel; and the tenth producer of oil. The Chinese manufacture computers, electron microscopes, nuclear missiles, and an enormous variety of machinery. They are now acquiring a petrochemical industry, have options on the Concorde supersonic airliner, and within a few years will be able to manufacture advanced aeronautic equipment of their own. In terms of China's National Product, continued growth at current rates would give China a Product as large as that of the United States by the early part of the next century. This growth has been accompanied by fitful, but at times rapid, expansion of trade, and this is a second reason for interest in China's economy. China's trade is less than 1 per cent of the world's total; but as an importer of steel, chemicals, and equipment from Japan, of grain from Canada and Australia, and of a variety of goods from Europe and America, China has increasing weight. Indeed, uncomfortable as it is for all parties, the interdependence between China and the rest of the world is such that China's harvests can change the price of our bread.

Concern about China's economy has also been stimulated by visiting intellectuals and politicians, many of whom have been very impressed by China's achievements. For example, China has been described as the society where things 'work' (J. K. Galbraith); where there is 'no competition' (Mrs Jacob Javits); where there is 'total freedom from inflation and material and moral pollution' (Mr Denis Healey); and where the people are 'less anxious and ill-tempered than we are' (Mrs Joan Robinson).[1] The impact of these reports has spread like ripples on a pool, touching the curiosity of a wide audience, of whom few are likely to have the opportunity of visiting China, or of verifying these claims for themselves. In addition to visitors there are scholars whose study of the non-Chinese world has led them to think that the Chinese experience may have wider application, and who suggest that China may have found remedies for the dehumanization of industrial work, for the evils of inequality, for excessive urbanization, and for the wider problem of creating a viable civilization on a basis of finite resources.[2]

Finally, there is the interest of those who believe that China's progress is a matter of global concern, even when this is defined in the narrowest way. This approach can be understood only if we take account of the reverse side to the industrial successes sketched above. In the past twenty years, for example, population growth has kept the proportion of the population living in the countryside unchanged and has absorbed nearly all the gains that might have accrued in the form of higher living standards. (Consumption of grain and cotton cloth have increased slightly, if at all, since 1957.) Another indication of China's present backwardness (familiar to visitors) is provided by the long processions of men and women that move in and out of the cities pulling heavy, laden carts. Starting in the dark before dawn, often in freezing atmospheres, the inward carts carry food, the outward ones nightsoil. This intense physical effort remains a commonplace in an economy that, in some respects, is close behind the most advanced contemporary technology. It can be argued that overcoming this backwardness, even keeping abreast of the demands of population growth, will be extraordinarily difficult, and that if China's vast experiments fail it would be folly to imagine that the consequences will be contained within China. Many would add that to ignore such failure would be immoral, even if the consequences could be contained. In this view the future of China's population seems materially and morally inseparable from our own.

In response to these pressures and interests, university and government research has expanded. A list of all the important books on the Chinese economy given to me in 1963 contained six authors. A comparable list today would contain sixty. The result of all this effort, however, has all too often been studies that are specialist and extremely lengthy. For example, the latest excellent compilation prepared for the Joint Economic Committee of US Congress (1975) is half a million words long, of variable technical difficulty, and contains contributions that contradict each other.[3]

It must be added that since 1972 much official research has not been published at all. In some cases this reflects the unwillingness of governments and international organizations to act in ways that they believe will offend the Chinese (e.g. by publishing estimates that contradict Chinese claims). In other cases the Chinese have requested that reports containing material on China — however flattering — be shelved. In this way we have recently lost reports on China's population, agriculture, and education.

The purpose of this book, therefore, is to reduce our present knowledge of the Chinese economy to manageable proportions. The result will not answer many of the deep questions raised above. It will, I hope, provide a starting point and a minimal factual framework from which enquirers can proceed to better things. This factual framework is organized around three questions. How large is the Chinese economy? How is it organized? In which direction is it moving? The latter is a particularly important question. I at first attempted to limit the book to the 1970s but this proved impossible. The Chinese economy is a dynamic phenomenon whose properties have been shaped by history. As the text stands, lack of historical content — pre- and post-1949 — remains a weakness, but materials on the 1950s and 1960s are now included. Also, each chapter is prefaced with quotations that illustrate that in many respects an enquirer into twentieth-century China finds much that was reported by enquirers two and three hundred years ago.

In writing each chapter I have asked myself the question: 'What is the minimum information that a professional or serious student would need to know about this topic—assuming no previous knowledge of China?' I was helped in defining the answer to this by talking to businessmen, diplomats, journalists, civil servants, students, teachers, and to others who were just interested. I did find, however, that following this approach raised two difficulties. One was that addressing a varied audience required that the interests of one group had often to be set against those of another. The result is a compromise, and the reader who feels that I have fallen short in detail or depth, or have taken a topic too far, should bear this in mind. The other problem was that in writing about China there is a natural tendency to choose subjects for which materials are available: in this way a smooth and consistent result can often be produced. But if one's starting point is a series of basic, *a priori* questions, then the answers are necessarily very variable in quality. Thus it is relatively easy to write about the steel industry, but hard to say much about the standard of living. There is no solution to this.

Sources and notes

The sources used fall into four categories:
(1) Original (mainly Chinese language) books, newspapers, journals, and documents of various kinds. Also translations of monitored Chinese radio broadcasts (British and American).

(2) English language materials published in China. (Journals, magazines, and books.)
(3) Secondary sources (mainly in English) published outside China. These include books, journals, Western and Asian newspapers.
(4) Interviews (and transcripts of interviews) with Chinese informants. Conversations with many of the numerous businessmen, scholars, students, politicians, and others who have visited China (particularly during the past five years). This type of material was used in conjunction with impressions formed on my own visits.

The policy followed in writing the notes is as follows. For each chapter I have indicated the main English language sources available for the study of the topics covered. For statistics and quotations, citations are almost always provided. Other notes provide information that I felt would be out of place in the main text, as well as the sources of relatively unknown pieces of information. The notes are thus primarily designed to help the general reader; not to provide an academic defence of the text for eavesdropping specialists familiar with Chinese sources.

The problem of statistics

Between 1949 and 1960, and since 1971, the Chinese have published economic statistics. Those published for the earlier period are particularly abundant. With their aid it is possible to study local and national developments, and to analyse individual sectors and industries in detail.[4] Statistics published since 1971 are far less detailed and there has been no resumption of publication of statistical and economic journals of the kind that disappeared in 1960. The interpretation of the available figures, and the construction of estimates to fill in the eleven-year gap, has exercised several very clever analysts. In particular, Dr R.M. Field and his team in the Office of Economic Research at the Central Intelligence Agency, Dr J.S. Aird and Mr J.P. Emerson at the US Department of Commerce, and Professor Nicholas Lardy, now at Yale University, have made available a collection of statistics that are landmarks in the history of Chinese economic studies. These are the most widely used and generally reliable series we have, and I have drawn on them extensively. Nonetheless, there are three points about these statistics that I have to make. First, I believe that Field's index of industrial production includes figures for 1960 that may be a little too high. The data for that year include claims of a 'Great Leap' variety; they often refer to outputs that were of low, even unusable quality. If these factors are inadequately discounted, the contrast between the rapid growth of the 1950s and the slow growth thereafter appears too sharp. Thus, although I have used the CIA series, this qualification should be borne in mind—particularly in the chapter on industry.

Secondly, in the case of agricultural data, I have been unable to accept many of the CIA or US Department of Agriculture grain estimates.[5] The essential reason for the confusion that has arisen in these is that the American analysts have tried too hard to reconcile their first estimates for the 1960s and early 1970s with an evolving view of the official Chinese claims for the 1970s. Where necessary, I have therefore made use of grain estimates supplied to me by Professor K.R. Walker, whose own research on this topic is being prepared for publication.

Population statistics are the third problem. Chinese statements are few and questionable, and the only consistent data we have are a series of estimates prepared over many years by Dr J.S. Aird. In autumn 1976 Dr Aird produced an important new series that incorporated his latest thinking on this subject.[6] I have accepted these, subject to a minor qualification explained in the text. I am aware of the weaknesses of this solution, but see no alternative at present.

Acknowledgements

The preparation of this book would have been impossible without the generous, unstinting assistance of many people. Much of this assistance has taken the form of conversations, but I have also received a flow of documents, articles, and materials of various kinds. In particular, I should like to thank Professor K.R. Walker, who has provided me with complete access to his encyclopedic materials on Chinese agriculture as well as with many other useful ideas and pieces of information. I have also received invaluable help from Mr Dick Wilson, Editor of *The China Quarterly;* Professor Dwight Perkins, Harvard University; Professor Ezra Vogel, Harvard University; Professor Michel Oksenberg, University of Ann Arbor; Professor Nicholas Lardy, Yale University; Mr John Dolfin, Universities Service Centre, Hong Kong; Professor Bruce Reynolds, Union College; Mr David Goodman, Mr Peter Nolan and Mr Lars Ragvald, former Fellows of the Contemporary China Institute; Mr Nick Ludlow and Mr Howell Jackson, National Council for US:China Trade, Washington; Mr J.P. Emerson and Dr J.S. Aird, Bureau of Economic Analysis, US Department of Commerce; Mr C. Liu, US Department of Agriculture; Dr Robert Michael Field, Office of Economic Research, Central Intelligence Agency; the Editor, *Current Scene;* Mr Kayser Sung, Editor of *Textile Asia;* Dr Hans Heymann Jr, The Rand Corporation; Mr Roderick MacFarquhar, MP; Mrs Caroline Oakman; Mr Peter Marshall, the Sino-British Trade Council; Mr Shigeru Aoki, Asian Affairs Research Council, Tokyo; Mr Tatsu Kambara, The Japan

Petroleum Development Corporation, Tokyo; and Mr Tatsuo Mizuno. For information on textiles, I am grateful to Mr Bob Rutley, on chemicals to Dr Sydney Dorling, and for materials on oil to Professor Edith Penrose.

I must emphasize, even more than is usual, that none of the above have any responsibility for the text. I have read and taken advice as widely as possible, but I have drawn my own conclusions, some of which might be rejected by those who have helped me.

On practical matters, I wish to express thanks to Colonel W. Baynes, Assistant Secretary responsible for the administration of the Contemporary China Institute, and to Sir Cyril Philips, who was until recently the Director of the School of Oriental and African Studies. Few institutions in the world provide their staff with the resources and stimulation necessary to undertake work of this kind; under Sir Cyril, the School became one of them.

I am indebted to my typists. Miss Avril Norton and Mrs Rosemary Allen typed all the early drafts. The final draft was typed by Mrs Patricia Pettitt—truly a professional's professional. Finally, I should like to acknowledge the encouragement and assistance of Mr Antony Wood of the firm of Paul Elek.

C.H.

Introduction

'To give the Reader a general Idea of this charming country, we cannot do better than quote the Words of a late Author, who, in his Account of China, writes as followeth:

"China is justly reckoned the finest Country in the World. It is exceeding fruitful; the Mountains themselves being cultivated to the Top. It produces, in many Parts, two Crops of Rice, and other Grain, with Variety of uncommon Trees, Fruit, Plants, and Birds. It abounds with Cattle, Sheep, Horses and Game. It is full of large navigable Rivers, and Lakes, stored with Fish. Its Mountains yield Mines of Gold, Silver, Copper, brown and white, etc. with Plenty of Coals everywhere. Pe-che-li, Kyang-nan, and Shangtong, are mostly plain, and cut into infinite Canals, like Holland. Being of great Extent in Latitude, the Northern Provinces are cold, the Southern hot; but the Air generally good. In short, China far exceeds all other countries for Number of People, Cities, and Towns; the Morality, Civility, and Industry of its Inhabitants; the Excellency of its Laws and Government." '

A Short way to know the World, quoted in Thomas Astley,
A New General Collection of Voyages and Travels
(London, 1747)

In the past two hundred years economic life in a substantial part of the world has been transformed by industrialization. In Europe, America, the Soviet Union, and a number of other countries, industrialization has accelerated economic growth at unprecedented rates and changed irreversibly the ways in which people live, work, and relate to each other. Industrialization has also increased the world's trade and thereby posed new problems of mutual dependence and conflict to which no solutions have been found.

Since 1945 these processes have begun to spread to the rest of the world. The stimulus for this has come from many sources: from nationalism and the decolonization of Africa and Asia; from the

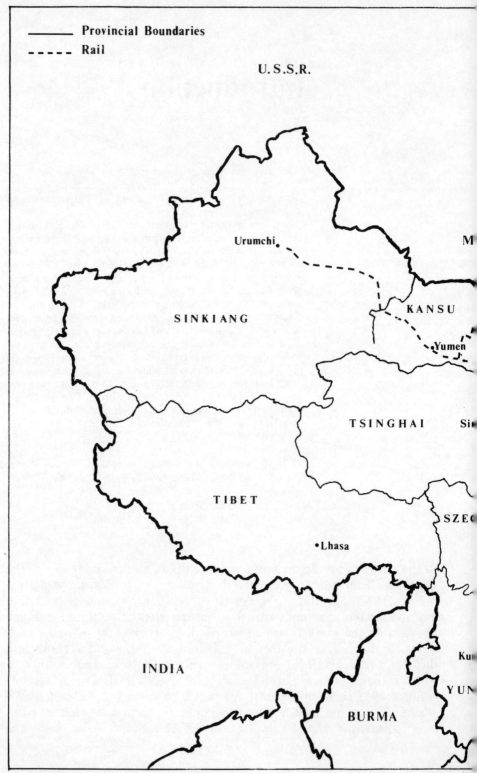

U.S.S.R.

M

Urumchi

KANSU

SINKIANG

Yumen

TSINGHAI

Si

TIBET

SZEC

•Lhasa

Ku

YUN

INDIA

BURMA

The Provinces and principal rail routes of China

spread of Communism and reactions to it; and from the technological requirements of modern war and diplomacy. These new industrializations, however, are taking place under conditions that differ from those of the 'early' industrial revolutions. Some of these conditions are more favourable to progress, others are less so. On the positive side, contemporary industrializing nations can draw cheaply and without risk from a vast stock of knowledge available in advanced economies. On the negative side, they have to combine industrialization with provision of employment and acceptable living standards for politically aroused populations whose initial living standards have been lower, and whose rates of growth have been higher, than those of the populations of the early industrializing nations. Typical incomes in the poorer developing countries are about half those found in Western Europe on the eve of its industrialization, while rates of growth of population are 2-3 per cent compared to about 1 per cent or less in the early industrializing nations. As a result, even in the relatively favourably endowed developing economies, employment and personal incomes rise only slowly; in the poorest, the nightmare of populations rioting in the streets for food has become reality.

The strains associated with contemporary industrialization have led almost everywhere to the creation of new economic institutions that, by expanding the State's control of the economy, attempt to improve on the slow incremental advance expected of *laissez-faire* systems. These institutions, however, have their own problems. For while they provide a means of sharply increasing an economy's rate of saving and investment, while they afford the planners direct control of the nature of the economy, they also deaden the willingness to work, to innovate, and to make sacrifices; and they create bureaucracies that are expensive and socially divisive. State control carries the additional risk that when the masters of the bureaucracies are ignorant, they make errors on a scale impossible in economies organized by less centralized and interventionist means.

China's economic progress and problems during the past twenty-seven years fit reasonably well into the patterns suggested above. It is true that China differs from many underdeveloped countries in having a long history of cultural, governmental, and economic achievement. Nonetheless, the Chinese leaders are uncompromising industrializers; they have had to struggle continuously with problems of food and population; and, as Communists, they are natural interventionists and planners and have experienced all the problems that this entails. At the international level too, China now shares with other developing countries a growing preoccupation with raw material prices, with the working of international economic institutions, and with general problems of world economic order.

THE ECONOMY BEFORE 1949

The Chinese economy in 1949 reflected two fundamental developments: a crisis in the long-term relationship between the growth of
population and the growth of the food supply, and the beginnings of an
industrialization that started during the First World War, and
continued thereafter in Manchuria and in a few major Treaty Port
cities such as Shanghai and Tientsin. Incomes throughout the economy
were extremely low and, according to the rudimentary estimates it has
been possible to make, it appears that investment in the period from
the 1920s to the 1940s was becoming increasingly insufficient to cover
even the wear and tear of the depreciation of the nation's stock of
capital.[1]

Much of this dislocation and lack of investment was due to war.
From 1927 the Chinese were fighting a civil war; from 1937 they were
fighting Japan. The effects were particularly important in agriculture
where the elaborate labour-intensive cycle of operations necessary to
maintain output at maximum levels was interrupted both by conscrip-
tion and by massive population movements from the countryside to the
greater security of the city. As a result of these developments,
agricultural output by 1949 had fallen to about two-thirds of the
highest previous level recorded.

China's agrarian problems were not, however, just a by-product of
war. In the perspective of centuries, we find that whereas from the
fifteenth to the nineteenth century agricultural improvements—both
the opening of new land *and* the achievement of higher yields—had
kept pace with population growth, from the early nineteenth century
onwards this was ceasing to be true.[2]

In the 1920s and 1930s much was written about China's agrarian
economy by Chinese and by interested Westerners. The picture was
uneven in that problems differed and were more severe in some parts
than in others. Nonetheless, most commentators noted that the major
causes of rural poverty were fragmentation of land holdings, ignorance
of modern agronomic techniques, and lack of Government investment
in large-scale transport, water control, and land reclamation.

Many suggestions were made to improve this situation; and indeed
the best of the pre-war analysts (such as T.H. Shen) set out with
remarkable foresight the *technical* reforms that would be needed (i.e.
development of water control, improved seeds and varieties etc.).
There was, however, little agreement on the best *institutional* framework for China's agriculture. Some advocated a land reform that
eliminated tenancy, others wanted locally organized cooperatives,
others looked to the example of the Soviet Union and advocated large-
scale, mechanized collectivization.

Although industry was also adversely affected by war in the late 1940s, the progress of this sector from 1914 to the mid-1940s had been quite impressive. From 1912/14 to 1941/43 industry grew at between 7 per cent and 8 per cent per annum.[3] Light industry developed in coastal Treaty Port cities such as Shanghai, Tsingtao, and Tientsin; while, particularly after their seizure of Manchuria in 1931, the Japanese built up a network of mining, metallurgical, and power industries which was to become the foundation for the Communist industrialization drive in the 1950s. In spite of this start, it could not be said that China had experienced (except in limited parts of the North-East) an 'industrial revolution'. This point is most vividly illustrated by the statistic that out of a population of five hundred million, employment in industry was at most two millon.

China's pre-1949 economic situation did not reflect any peculiar characteristics of Chinese culture or of the Chinese people. It was the result of the intrinsic difficulties of initiating growth over a vast and varied geographical area: an area whose traditional form of government was in a state of decay and collapse, and which lacked the means by which radical change could be transmitted from Central Government to villages and households.

The other major obstacle to economic improvement was that the time of China's first efforts at planned industrialization in the 1930s unluckily coincided with unfavourable international developments: in particular, with a world-wide depression that made it difficult for China to expand foreign trade effectively, and with a crisis in Japan's economic development which led Japan to attempt to capture the Chinese economy for Japanese ends.

DEVELOPMENT SINCE 1949

China's development since 1949 has been uneven. The first phase, which lasted from 1949 to 1952, was a minor one. This was a phase of recovery and rehabilitation during which the Party took control of the monetary, fiscal, and trade systems, and implemented a Land Reform. The Land Reform was a traumatic event which eliminated the political and economic power of the landlords and distributed land and other assets to the rural population. It did little to remedy the underlying reasons for agriculture's failure to grow adequately, although the resumption of peace, and, possibly, the incentives now offered to the individual peasants, led to a rapid recovery in agricultural output to the best pre-1949 levels.

In industry the Party was more conservative. Drastic nationalization was avoided and a fairly positive approach was taken towards existing private industrial firms. By 1952 most industries were back to, or approaching, full capacity, and at this point it was necessary for the Party to decide upon its long-term strategy for improving China's economic performance. The four phases of development since 1952 I label as follows:

(1) The Period of Fastest Growth (1952-59).
(2) The Great Depression (1959-61).
(3) Readjustment and the Cultural Revolution (1961-70).
(4) The Revival of Growth with Trade (1970-77).

Table 1: *Rates of growth of key economic indicators, selected periods, 1952-75*
(per cent per annum)

	I 1952-59	II 1959-61	IIIA 1961-75	IIIB 1965-70	IV 1970-75	1952-75
Industrial output	20.52	−21.6	16.32	9.5	8.79	10.51
Grain output	4.44	−14.44	5.92	3.56	2.51	2.01- 2.37
Total trade	13.62	−16.61	5.49	−.19	12.1	5.57
State Budget Revenue	17.46	−16.45	5.76	4.39	4.58	6.71
Gross National Product	6.69	−12.4	13.28	6.08	6.43	5.79
Gross investment	24.37	−16.25	9.3	7.16	10.72	10.93
Population						1.9-2.15

Notes:
1. The periodization of grain data is 1952-1958-1960-1965-1970-1975. The trend 2.01 per cent is a statistical measure (see Table 20), whereas 2.37 per cent is the rate of growth between the two years 1952 and 1975. The lower figure is the better measure of growth; the higher figure is the best possible interpretation that can be given to the official data and comments.
2. For trade, the 1974 data are the last available. For gross investment, 1973 is the final year.
3. Total trade data are at constant prices.
4. Variations of growth of State Budget Revenue *within* the period 1959-70 are estimated.

Sources: Industry and Gross National Product, CIA, *Handbook of Economic Indicators* (1976), p.3. Trade, JEC (1975), p. 645, and price data for 1974 from Japanese sources. Grain, Table 19. State Budget Revenue, data for 1952 and 1959, N.R. Chen, *Chinese Economic Statistics*, p. 441; for 1970, *Basic Knowledge in Political Economy* (Shanghai, 1974), Vol. II, p. 195; for 1975, New China News Agency, quoted in *Survey of World Broadcasts*, September 17, 1975, FE/W/844/A/2. Gross investment is Gross Domestic Fixed Capital Formation from a set of provisional estimates by R.M. Field, *Real Capital Formation in the People's Republic of China 1952-1973* (Washington, 1976). Population, Table 2.

The Period of Fastest Growth (1952-59)

This includes the First Five Year Plan (1952-57) and the Great Leap Forward (1958-59). As Table 1 shows, output of industry and grain grew nearly twice as rapidly as their respective long-term trends during this period, while trade and the State Budget Revenue grew nearly three times as fast. This exceptional performance reflected many factors. In industry most of the growth during the Plan was the result of more

Figure 1: *Major Economic Trends, 1952-75*
(1952=100)

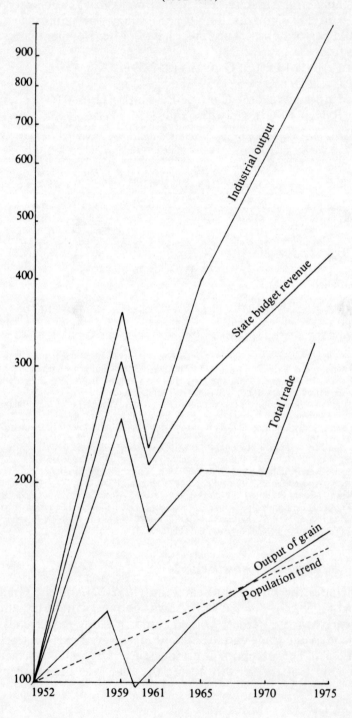

intensive use of existing plant. Then, during 1958 and 1959, there was an upsurge of output from new plants constructed with Soviet assistance during the Plan. At the same time there was an additional expansion of output as a result of the revival of small-scale industry and of the exceptionally intensive efforts by the workforce that were made in the Great Leap.

In agriculture, growth was rapid partly because the process of post-war recovery was not fully exhausted by 1952, and partly because 1958 (which I have taken as the final year) was climatically exceptional. The expansion of State Budget Revenue (at a pace three times as fast as the Gross National Product) reflected the expansion of the power of the State over the economy. Finally, the rapid growth of foreign trade reflected the policy of expanding industry by means of imports of plant, machinery and equipment.

During this period there were drastic changes both in the economy's organization and in the pattern of its development. In late 1952 the Chinese adopted Soviet policies towards both the pattern of economic growth at which they were aiming, and the type of institutions that they would create to achieve this. The whole strategy was summed up in the *First Five Year Plan (1953-57)*.[4] The Plan started in January 1953, although final details were not agreed (and the Plan was not published) until July 1955. The Plan is an interesting document, which we have in full.

The most revolutionary proposal implicit in the Plan was to raise (to about 20 per cent) the share of the nation's resources to be invested, and to use these resources for the development of heavy industry. The *acquisition* of investment resources was to be achieved by: (a) imposing compulsory purchase and taxes on agriculture and private industry; and (b) by earning high profits in State-owned industry. The controlled *allocation* of resources was to be made by establishing a Soviet style apparatus for the central planning of State industry, wholesale, retail, and foreign trade. Foreign trade control was particularly crucial, since the strategy adopted required that China sell agricultural products to pay for industrial goods and materials supplied by the Soviet Union. It is important to note that the Plan did not call for immediate nationalization of private industry and commerce.

In the countryside, Land Reform had left agriculture as a sector composed of private, small-scale plots and farms. The Plan envisaged no drastic change in this, although it did envisage the *gradual* expansion of Lower Stage, and later of Higher Stage Agricultural Producers Cooperatives. Both types of cooperative involved the pooling of land and other major assets. The difference between them was that in the smaller, Lower Stage Cooperatives, peasant incomes were related to work done *and* to their contributions to the Cooperative (i.e. of land, draught animals and other assets); in the Higher Stage Co-operative incomes were to reflect only work done (contributions of land and assets to be regarded as gifts to the Cooperative).

According to the Plan, getting peasants into Higher Stage Co-operatives would take fifteen years. By the end of the Plan only a third of the peasants were expected to be in Lower Stage Cooperatives, and only a handful were to reach the Higher Stage. This was parallel to the similar gradual timetable worked out for the peaceful socialization of private industry, handicrafts, and retail commerce. The other important aspect of the Plan for agriculture was that, apart from some major works in water conservation, investment in agriculture was to be financed and organized by the peasants themselves.[5] Thus from the point of view of the Central Government the Plan was a gamble, since it relied on a relatively unplanned and unsupported agricultural sector to supply the growing food and raw material needs of industry and the total population.

It is worth mentioning that this strategy was by no means the only one that might have been adopted. Among the Chinese leaders there were some who argued that the pace of growth should be slower, and that China should specialize in agriculture and light industry rather than make a headlong dash to establish heavy industries. The strategy adopted was chosen because it had the support of Mao, and of those who were particularly concerned with establishing industries capable of sustaining a modern system of defence.[6]

The First Plan had been published only three weeks (July 1955) when Chairman Mao made a speech that completely upset the timetable for the economy's reorganization, and reversed fundamental policies incorporated in the Plan. In the speech (*On the Problem of Agricultural Cooperativization*) Mao called for an immediate accelera-tion of agricultural cooperativization. During the following eight months he also called for early collectivization of industry and com-merce, for measures to reduce the emphasis on heavy industry, and for a reduction of the strict central control of the economy. The most far-ranging of all these speeches was that entitled *On The Ten Major Relationships* (April 1956). This was not published at the time, but was issued in a revised form over twenty years later by Mao's successor in December 1976 (Appendix C). The new strategy in these speeches reflected Mao's conviction that a faster rate of growth could be achieved only by complete, immediate public ownership of the economy, and by the adoption of a flexible approach to planning. The strategy also implied that a more socialist form of society could be established *without* waiting for the gradual creation of the wealth to support it.

This new line was prompted partly by Mao's anxieties over the slow growth of agriculture, and partly by his growing conviction that in China—a country more backward, more populous, and more agricultural than the East European economies—the entire 'Soviet model' was inappropriate. On the agricultural question he was right to be anxious. The harvest of 1954 was poor, and unsuccessful attempts at collectivization in 1954 and early 1955, combined with the imposition of new forms of taxation, had created a serious situation. The peasants and cadres were demoralized, and although the Plan set a growth target for grain of 4.6 per cent per annum, during its first two years (1953-54) growth had been only 1.7 per cent per annum. The cotton situation was even worse. The Plan was that output should increase at 4.6 per cent per annum, but by 1954 output had *fallen* by 20 per cent from the level achieved in 1952. By spring 1955 lack of raw cotton had reduced the cotton industry to operating at 25 per cent below capacity. Indeed, it is no exaggeration to say that by mid-1955 agriculture's performance was beginning to undermine the credibility of all the industrial targets of the First Plan.[7]

Mao's impact on agricultural collectivization was dramatic. By March 1956 over 90 per cent of the Chinese peasants were in Co-operatives, and by 1957 virtually all were in the 680,000 Higher Stage Cooperatives. Thus a revolution planned to take fifteen years was completed in little more than one. The results, however, were unsatisfactory. Mao's expectation that changes in ownership and organization would produce immediate economic effects was belied by events. In autumn 1957 it was apparent that the growth of agriculture was still too slow, that urban unemployment was serious, and that relations with the Soviet Union (on which industrial assistance depended) were worsening. This crisis led Mao to launch the most extraordinary economic adventure that the world has ever seen—the Great Leap Forward of 1958. Abandoning all caution (and all Soviet advice) Mao took his argument one step further. He now urged that spectacular development could only be achieved if changes in ownership and organization *were combined with* a radical psychological transformation of the population—a transformation that would stimulate people to work more intensively, more creatively, more selflessly. If this could be achieved, Mao anticipated a wave of investment and development—a Great Leap Forward.

Apart from this central theme, the Great Leap embodied many other ideas and policies. For example, the Leap encouraged local initiatives, especially in developing small-scale industry and local economic self-sufficiency. This policy followed from Mao's conviction that Central Government bureaucrats were ill-informed of local conditions, and that neither they, nor the Party, nor he himself, had an infallible grasp of the laws governing the success or failure of human enterprises. The way the Leap was organized also reflected Mao's belief that chaos and imbalance were progressive, i.e. that a surge of activity in one area or sector created tensions that stimulated progress elsewhere.

In narrower economic terms, the Leap can be seen as a movement to improve employment and to make use of underutilized local resources such as coal and iron ore. It was also an attempt to narrow the gap between industry and the large-scale urban economy on the one hand, and rural life and the primitive handicrafts of the countryside on the other.

It is not often realized that, although the final Leap was sudden, many of its industrial policies had been in the making for two to three years. The decentralization regulations (which were a key to expanding local initiative) were mostly prepared during 1957; while plans for the expansion of small-scale industry and for increasing local self-sufficiency were both included in the drafts of the *Second Five Year Plan*—preparation of which began two years before the Leap. The Leap, however, took these policies to extremes that no one had previously contemplated, and added to them Mao's new conviction that with the new ingredient of proper motivation, progress at incredible speed was possible. All of this reflected Mao's determination to solve China's problems by finding 'another way' than that followed by the Soviet Union, a way appropriate to a country that had become the new centre of world revolution.[8]

In agriculture, the framework for the Leap was a new form of agricultural organization — the People's Commune. The typical Commune was a grouping of twenty to thirty Higher Stage Cooperatives; thus whereas in the Cooperatives the framework of peasant life had usually remained the relatively familiar village, it could now in some cases become an organization of up to 50,000 people incorporating villages and regions with which many peasants were unfamiliar. In many instances the Commune also revolutionized family life by introducing public mess halls, and there was a widespread campaign to limit incentives by paying incomes in relation to need as well as to effort.[9]

The atmosphere during the summer of 1958 was extraordinary. Officials who for years had made cautious, pragmatic speeches about China's economy suddenly announced that grain, steel, and other commodities could be produced in almost unlimited quantities. Mao himself, visiting a Commune in August, advised the peasants that the time had come when the surplus of food grains might prove impossible to dispose of.[10] By December there was some awareness that the Leap was running into problems. Nonetheless, a Party meeting held in that month published the most amazing claims for 1958. These included grain production of 375 million tons — more than double the output achieved in 1957. And at the same meeting the targets set for 1959 indicated that the Leap was to continue. Steel output was to rise from 11 to 18 million tons; coal from 270 million to 380 million; and grain from 375 million to 525 million.[11] As the Leap went on into 1959, administrative confusion deepened and the consequences of strain, of the misuse of resources, and of sheer human exhaustion, became increasingly serious. When the end came it coincided with the withdrawal of Soviet assistance and a succession of natural disasters. The results were appalling; the Period of Fastest Growth concluded with disaster.

The Great Depression (1959-61)

Table 1 illustrates the decline of the Chinese economy during the Great Depression. The plunging line on Figure 1 tells the same story. Missing from both are the effects of the Depression on fertility, mortality, and population change; also missing is any indication of its human consequences. The former we shall never know, but we do have some conception of the latter from eyewitness accounts. Some of these accounts have become available only in the 1970s, although documents acquired by American and Taiwanese intelligence in the 1960s give a graphic picture of the tragedy. They describe the closure of factories, the collapse of agricultural organization, and a population that in many parts of China was wandering around stupefied with malnutrition and searching desperately for edible roots, tree barks, and natural life of any kind. As one provincial report put it, 'The Province of Honan is covered in darkness'.[12]

By 1960 Mao and the Party leadership began to make fundamental changes. The most important was the priority given to the development of agriculture. Resources were ruthlessly allocated to the chemical fertilizer industry, and machinery plants all over China were converted to the production of agricultural equipment. Incentives to the peasants were increased and this required radical changes in the Communes. At first, the smaller Brigade (previously subordinate to the Commune, and frequently equivalent in size to the old Higher Stage Cooperative) was made the main unit of planning and accounting. Later, in autumn 1962, the Team (which had been the smallest component of the Commune and which was usually equivalent to a village) was given this central role. Moreover, in many parts of China collective organization was completely dismantled and the land was handed over to family management on condition that certain basic tax and state purchase targets were met. These institutional reforms were described in the *Sixty Articles of Commune Management*, which in its revised version of 1962 is still the main official guide to Commune organization.[13] In an attempt to undo the damage caused by successive experiments with agriculture, the *Sixty Articles* stipulated that in crucial respects agricultural organization was to remain unchanged for thirty years.

Another key document, which was circulated in 1961, was the *Seventy Articles on Industrial Policy.*[14] These were an attempt to remedy the administrative chaos into which industrial enterprises had fallen during the wild years of the Leap. Both the *Sixty* and *Seventy Articles* may be regarded as part of a complete reversal of the Great Leap, the essence of which was expressed by Mao in the sentence: 'In everything we will start out from reality' (1961).[15]

In spite of his own flexibility, Mao found that political retreat from the Great Leap Forward was difficult. Not only was he criticized by his senior colleagues; but local leaders responsible for handling the day to day situation were scathing about him and his Great Leap Forward. 'A blind man riding a blind horse' was one description, and accusations thrown up in the Cultural Revolution claimed that Provincial leaders after the Leap were openly saying that they were 'too busy to read Mao's thought', and that the best political action was 'growing potatoes' and 'applying fertilizer'. For a while Mao had to tolerate this, but later he sought revenge in the Cultural Revolution.[16]

Readjustment and the Cultural Revolution (1961-70)

From 1962 to 1964 the Chinese economy improved slowly but surely. Central control was reasserted in many spheres; planning was cautious; output rose; trade was restored; and the standard of living began to regain the level reached at the end of the First Five Year Plan. In everything moderation and proportion were the keywords. In December 1964 Chou En-lai addressed the Third National People's Congress. He reported the recovery of the economy and urged that China pursue the 'Four Modernizations' (of industry, agriculture, defence, science and technology). Chou also urged that trade be expanded and that foreign technology be studied. In 1965 China's economic position improved further. Self-sufficiency in oil was achieved, and debts to the Soviet Union were finally cleared off. Visitors to China in the autumn of that year have described a calm, confident, and prosperous atmosphere.

Politically, however, the situation remained difficult. Mao believed that the retreat from the Leap had led to corruption, to selfish anti-socialist economic behaviour, and to the entrenchment of his enemies (notably Liu Shao-ch'i and Teng Hsiao-p'ing) in the bureaucracy. As early as 1962 he had launched a Socialist Education Movement to correct these tendencies in the countryside, and in 1964 Mao supported moves to enhance the role of the People's Liberation Army in trade and industry. By mid-1966 the revival of the economy finally made it possible for Mao to launch a campaign against his enemies in the Party and State administrative apparatus without risking disastrous economic consequences. Thus, unlike his Leap, Mao's Cultural Revolution was *not* launched to remedy economic problems. It was mainly a political struggle, although economic issues were argued about and the economic crimes of Mao's enemies were condemned.

The Cultural Revolution had two economic consequences. One was that general dislocation led to a decline in industrial output in 1967—the first for many years; the other was that it halted the tentative revival of foreign trade (Fig. 1). Between 1963 and 1965 China renewed imports of large industrial plants, but between 1966 and 1970 trade was frozen at existing levels. Outbreaks of anti-foreign hysteria (such as the burning of the British Embassy and the maltreatment of foreigners) created a climate within which new trade possibilities could not be explored. From mid-1968 the economy began to make progress again, although by the end of the 1960s it was encountering problems for which there were no purely domestic solutions.

The Revival of Growth with Trade (1970-77)

In the early 1970s the Chinese economy reawoke after ten years of isolation. Six years of this were accounted for by the struggle to recover from the Great Leap and the Soviet withdrawal, and four by domestic political strife. The planners faced a series of problems. The first was the general disarray into which planning and economic institutions had fallen. Responsibilities had been blurred; skilled managers and workers had been removed to unskilled posts as punishments; and the relationship between the central and local authorities was confused. Secondly, agriculture had responded well to the investments and new policies instituted in the 1960s, but was approaching a point where further growth required investment and fertilizer supplies on a larger scale than could be provided domestically. Thirdly, in industry two areas were particularly important. Among established industries, transport, iron and steel, and coal all required modernization. Without this, there was danger that any of these could seriously constrain the entire industrial sector. In addition, the remarkable growth of China's oil industry called for a complementary petrochemical sector; a sector with an enormous potential for the modernization of the whole economy. The plant required for this was of a sophistication beyond anything that China could produce at reasonable speed or cost from its own resources.

Against this background Premier Chou En-lai, and later Vice-Premier Teng Hsiao-p'ing (rehabilitated after his fall in the Cultural

Revolution), renewed Chou's strategy originally outlined in December 1964. Chou proposed that China should again pursue 'the Four Modernizations', first in a new Five Year Plan, and then in a series of longer-term plans extending to the end of the century. Expansion of foreign trade (particularly the renewal of imports of machinery and plant) was an important part of the strategy, and this expansion was facilitated by the diplomatic offensive launched in 1972, as a result of which China renewed links with the United States and opened full diplomatic relations with Japan and many other countries. The strategy also called for the reimposition of central planning and more positive policies for training and rewarding manpower which initiated a revival of the universities, all of which had been closed during the Cultural Revolution.

These proposals were given formal approval at the National People's Congress in January 1975. It was, however, clear to foreign observers at the time that a powerful faction opposed Chou's plans, and that conflict was affecting the economy at every level. Opposition to the Plan was reflected in a campaign to 'criticize Lin Piao and Confucius'. This campaign, which started in August 1973, took the form of attacks on Lin Piao and the historical figure of Confucius, which were actually veiled attacks on Chou, Teng, and their associates. In 1975 the media also began to publish strong attacks on central planning and on the use of foreign trade to develop industry. There was particular criticism of the policy of using oil to pay for imported machinery.[17] During these campaigns the domestic organization of the economy deteriorated. In 1974 strikes and disruption affected the railways and the steel industry, and in the summer of 1975 the *People's Daily* summed up the state of the economy as follows:

. . . on the pretext of cooperation between enterprises the State plan is ignored. And not only is there barter between enterprises, there is extortion and racketeering . . . in the villages too, things are not being done according to the State plan and regulations. The peasants sow what they like; they indulge in free trade; and still less tolerable are instances of corruption, theft, speculation, exploitation, and the illegal hiring of labour.[18]

After Chou En-lai's death in April 1976, his opponents secured the second fall of Vice-Premier Teng Hsiao-p'ing, and in the campaign against Teng revelations were made that provide further insight into Chou and Teng's view of the economic situation in the early 1970s. Consider, for example, this comment attributed to Teng:

. . . for the past twenty-five years our industry, agriculture, defence, science and technology [i.e. the Four Modernizations] have not been developed. For twenty-five years we have been saying, 'the situation is excellent', but now we are all tired of this. Nobody believes it.[19]

Teng's detailed analysis of the situation was broadly that outlined at the beginning of this section, although he particularly emphasized 'the crisis of knowledge'—a reference to the havoc wrought in the educational system by the Cultural Revolution. To remedy the situation Teng advocated Chou's programme, with special attention to the need for central control of industry, for use of foreign technology, and for attention to wage incentives.

THE CHINESE ECONOMY AFTER MAO'S DEATH

Mao died in September 1976 and his death was immediately followed by signs of a decisive new phase of economic policy. The critics of Chou's programme were almost immediately (and for the first time) identified as the 'Gang of Four' (i.e. Mao's widow Chiang Ch'ing, Chang Ch'un-ch'iao, Wang Hung-wen and Yao Wen-yuan). The Gang, whose members had risen to prominence in the Cultural Revolution, were arrested and accused not only of attempting to seize power, but of disrupting the economy. Specifically, they were reported to have undermined agriculture in six Provinces, to have sabotaged the iron and steel industry 'for years', to have interfered with transport, and to have permitted 'corruption, embezzlement, speculation and black marketeering to spread unchecked'.[20] The Gang were also accused of opposing the policies of controlling the economy by central authority, of training skilled and high level manpower, and of expanding foreign trade and China's maritime fleet.[21]

The disgrace of the Gang has been very important economically, since it has been possible to blame them for many economic troubles, to admit that past achievements have been inadequate, and to chart a clearer course for the future. This situation was explained by Chairman Hua at the National Conference on Learning from Teaching in Industry in May 1977. At this Hua said:

However, as a result of interference and sabotage by Liu Shao-ch'i, Lin Piao and the 'gang of four', our construction achievements are not great enough and the tempo of growth has fallen short of what we once anticipated. This is a bad thing, yet it can be turned into a good thing.[22]

This speech echoes earlier statements which show that the agricultural problem remains critical. An authoritative indication of how criticism of the Gang allowed official awareness of agricultural difficulties to be expressed more openly can be obtained by comparing statements by Vice-Premier Chen Yung-kuei before and after the fall of the Gang. In 1975 Chen made a major speech on the agricultural situation in which the most he could admit was that agricultural progress had 'by and large' met China's needs although it was still 'not fast enough'.[23] When he spoke again in December 1976 Chen said:

We must take note of the fact that the interference by Liu Shao-ch'i, Lin Piao and the Gang of Four was serious and that *the tempo of agricultural development has fallen far short* of the demands of the great strategic principle 'Be prepared against war, be prepared against natural disasters, and do everything for the people', and the requirements of our country's socialist revolution and socialist construction.[24]

Nothing could be franker than this, and Chen's comment is supported by the data on grain output. There has been at best a very small increase in grain consumption since the 1950s, and data for 1970 to 1974 show only erratic improvement. The fact that (as of spring 1977) there are still no official data for 1975 and 1976 suggests that growth in those years was at best marginal. We do not of course know what precisely has been happening to population in the 1970s. The best estimates suggest a rapid decline in the rate of increase, but the rate remains positive and is probably at least 1.5 per cent per year (see Chapter 1).

The agricultural situation has been complicated by changes in world trade. Both the slowing-up of trade expansion and inflation have been damaging to China. Inflation has increased the cost of importing food while decline in demand has made the expansion of China's exports very difficult. This has been particularly so in the case of manufactured exports where the quality is such that sales to developed countries are difficult to expand even under favourable conditions. As a result, China incurred substantial trade deficits in 1974 and 1975 (see Chapter 5).

Finally, during 1976, in addition to the chaos and confusion now blamed on the Gang of Four, the Chinese economy had to cope with the impact of a major earthquake in the Tangshan-Tientsin region. The details of this remain secret, but it seriously affected the coal mining and metallurgical industries and made the transport situation even worse than it was before.

Chairman Hua's economic policies

Chairman Hua spoke frequently on economic affairs in late 1976 and 1977. Most of the speeches were at special conferences each designed to lay guide-lines for key sectors such as industry, agriculture, and defence. This process culminated in the proceedings of the Eleventh Party Congress in August 1977 during which the new policies were spelt out in great detail and appointments were made to key positions.

The general political framework for the new policies was explained by Hua in his *Political Report* to the Congress. In this, he argued that the Congress marked the definitive conclusion to the Cultural Revolution. Mao, Hua reminded the Party, had seen the Cultural Revolution as 'a great disorder across the land that leads to great order'. The disorder must now end, Hua said, so that a healthy order might be established.

The emphasis on order and unity was not new, but was part of a tightening of central control and discipline that started immediately Hua came to power. For example, an early quotation from Hua stated:

The individual is subordinate to the organization. The minority is subordinate to the majority. The lower level is subordinate to the higher level. The entire membership [of the Party] is subordinate to the Central Committee.[25]

This statement has a flavour that stands in distinct contrast to Mao's position, which, while acknowledging the need for central supervision, always left more room for the importance of spontaneous local initiatives. This statement (and the detailed public criticisms of the errors of the Gang of Four) suggested that China's pattern of economic control would move back in the direction of the Soviet style of the 1950s — with the modification that the military role in the economy might be more important than it was in that period.

This emphasis on control was accompanied in 1977 by a campaign of education in which the cadres were told of the supreme and indispensable importance of developing production. This was difficult, many cadres apparently adhering to the view that 'good politics' should come first and production second, and believing that developments in thinking and organization can of themselves have decisive effect on production. The condemned views echoed traits in Mao's thinking, and Hua's new policy was a reversion to the theory that thinking and organization must not get too far ahead of the development of production, and that attempts to accelerate premature change are likely to be unsuccessful.

At the very top, new policies were to be implemented by rehabilitated and promoted officials who in the past were noted for their pragmatism, preference for order, and economic expertise. The rehabilitation of Teng Hsiao-p'ing is well known; equally important, however, was the promotion of economic specialists such Yu Chiu-li, Fang Yi, and Li Hsien-nien.

Within this new political framework, Hua envisaged 'a new period of development'. He admitted that production had been 'stagnating or even falling', and demanded a drive to reverse this. This drive, however, while accompanied by rhetoric associated with the Great Leap, was to retain the framework of priorities in which agriculture is placed first, light industry second, and heavy industry third.

The policies adopted by Hua towards agriculture, population, industry, and foreign trade have been largely those developed by the Chou-Teng group in the early 1970s. Agricultural mechanization is to be pushed ahead and the areas of 'High and Stable Yields' (see Chapter 3) are to be expanded to cover about half of the total arable area by 1980. Related to agriculture and food are population policies and in this field Chairman Hua has been reported as giving strong personal support to measures to limit fertility.[26] Industry is of course to remain very important and a number of articles in the Chinese press have emphasized that Hua's policy of military modernization will depend on the speed of industrial development. Both industrial and defence policies point towards a continuation of a favourable attitude towards the use of foreign technology in all its forms. Again, this theme was established very early in Hua's administration. On New Year's Eve 1976, for example, the State Council gave a prestigious reception for foreign experts to 'extend thanks' for their contribution to socialist construction in China. And in January 1977, there appeared a remarkable report of the completion of an imported ethylene plant in Peking. This plant was described as having been

built in the spirit of self-reliance and independence by Chinese workers, cadres and technicians who made the general layout and did the designs for civil engineering work and underground projects . . . in line with the principle of 'making foreign things serve China'.[27]

If installing and adapting foreign petrochemical plants is self-reliance, then clearly there are no *technical* limits to what is politically acceptable in foreign trade. There will, of course, be financial limits, but again, significantly, the policy of using oil to pay for imports of machinery is now described as a policy 'approved by Chairman Mao himself'.

The development of technology calls for expansion of the number of skilled people capable of using, adapting and developing it. To secure this in late 1976 and in 1977, there were indications of a much more positive policy towards education and the development of human resources, and also of a commitment to stimulate productivity with material incentives. In education, formal educational training, and even theoretical research work, were prominently encouraged, and extreme educational practices associated with the Cultural Revolution were abandoned or modified. Hua also inaugurated a campaign to encourage China's most skilled people, who in the past had been 'repressed and stifled', to participate in education and work in a more confident and persistent way. This campaign included a promise that the 'Hundred Flowers' would bloom again (i.e. that people would speak frankly and admit their differences).

To get the most from the development of human skills and the mobilization of the whole workforce, clear incentive policies are required. New trends in incentive policy have been indicated in many ways. First, Vice-Premier Chen Yung-kuei, in the speech referred to earlier, confirmed the policy that in years when incomes in the People's Communes increase, at least 90 per cent of the Commune members must receive an increase in income. Secondly, Hua promised a rising standard of living at the Eleventh Party Congress. This emphasis is distinctly different from Mao's ambiguity on the question of living standards, and from the definite hostility to material incentives expressed in China in the mid-1970s (see Chapter 6).

None of these policy developments is surprising and indeed, none of them is novel. In the past they have generally been associated with economic progress, and the pressure to maximize this has never been more powerful. *Internally*, China's population growth requires increases in agricultural output that in turn require industrial supplies of chemicals and machinery. *Externally*, defence needs continue to impel the Chinese to push their energy, metallurgical, machinery, and electronics industries as near the frontiers of modernity as possible. In order to achieve this, centralized planning, the development of human resources, incentives, learning from abroad, and involvement in the world economy, are all indispensable. We can be sure, too, that in different ways these pressures will continue to have far-reaching consequences for China's politics and culture in the broadest sense.

ADDENDUM

Late in the preparation of this book figures became available that made it possible to summarise the state of the Chinese economy at the end of 1976. These are presented below.

China's Economic Indicators, 1976

GNP (billion US$)	300 (62)	Coal (mmt)	448 (38)
Population (million)	916 (2)	Crude oil (mmt)	83.6 (38)
GNP per head	327 (62)	Crude steel (mmt)	23 (43)
Grain (mmt)	285 (19)	Foreign trade (billion US$)	12.9 (49)
Cotton (mmt)	2.3 (25)	Exports (billion US$)	6.9 (49)
Index industrial output		Imports (billion US$)	6.0 (49)
(1960 = 100)	259 (32)		

Notes:
1. mmt = million metric tonnes.
2. Figures in brackets refer to table numbers for earlier years.
3. Foreign trade data are a revision of those in table 49.
Sources: Estimates based on sources cited in tables and, National Foreign Assessment Center, *China: Economic Indicators* (Washington, October 1977), table 1.

1
Population and Human Resources

'Yet, notwithstanding the great Sobriety and Industry of
the Inhabitants of China, the prodigious Number of them
occasions a great deal of Misery.'

Thomas Astley, *A New General Collection
of Voyages and Travels*

There are four aspects of a country's population of particular
importance: its size, its geographical distribution, its quality, and its
employment. Size and growth are important because of the pressure
they put on food, goods, services, and jobs. People demand to be fed
and to be provided with commodities; they need services — especially
Government ones — and when they reach working age they need jobs.
Failure to handle population pressures usually leads to disorder and
political collapse; such collapses are often accompanied by a temporary
decline of population, and followed by the emergence of a social
system capable of managing a larger population. The Communist
Party came to power at what appeared to be the end of a long crisis of
over-population. But since 1949, it has itself had to grapple with a
further spurt of population growth. The pace of this had no Chinese
historical precedent, but it is similar to the population explosions that
have been occurring during the past thirty years in other poor countries
in Asia, Africa, and Latin America.

Neither a big population, nor a high rate of growth, is intrinsically
undesirable. Their significance depends on the efficiency of a society's
economic organization; on the availability of natural resources and
capital equipment; and, above all, on the skills of the population in
question. Throughout the world the highest average incomes tend to be
found in big cities. These large, densely settled populations achieve
high living standards by applying their skills in economic activities that
are specialized and coordinated to a degree that more scattered
populations seem unable to achieve. Thus we cannot predict the effect
of population growth on human welfare unless we understand the ways
in which such growth will affect growth of other resources, the skills
and location of the workforce, and the efficiency with which resources
are put to work.

Chinese policy towards population has fluctuated. In the 1950s Mao believed that Western descriptions of China as 'over-populated' reflected a reactionary outlook that failed to take account of the economic potential of China after a revolutionary transformation took place. Indeed, in 1949 Mao wrote: 'It is a very good thing that we have a large population: and we are perfectly prepared to cope with several times the present population.' Later he modified this view and by the 1970s Mao fully endorsed population control. The current view was summed up in 1971 by Vice-Premier Li Hsien-nien who said: 'We are racing against time to cope with the enormous increase in population.'[1] Let us now turn to the problem of measuring the Chinese population.

THE SIZE AND RATE OF GROWTH OF THE CHINESE POPULATION

The Chinese data

There have been numerous attempts to estimate the size of China's population, but it is generally agreed that the only starting point for a realistic figure is the official Census of 1953-54. Historians have used earlier data to construct outlines of the long run trends of population change, but the 1953 Census was the first count that approached modern standards of enumeration. The Census was undertaken because information about population was needed for the preparation of the First Five Year Plan. Even simple planning required some knowledge of the size, age structure, rate of growth, and geographical distribution of the population. Preparation for the Census started in 1952, and returns were to relate to midnight, June 30, 1953. However, the practicalities of enumeration and checking were immense, and by the end of 1953, less than a third of the population had been counted. The final result, announced in November 1954, was a total of 583 millions, excluding Taiwan.

Demographers have differed about this census. Some have argued that its organization and execution were so inadequate that its results cannot be used at all. However, John Aird (the most authoritative analyst and critic of official sources) has written that 'with all its defects . . . the reported 1953 Census total of 583 millions is probably the nearest approach to a reliable population figure in the history of China.'[2] Nonetheless, Aird has argued that the Census figure probably underestimated the population by at least 5 per cent.

Since the Census, population changes have occurred with great speed. Growth appears to have accelerated in the 1950s, come to a halt in the early 1960s, and then to have resumed its upward movement. In addition, geographical shifts in the distribution of the population have occurred as millions of migrants moved into the cities in the 1950s, and then, starting in 1955, millions of peasants and young graduates were sent to the countryside in a series of *Hsia Fang* ('sending down') campaigns.

Our knowledge of these later changes is impressionistic. Various post-census estimates of population change were published in the later 1950s, but their accuracy is questionable. In 1964 there was a check of the registers of births and deaths. Indeed, Chinese refugees who participated in this claim that the check was a Census. This seems improbable; but, whatever the check's precise character, official statements started quoting some new population figures.

The next population figures to appear were in reports published between November 1967 and September 1968, which described the establishment of new Revolutionary Committees in cities, in Provinces, and in the Autonomous Regions. Although these figures were given rather casually, careful inspection suggests that a number were new estimates (presumably based on the population registers), and not simply mechanical updatings of old figures.

In the 1970s many local population figures have been published, and there have been two important statements about the total population. The first is actually a group of statements by Chou En-lai and others to the effect that, between 1949 and 1974-75, China's population increased by 60 per cent. If we accept the 1953 Census total, this implies a total of about 868 millions for 1974.[3] The second statement was a comment by Vice-Premier Li Hsien-nien, made in the course of an unusually frank interview with Egyptian newsmen. The key passage is as follows:

Some people estimate the population of China at 800 millions, some at 750 millions. Unfortunately, there are no accurate statistics in this connection. Nevertheless, the officials at the supply and grain departments are saying confidently, 'the number is 800 millions.' Officials outside the grain department say the population is '750 millions only,' while the Ministry of Commerce affirms that, 'the number is 830 millions.' However, the planning department [State Planning Commission?] insists that the number is 'less than 750 millions'.[4]

A summary of these figures, together with the rates of growth implied, is shown in Table 2.

US Department of Commerce estimates

Official data and the statements mentioned above leave many unanswered questions. There are the problems of the 1953 Census; the difficulty of reconciling conflicting official totals; the incompatibility of various reported totals with reported rates of growth; the improbabilities of official age and sex data; and inconsistencies between official statements about birth and death rates. Above all, the

Table 2: *Population estimates, 1949-2000*
(millions)

	1949	1952	1957	1964	1971	1974	1975	1980	2000	Rate of growth (per cent p.a.)
Official sources										
State Statistical Bureau	542	575	646							2.43 (1949-57)
Chou En-lai (1975)	542					868				1.9 (1949-74)
Revolutionary Committee Reports	542			717						—
Li Hsien-nien (1971)	542				750-830					—
Combined official series	542	575	646	717	750-830	868				1.9 (1949-74)
Western estimates										
US Dept Commerce (1976) (a)	538	570	640	734	860	917	935	1008	1329	2.15 (1949-75)
US Dept Commerce (1976) (b)	543	576	647	742	870	926	943	1014	1338	
Preferred series	538	570	640	718	841	894	901			2.00 (1949-75)

Notes:
1. Official sources quote population totals at the end of the year.
2. US Department Commerce (a) series is mid-year; while (b) is end-year, for comparability with official Chinese sources.
3. The preferred series is mid-year, and deviates from Aird after 1960. In the text, end year data for population are usually used since they combine with end year data for grain, urban population, etc.
4. These data exclude Taiwan, Hong Kong, Macao, and Chinese living in other foreign countries.

Sources: Statistical Bulletin (Ch.), 1957, No. 11, pp. 24-25; *Ten Great Years*, p. 8; *Foreign Broadcast Information Service*, No. 230, November 30, 1971; J.S. Aird, JEC (1967), pp. 341-406; J.S. Aird, JEC (1971), pp. 220-331; CIA, *Economic Indicators* (1976), p. 7.

lack of a proper census since 1953 throws doubt on all recent Chinese statements — except of course the sceptical statements of Li Hsien-nien. In the face of all this, the US Department of Commerce have made their own estimates of the age and sex structure of the population, and a range of estimates of the rates of births, deaths, and natural increase. Combined with alternative estimates of the 1953 population (based on alternative views of the degree to which the population was under-counted), these estimates yield a series of population totals that start in 1949, pass through the present, and extend into the future. Table 2 includes some of the most recent of these estimates.

What conclusions can we draw from this conflicting evidence? The Chinese statements surely indicate that lack of firm, official information reflects genuine uncertainty rather than secrecy. Demographers agree that without regular censuses, detailed information about populations cannot be obtained. Some even advocate the need for censuses at five year intervals. Yet in China there has been no such census for over twenty years.

In spite of this it is worth observing that the range of figures for the *growth* of population is not all that wide. Chou En-lai's 60 per cent growth represents 1.9 per cent per annum, and the latest Department of Commerce estimate is 2.15 per cent. However, if these differences are compounded over twenty-five years and linked to alternative estimates of the 1953 population, the final difference in estimates of the current population can be up to 200 million — a figure not far short of the total population of the Soviet Union!

I believe that a figure close to the lower growth rate of 1.9 per cent per annum is the more likely, for the following reasons. If the growth of the population is broken down into periods, most agree that growth in the 1950s and since the mid-1960s has been above 2 per cent per annum. A lower rate would be incompatible with what we know (from China and elsewhere) about the way in which population growth is affected by general political security, by food supply, and by public health improvements. The essential difference between 'high' and 'low' estimates, therefore, concerns the early 1960s. High estimates assume a slight pause in the rate of upward movement, while low estimates imply that the Great Depression of 1959-61 led to a serious population setback. Such a setback would seem indeed to have occurred. The Chinese are understandably reticent about this. A 30 per cent drop in food output, the collapse of central government administration, thousands of factory closures, and severe unemployment are none of them matters to discuss openly. But they did occur, and a Malthusian check to population growth between 1960 and 1963 is the one way in which we can reconcile an *underlying* rate of growth of over 2 per cent with Chinese statements of the current size of the population. A modern parallel to China's population setback in the 1960s is the drop in the population of the Soviet Union in the three years 1920, 1921, and 1922. As in China, this decline reflected a crisis in food output and distribution, and occurred in spite of an average level of food availability higher than in China. Thus in Table 2, I have accepted the US Bureau of Commerce series, *subject to amendments based on the assumption that there was no growth of population in 1961 and 1962.* This small qualification enables us to reduce the difference between the Bureau's estimates and Chinese statements to about 3 per cent, and leaves us with an estimate for 1974/1975 of about 900 million.

Table 3: *Rate of growth per annum of the Chinese population, selected periods, 1400-1975*

Period	1400-1700	1700-94	1794-1850	1850-1949	1949-75
Rate of growth (per cent)	0.28	0.79	0.6	0.22	1.9-2.15

Sources: Ho Ping-ti, *Studies on the Population of China, 1368-1953,* pp. 257-78; as Table 2.

The significance of these figures can be seen from Table 3, which shows that population has been increasing for most of the past six centuries. There was a big spurt in the eighteenth century; in the nineteenth century, growth dropped in response to a crisis of over-population; but the rate of increase in the past twenty-five years is more than double the peak historical rate of 0.79 per cent per annum, and about ten times the rate recorded for the previous century! In this context the difference between increases of 1.9 per cent and 2.15 per cent per annum falls into perspective. Whether the upper or lower figure is correct, the growth is unprecedented, and must, if catastrophe is to be avoided, be accompanied by unprecedented economic progress. Let us now consider the reasons for this acceleration.

Fertility and mortality

Table 4 shows rates of births and deaths from 1953 to 2000, and the resulting rates of natural increase. Table 5 provides a valuable comparative perspective by showing comparable information for Taiwan. It will be seen that the main differences between US Department of Commerce and official statements about births and deaths are that the Department believe the Chinese to have understated the birth, death, and natural increase rates in the 1950s. Both sets of figures agree that birth and death rates are now falling.

The decline in death rates reflects improved medical and social services, improved production and distribution of food, and the cessation of wars. All of these work in the same direction, and have, on the Bureau's figures, reduced the death rate by 56 per cent in twenty-two years.

The factors governing births are more varied and conflict in their effects. In favour of *declining fertility* we have positive Government programmes for reducing births. These have been especially important since 1971. There has also been a rise in incomes and an increase in the proportion of the population living in cities, both of which have been associated with declining birth rates in every country for which detailed information is available. Fertility must also be reduced by the separation of spouses resulting from labour allocation, and by the development of social services and collective institutions such as Communes—a development which, by removing some of the responsibility for the old from the young, lessens the incentive to have children to care for one in old age.

In spite of all downward pressures on births, the rate of decline in the birth rate between 1953 and 1970 was only 1.35 per cent per annum. This was less than half the rate of decline in deaths and suggests that there must have been some powerful influences working in favour of *high fertility*. One of these has been the peace and relative stability of livelihood which, in the 1950s and since the mid-1960s, may have increased the propensity of families to have children. But perhaps most important of all, 80 per cent of the population still live in the countryside where traditional values are most potent and where, even after collectivization, the peasants continued to perceive large families as being in their economic self-interest. The evidence cited in Chapter 6 suggests that large families are relatively better off than small ones, and this is explained by the fact that children begin to make a productive contribution at five or six years of age; a contribution that is still only marginally reduced by compulsory junior schooling. Since the early 1960s the peasants will also have been influenced by memories of the Great Depression, during which Communes collapsed, land was returned to households, and the State was forced to rely on families to plan production and to supply grain to feed the city populations. It is these factors that made the birth rate so resistant to efforts to reduce it.

Table 4 describes an amazing decline in birth rate since 1970. The rate of decline is estimated to have more than trebled in five years! If true, the explanation for this must be that the current campaign to reduce fertility is being successful. It is certainly fiercer, better organized, and technically more sophisticated than anything that has preceded it. The campaign also carries unprecedented political force. According to a State Council Directive of 1971, 'planned birth is an important matter which Chairman Mao has supported for many years.' Since 1971 the whole force of society has been mustered against couples who marry too young (28 years old for males and 25 years old for females) or who have more than two children if a city family, or three if they live in the countryside.[5] It is particularly significant that in the countryside compliance with offical population policy is now linked to plans to produce and *consume* food. This is revealed by articles that describe how Brigades and Teams combine the making of plans for production and consumption of foodgrain with plans for marriage and child-bearing.[6] The implication is that no allowance in the food is made for unplanned births. This measure has been supplemented by a change in the rules governing the distribution of land for peasants' private plots. The old practice was to give larger households larger plots; now, in some areas at least, no additional land

Table 4: *Births, deaths and natural increase, 1953-2000*
(per cent)

	Births	Deaths	Natural increase
Official sources			
1953	3.7	1.7	2.0
1957	3.4	1.1	2.3
1973/1974			2.0+
US Dept Commerce Estimates			
1953	4.5	2.25	2.25
1957	4.13	1.8	2.33
1970	3.57	1.23	2.34
1975	2.76	0.98	1.78
1980	2.15	0.82	1.33
2000	2.2	0.83	1.37

Sources: Official data quoted in J.S. Aird, JEC (1967); US Department of Commerce estimates are from CIA, *Economic Indicators* (1976), p. 7.

Table 5: *Births, deaths and natural increase in Taiwan, 1953/55-74*
(per cent)

	Births	Deaths	Natural increase
1953/55	4.51	0.87	3.64
1974	2.34	0.48	1.86

Source: Tzong-shian Yu, *Population Change and Investment Allocation in Taiwan,* Institute of Economics, Academia Sinica (Taipei, 1975).

is,allocated to households of more than five persons.[7] These measures must have dramatically reduced the economic incentive to childbearing.

However, even if the Chinese succeed in achieving further falls in fertility, the favourable effects of these on the growth of population are likely to be offset by continued reductions in *mortality*. Thus, if there is steady economic progress, population growth seems likely to remain positive for as far ahead as one could attempt to predict, and total population is likely to exceed 1,300 million by the year 2000. The only alternative future is one in which economic failure would reduce population growth by the same mechanisms as those that operated in the early 1960s.[8]

To sum up: estimates of birth and death rates are speculative, but the present rate of natural increase is probably still 1.5 per cent to 2 per cent per annum. In the future, continued economic progress is likely to reduce mortality at a steady rate, so that even if campaigns for birth reduction continue to succeed, population growth is likely to continue for a generation.

URBAN GROWTH AND GEOGRAPHICAL DISTRIBUTION OF POPULATION

In countries that are now rich, growth and industrialization have been associated with urbanization. Since the Second World War developing countries have departed from this pattern in the sense that the redistribution of population to the cities has occurred *far more rapidly* than the growth of industrial and other modern forms of employment can justify. This urban growth has been accompanied by growing numbers of urban residents with no employment, or employment only in 'marginal', low income jobs. The following paragraphs analyse both the extent to which China's experience conforms to this pattern, and how successful the Chinese have been with their unique, 'anti-city' policies.

Table 6: *Urban population growth, 1949-74*
(millions)

	1949	1957	1974
Urban population	58	100	171
Total population	543	647	902
Urban as a percentage of total population	11	15	19

Note: Data are end-year.

Sources: Estimates based on data in *Statistical Work* (Ch.), 1957, No. 11, pp. 24-25; *Enlightenment Daily* (Ch.), October 7, 1963; *Peking Review,* 1972, No. 41, p. 12; and the same, 1976, No. 14, p. 14.

Tables 6 and 7 show the changing pace of urbanization. Between 1949 and 1957 urbanization was very rapid. In this period the urban population grew at over 7 per cent per annum—nearly three times the rate of growth of the total population. Individual cities had spurts far above this average. For example, Taiyuan, in North-West China, grew at 19 per cent per annum (1949 to 1957); Soochow, in East China, grew at 16 per cent (1949 to 1957); and Lanchow (the centre of China's nuclear effort) grew at 17 per cent (1949 to 1956). The population of Loyang jumped from 120,000 to 370,000 during the first two years of the First Five Year Plan; and even Canton, for which little was planned in the way of industrial development, grew at 10 per cent per annum during the Plan. At the apex of this gigantic, exploding urban system was Shanghai, which in 1957 had a population of about seven millions.

Since 1957 useful statistics on the urban population have been scarce, and such data as we have are difficult to interpret. In the late 1950s many cities enlarged their boundaries to include adjacent rural areas. In this way Shanghai grew from seven to ten millions at a stroke.[9] Uninformed observers (including those of the United Nations) have quoted statistics of urban 'growth' that reflect these boundary changes. In estimating current urban populations we also have to take account of 'sending down' campaigns that have reduced the urban population by millions. A striking report in 1964 referred to '30 millions' being sent to the countryside;[10] in 1976 references were made to the '12 million' school graduates who had been sent to the countryside since the Cultural Revolution.

In the 1970s the Chinese have on several occasions reported their urban population as a percentage of total population. Since the authorities are usually most scrupulous in their distinction between 'proper' and 'rural' urban population, I believe this figure (19 per cent-20 per cent) provides a guide to the current size of the urban population, using definitions comparable to the 1950s. If this is so, since 1957 the growth rate of the urban population has fallen *by more than half*. Urban growth is still higher than the total population growth, but the gap has narrowed dramatically (Table 7).

Table 7: *Rates of growth per annum, urban and total population, 1949-74*
(per cent)

	1949-57	1957-74
Total population	2.21	1.97
Urban population	7.05	3.21

Note: About two-thirds of the 'urban' population in the 1950s were people living in urban places of 20,000 inhabitants or more.
Sources: As Table 6.

Table 8: *China's 'large' cities, 1958, 1970s*
(millions)

In size order, 1958		*In groups, 1958, 1970s*		
		Region	*1958*	*1970s*
Shanghai	6.9			
Peking	4.1			
Tientsin	3.3	*North China Plain*		
Shenyang	2.4	Peking	4.1	4.1
Wuhan	2.2	Tientsin		
Chungking	2.2	(pre-July 76)	3.3	3.3
Canton	1.9	Tangshan*		
Dairen	1.6	(pre-July 76)	0.812	1
Harbin	1.6			
Nanking	1.4	*Manchuria*		
Sian	1.4	Shenyang	2.4	2+
Fushun	1.2	Dairen	1.6	n.a.
Taiyuan	1.1	Harbin	1.6	2
Tsingtao	1.1	Fushun	1.2	n.a.
Chengtu	1.1	Tsingtao	1.1	1+
		Anshan**	0.833	n.a.
		Changchun*	0.988	1.3
		Central China		
		Wuhan	2.2	2.5
		Chengchou**	0.785	n.a.
		East China		
		Shanghai	6.9	5.6-6
		Nanking	1.4	1.7
		Hangchow**	0.794	
		North-West		
		Sian	1.4	1.5
		Taiyuan	1.1	n.a.
		Lanchow*	0.732	1-2
		Tsinan*	0.882	1+
		South-West		
		Chungking	2.2.	n.a.
		Chengtu	1.1	1+
		Kunming*	0.9	1.3
		South		
		Canton	1.9	2+

Notes:
1. * denotes cities reported to have moved into the one million class since 1958. Five cities are reported to have made this transition, bringing the total number of cities in this class to twenty. Three more have probably moved into this class, denoted by **.
2. Peking data for 1970s are estimated from visitors' reports of total population and an official statement that 46 per cent of Peking's population is rural, *Peking Review,* 1975, No. 40, p.29.

Sources: Morris B. Ullman, *Cities of Mainland China: 1953 and 1958,* US Department of Commerce (Washington, 1961). Post 1958 data are mainly travellers' data collected by the Foreign Demographic Division, Bureau of Economic Analysis, US Department of Commerce.

Table 8 lists the cities that have been reported as having populations of more than one million inhabitants. There are at least twenty of these; five more than in 1958. Seven cities are thought to have populations of more than two millions.

The contrast between the rapid growth up to 1957 and the slowing down since then suggests that *the nature* of growth has changed. It has. In the 1950s *migration* into the cities accounted for 50 per cent to 60 per cent of their population increase; the balance was supplied by the natural growth of the urban population. Since then the volume of migration has been greatly reduced, and its contribution to urban growth must now be quite small.

Policies towards urban population growth

When it first came to power, the Communist Party regarded urbanization as a good thing.

The peasants are the future industrial workers of China [said Mao], and tens of millions of them will go into the cities. For if China wants to construct large scale, indigenous industry, and to build a great number of large modern cities: then she will have to undergo a long process of transformation in which the rural population become the residents of the cities.[11]

During the First Five Year Plan it was intended that urban growth should favour further development of Manchuria (a region already urbanized by the Japanese before 1949); and the establishment of new cities in the North and West, and in other regions in the deep hinterland. At the same time restrictions were placed on the economic development of the seaboard cities, to the extent in some cases of removing both plant and workers to the more favoured areas. In the late 1950s urban policy underwent two changes. In 1956 interest and investment in the seaboard cities were resumed because it was discovered that the high costs of developing new cities in remote areas made a more balanced policy sensible. Mao himself went so far as to describe the period before this change as 'the seven years that were wasted'.[12] In 1958 a further policy was introduced, one that has persisted to this day. This is the policy of developing 'small and medium' cities. In conversation, Chinese officials give varying definitions of these city types, but an authoritative article published in 1958 described the policy in the following terms. 'Small cities' have populations of up to 300,000, and are to be 'generally developed'; 'medium cities' are those with populations of 400,000 to 700,000, and are to have 'limited development'. Anything bigger is a 'large city', and is to be 'generally restricted'. Special emphasis is put on control of cities with populations of a million or more.[13]

The rationale of this policy has varied. At first, the case for small and medium cities was their 'cheapness'—cheapness in the sense that the costs of administration and public works are lower in them than in large cities, and that the development of big cities puts pressure on transport. In the mid-1960s the emphasis switched to the strategic argument; concentrations of population were to be dispersed as a precaution against war (fear of which was powerful during the Vietnam War). Recently a new argument has appeared, to the effect that large cities are the natural location for heavy industry, while small and medium cities are appropriate for light industry and industries with close agricultural links. In this way urban policy has been related to the policy of putting agriculture first.

These experiments in urban planning are of great potential interest. But although China appears to have achieved more effective control of population movement than any other country, the net effects of this are difficult to judge. There has certainly been discrimination between cities, although the basis of this is not always clear. Many 'small' and some quite substantial 'medium' cities (Foshan and Chuchow for example) have indeed been reported as growing at 5 per cent to 6 per cent per annum, but others in the same class size (Kweilin, Changsha, and Tsinan) have reported growth of only 1 per cent to 2 per cent per annum. Among the 'large' cities, implementation of the restrictive policy is more obvious. Shanghai and Canton have actually reduced their size slightly; others in the 'one million' category such as Tientsin and Sian have had their populations stabilized; while even those just below the million class which have grown, have only done so at very modest rates.

In judging China's achievement in urban control, the first point to note is that when we look at the *comparative* pace of urban and industrial growth, we find the decline in the speed of urban growth (54 per cent down since 1957) closely reflects the decline in the rate of industrial growth (42 per cent down). Thus, although the Chinese have *not* been achieving 'industrialization without urbanization', they have, by controlling migration, reduced increases in urban population to a rate appropriate to the slower speed of industrial expansion. The second and even more impressive point is that in some 'large' cities the planners have succeeded in combining stable or declining populations *with continued economic growth*. This has been done by drawing labour for industry from the ranks of the non-employed, and from people in 'marginal', low productivity occupations.

Current urban trends reveal a pattern that was not predicted in any known policy statements. This consists of: (1) the inexorable expansion of the Peking-Tientsin-Pohai Gulf urban-agglomeration; (2) the decanting of part of Shanghai's population into cities in East China relatively close to the city; and (3) the continued growth of cities in Manchuria. Thus China's urban population is concentrating in three industrial regions centred on Peking, Shanghai, and Manchuria. Within this framework some 'large' cities with static populations may actually be growing in importance because of the leadership they exercise in these regions. It may be that by limiting *individual* city size, but allowing the development of densely urbanized industrial *regions,* the Chinese are capturing the advantages of big cities without incurring all of their problems and costs.

Other changes in the distribution of population

Historically, China's migrations have reflected the pressure of population on agricultural land. Cultivable land in China is very scarce; only 10 per cent of the surface area is cultivated at present and not more than 15 per cent has ever been considered potentially available. Most cultivable land is in the South and South-West, along the Eastern seaboard, and in Manchuria.

The density of China's population can be seen in international perspective from Table 9. The left-hand column shows China's population to have nearly three times as much land per head as Taiwan's, twice as much as Japan's, and slightly more than India's. In the right hand column—which shows the relationship between population and *cultivable* land—China's land scarcity is more obvious. Population density is still less than half the Japanese level, but is *seven* times that of America and the USSR. The implications of land shortage for China are more serious than for industrialized populations, since

Table 9: *Population density in China and various countries, 1965*

Persons per hectare (total land)		Persons per hectare (cultivated land)	
Taiwan	3.3	Japan	16.3
Japan	2.7	Taiwan	12.0
UK	2.2	UK	7.7
Ceylon	1.7	China	7.3
India	1.6	Ceylon	5.5
China	1.3	Indonesia	5.8
Pakistan	1.2	Pakistan	4.0
France	0.9	Thailand	3.1
Indonesia	0.7	India	3.0
Thailand	0.6	France	2.2
USA	0.2	USA	1.0
USSR	0.1	USSR	1.0

Source: National Academy of Science, *Rapid Population Growth* (Baltimore, 1971), p. 13.

the latter can obtain food in exchange for industrial exports—an option not yet open to China on a large scale.

Chinese migrations have followed two main routes. In the first (a movement from North to South), migrants developed the fertile Yangtze river region, moved on into Hupei, Hunan, Szechuan, Kwangtung, and finally reached Yunnan, where China's South-West frontier faces Burma. These southerly movements lasted from the eighth to the thirteenth centuries, and began again in the eighteenth. By the nineteenth century there remained only slight scope for migration based on new agricultural regions. South China was 'full'. This left one further area for viable migration—Manchuria—to which might be added some longer-term possibilities in the North-West.

Manchuria, a region rich in arable land and other resources, was preserved for two centuries for use by China's Manchu aristocrats; it was therefore 'closed' to migration by the mass of the Chinese population. But from 1860 migration from the poor, densely populated provinces of central China began on a large scale. This continued up to the outbreak of the Sino-Japanese war in 1937, and, under Japanese rule, migrants were attracted to Manchuria not only by its agricultural potential but by the new economic possibilities opened up by Japanese industrialization.

Since 1949 the 'filling up' of Manchuria has been resumed. In addition, the Government has encouraged migration to the other empty regions of China: Inner Mongolia, Kansu, Tsinghai, and Tibet. Some of these migrations have been political, but for the most part they reflect the age-old search for land and new opportunity. The difference between present and past migrations is that now it is the Government, not the individual, which sees the benefits and controls the direction.

Table 10 summarizes recent evidence of the way in which the growth of population in different Provinces reflects differences in cultivated land per head. In column one Provinces are arranged in order of cultivated land per head. At the top, Inner Mongolia is rated as 100 per cent; other Provinces are scored proportionately. This measure of population pressure is then related (in column two) to changes in population growth. Provinces with a plus are those that have had population growth *above the average*; those with a minus have grown at a rate *below average*.

Two features of this Table stand out at once. The first is the *size* of variations in cultivated land per head—the top scorer, Inner Mongolia, having seven times as much land per head of the population as the bottom Province, Chekiang. The second is the remarkably consistent way in which population tended to grow fastest in Provinces with most 'room'. This can be seen if a line is drawn in the Table under the Province of Liaoning. We then have a top group of nine where the

Table 10: *Population density and population change in China's Provinces and Autonomous Regions, 1950s-70s*

Province/Autonomous Region	Index of arable land per head (1952)	Population growth greater (+) or smaller (−) than average
Inner Mongolia	100	+
Heilungkiang	78	+
Kirin	58	+
Kansu	49	+
Sinkiang	46	+
Shansi	46	+
Shensi	41	+
Hopei	34	−
Liaoning	33	+
Honan	29	−
Anhwei	27	−
Shantung	23	−
Kiangsi	21	+
Hupei	21	−
Kiangsu	19	−
Yunnan	19	+
Kwangsi	18	+
Kweichow	16	+
Fukien	16	+
Szechuan	16	−
Hunan	15	−
Kwangtung	15	−
Chekiang	14	+
Average	26	

Note: In this exercise, 7 out of 24 Provinces do not fit the pattern; a similar exercise using 1960s data found only 5 out of 24 Provinces misplaced. The 1960s data are in R.M. Field, *The China Quarterly*, No. 37 (1967), pp. 158-63.

Sources: Figures for cultivated land per head supplied by Professor K.R. Walker; 1970s population data, *Current Scene*, 1976, No. 11, pp. 6-19.

average area of cultivated land per head is more than double that of the bottom group of thirteen. These Provinces are mainly in the North and North-West and with one exception have experienced population growth above average. Of the bottom group, eight of the thirteen scored below average population growth.

Thus although the quality of these population data is debatable, the pattern of change makes such obvious economic sense that it is hard to believe that they do not reflect actual trends.

To what extent these variations in population change reflect variations in *natural* population growth (as distinct from *migration*) we cannot know. It is likely that both changes work together.[14] However, we can be sure that from the point of view of the densely populated regions, emigration affords only minor relief to their population pressures. This is because there is no practical possibility of transfers of population on a scale that would equalize land resources per head in a short period of time. For many years to come the densely populated Provinces will have to minimize their rates of natural population growth, and raise their incomes by further economic and agricultural development. In the very long run the geographical balance of population will change, and those who fear that population pressure may propel the Chinese into wars of expansion can take comfort from the fact that China's own 'internal' frontiers still have generations of development ahead of them.

THE LABOUR FORCE

Size

The growth of population since 1949 has made the Chinese population a 'young' one. This means that the bulk of the population is either of working age (15 to 64) or is waiting to enter it. In 1976 an estimated 57 per cent of the population was of working age (15-59 for women, 16-64 for men) (Table 11). Some of these will be engaged full-time in domestic work or in education, and will not therefore need productive employment. But we must also take account of the fact that in poor rural communities children make a productive contribution long before they reach the age of 15. This means that a share of the 5 to 14 age group has also to be considered as members of the workforce.

Table 11: *An estimate of the age structure of China's population, 1975*

Age	Percentage of total
0-4	13
5-14	25
15-24	20
25-59	36
60+	6

Source: CIA, *Handbook of Economic Indicators* (1976), p. 9.

Table 12 estimates total employment for 1974. This is a crude estimate because we lack the surveys that are necessary to assess the agricultural, part-time, and female labour forces. Nonetheless, I believe that Table 12 gives an approximate picture of the situation.

Population and Human Resources

Table 12: *An estimate of urban and rural employment, 1974*
(millions)

Type of place	Rural	Urban	Total
Population	708	177	885
Employment	297	84	381
Per cent in employment	42	47	43

Notes:
1. The estimate of urban employment is based on: (1) data for total urban employment in 1957; (2) an estimate of the relationship between urban employment and industrial growth calculated from 1950s data; and (3) data on industrial growth, 1957-74.
2. Rural employment estimates are based on surveys made in the 1950s; US Bureau of Census estimate of age structure of the population and visitors' reports on trends in the proportion of the younger age groups engaged in full-time education in the 1970s.

Sources: Christopher Howe, *Employment and Economic Growth in Urban China 1949-1957.* Industrial output from R.M. Field, JEC (1972) and JEC (1975). Urban population Table 6 above.

The task of employing these enormous and growing numbers is prodigious. The Chinese report that 12 to 20 millions enter the labour force each year, and since 1949 at least 200 million jobs have been needed in addition to those left vacant by deaths or retirements. This figure of job 'requirements' takes no account of the aspirations of the older generation of women (especially those living in the cities) who have, since 1949, been encouraged by the Government to seek work outside the home.

The problems of employment creation

In common with other developing countries, the Chinese have had to recognize that even if the modern, industrial sector of the economy grows rapidly, the net effect on employment is small. Between 1949 and 1952 employment in the cities grew rapidly enough to absorb all new job seekers, as well as many of the three million urban dwellers who were unemployed in 1949. During the First Five Year Plan, however, although industry was growing at more than 14 per cent per annum and industrial employment at 8 per cent per annum, at least one million persons per annum were failing to find work in modern industry and services.[15] In China, as elsewhere, the cities were overwhelmed by demands for jobs from the natural increase of the labour force and from the flood of rural migrants. Migration to the cities continued throughout the 1950s, and was actually *increased* by early attempts at agricultural collectivization. The Lower Stage Co-operatives rationalized basic agricultural tasks, but their scale was so small, and their nature so limited, that they were incapable of creating the type of projects that would absorb surplus labour. Higher Stage

Cooperatives (1956 to 1957) also made matters worse, since by eliminating private ownership of land they removed one of the last incentives that had kept peasant households in the villages.

Unemployment in the late 1950s was compounded by the migration to the cities of workers' families. A survey of fifteen major cities revealed that between 1953 and 1956 a 28 per cent increase in basic workforce had been accompanied by a 70 per cent increase in the dependent, i.e. non-working, population.[16] The strains and costs of this became enormous, and during the First Plan it was estimated that proper provision of urban housing would take 70 per cent of the State's total annual budget for investment in industry.[17]

Employment oriented economic policies

Since the late 1950s the Chinese have attempted to remedy their employment problems by a series of drastic and imaginative measures. The most fundamental of these were the shifts of emphasis between different sectors of the economy, designed to increase the effect of economic growth on employment. Resources were moved from industry to agriculture, and within industry more emphasis has been given to light and small-scale industry, both of which use more labour than the heavy and large-scale sectors.

Institutional change These changes were likely to increase employment, but they needed time. To solve the immediate problem (created by accelerating migration) the Chinese in 1958 imposed *direct* controls over population and the labour force. Residence, travel, and employment were all made subject to new, stringent regulations aimed at stopping migration to the cities. Visitors to China can observe for themselves the formalities and security at main-line railway stations; and there is no doubt that house to house control is exercised with similar care in towns and villages. Also in 1958, the establishment of the People's Communes created new possibilities for employing the labour force in large-scale projects; as seen in Chapter 2, rational control and use of labour is still one of the Communes' most important functions.

The policy of 'sending down' The Government has been sending urban people to the countryside through its whole period of power. In the 1950s peasants who had fled to the cities for security during the civil war were sent back home. At the same time, thousands of political prisoners were sent to the sparsely populated North-East where they were organized in State Farms.

Since the mid-1950s 'sending down' has had three meanings: it has referred to the removal of rural migrants back to their villages (Co-operatives or Communes); it has described the practice of giving Government officials and staff in administrative positions first-hand experience of production; and it has referred to the despatch of graduating high school students to work in the countryside. The latter may be subdivided into migrations that are for life (like the thousands of East China youth who have gone to Sinkiang and Inner Mongolia), and those that are temporary—the young migrants being allowed to return to the cities after two or three years, often to continue their education.

'Sending down' is particularly important in 'large' cities, where it is used to keep the population stable. In its early stages 'sending down' created complex problems for the communities to which the migrants were sent, as well as for the migrants themselves. Today, planning is meticulous. The urban authorities provide migrants with cash to last them for their first year, and they even provide resources for housing them in the villages. Sums of cash taken by the migrants have been reported as being up to 600 *yuan*—a fortune by rural standards. Despite these improvements, residents report that when 'sending down' time comes round at the end of each academic year, the Chinese cities become tense; in the last resort, voluntary opting-out is rarely permitted.

How successful have Chinese employment policies been?

We have few hard data to judge the success of Chinese employment policies; but from what we do have we may say that, by comparison with the crisis of the late 1950s, the situation has improved in several respects. Table 12 estimates the 1974 level of urban employment. This is based on information about the growth of population and industry. My estimate for *all* urban areas is confirmed by evidence reported for a wide variety of individual cities. [18] It will be seen that the proportion of the city population now employed has risen from about one third in 1957 to just over half in 1974. Thus the growth in the proportion of 'dependants', which caused so much alarm during the First Five Year Plan, has not only been halted but actually reversed. It is true that many of the employed work in poor conditions for low wages (see Chapter 6), but these conditions are not worse, and are often better, than those found in the less privileged sectors of the cities of India, Latin America, and Africa.

The rural situation is probably less satisfactory. This is not surprising. The rural areas are being called upon to take the strain in the long period which must elapse before significant numbers of the agricultural population can be shifted to urban work or absorbed into rural industry. At present, a growing rural workforce continues to press on a limited area of cultivable land and, although many sensible ways of using this labour have been found, the productivity of additional workers is probably low.

In the 1970s the rural employment problem has revealed itself in numerous reports of illegal transfers to the towns and of the periodic collapse of labour control in the rural areas. An investigation in Hunan Province, for example, discovered that 'a lot of labourers freely went elsewhere to engage in sideline production, doing what they liked. The Brigade and Production Team cadres were only concerned about this labour force making money.' Another report, from Kwangsi Province, reiterated that urban employers 'may not sign contracts at will with rural Brigades and Communes, for the use of their labour.'[19]

It is probable that the 1975 campaign to copy the mass labour projects of Tachai reflects the need to find new ways of keeping the rural workforce at home. In underdeveloped countries where free movement of labour *is* allowed, the physical ghastliness and poor employment opportunities in the urban slums constitute a natural brake on the movement into cities. But in China, where urban conditions have not been allowed to deteriorate to the same extent, containing the pressures of an under-employed rural population is extremely difficult.

Education and skills

So far we have considered the population as a burden to which the economy must accommodate itself. Fortunately the *quality* of populations varies, and, by raising its skill level, a population can raise its capacity to support and improve itself. Indeed the difference between an advanced and a backward economy may lie more in the skills of its workforce than in anything else. The truth of this has been demonstrated by the post-war economic growth of Germany and Israel, both countries with skilled populations which, owing to historical circumstances, were temporarily deprived of capital equipment. Their astonishing progress provides a vivid economic example of the Maoist dictum that 'man, not weapons, is the decisive factor.'

A society imparts skills in many ways. Some of these are only imperfectly understood, and for this reason the easiest way to investigate the economics of learning is to look at the performance of the formal education and training systems. These systems are not the only channels through which skills flow, but they do have a central role.

The contributions of formal educational institutions to economic progress include the following:

(1) Training people to perform specific jobs and occupations.

(2) Forming attitudes and imparting skills that enable people to learn new jobs or new techniques in place of old ones.

(3) Providing a broad backcloth of knowledge that gives a person an understanding of his relationship to the economy and society at large, so that peasants, for example, can in addition to performing specific agricultural tasks, have some grasp of marketing, of the management of labour, and even of national agricultural policy—all of which will be relevant to their productiveness in a growing economy.

The educational system must also attempt to satisfy the social aspirations of the population *and*, if possible, mould them so that these relate closely to reality. In a poor country these functions have to be performed within narrow financial limits and within cultural, historical, and political influences that pose formidable barriers to reform.

It is not surprising that all this has proved too much for many developing countries. Some of them now have educational systems that produce too many graduates, provide qualifications of negligble economic relevance, and impart attitudes to work that encourage their high school and university graduates to spend long periods waiting for 'suitable' employment, rather than to take socially useful jobs immediately; while at the lower end of the educational system, many developing countries are also introducing universal primary and secondary education at immense and possibly unnecessary public cost. How have the Chinese handled all this? Does their experience hold any lessons for other countries?

The supply of school and college graduates   There are two ways of measuring the increase in a population's skill level. We may measure the supply of *graduates* the educational system produces, or alternatively we may measure the increase in the *number of people employed in jobs requiring skills and training*. In an economy where the educational system is a successful machine for producing employees in planned numbers and varieties, the stock of trained people supplied by education becomes identical with the stock of skilled labour in the workforce. In China, however, these two groups are very different; and to understand the manpower situation we have to look at each group separately and analyse the discrepancies between them.

In Table 13 the reader can examine increases in the numbers of graduates of higher educational institutions by major fields of study. The data cover the years 1949, 1957, and 1963. The latter was the year in which the numbers of graduates reached a peak. Table 14 shows the number of graduates from the whole educational system in 1957—the last year for which full data are available. This table also shows graduates as a percentage of the age group in the population.

Table 13: *Graduates of Higher Educational Institutions by major field of study, 1949, 1957, 1963*

	1949	1957	1963	1975	1980
Engineering	4,752	17,162	77,000	n.a.	n.a.
Agriculture and Forestry	1,718	3,104	17,000	n.a.	n.a.
Economics and Finance	3,137	3,651	3,000	n.a.	n.a.
Medicine and Public Health	1,314	6,200	25,000	n.a.	n.a.
Natural Sciences	1,584	3,524	10,000	n.a.	n.a.
Education	1,890	15,948	46,000	n.a.	n.a.
Humanities	2,521	4,294	n.a.	n.a.	n.a.
Other	4,084	2,117	n.a.	n.a.	n.a.
Total	21,000	56,000	200,000	65,000 (est.)	200,000+ (est.)

Notes:
1. Definition of Higher Education given in text.
2. Estimates for 1975 and 1980 are based on visitors' reports to institutions that indicate graduates running at a third of the level of the 1960s.

Source: J.P. Emerson, *Administrative and Technical Manpower in the People's Republic of China,* US Department of Commerce (Washington, 1973), p. 89.

Table 14: *Number of graduates by level and type of school, 1957*

	Total	Graduates by percentage of their age group
Higher Education	56,000	0.5
Specialized Secondary Schools	146,000	1.3
Senior Middle Schools	203,000	1.8
Junior Middle Schools	1,096,000	6.8
Primary Schools	12,307,000	76.4

Source: J.P. Emerson (1973), p. 97.

It will be seen that the numbers of trained people grew very rapidly in the 1950s and in the early 1960s. The total number of graduates from higher education increased by over 13 per cent per annum between 1949 and 1957, and by 24 per cent per annum between 1957 and 1963. Table 13 also indicates the magnitude of the collapse brought about by the Cultural Revolution. For the eight years between 1967 and 1974 hardly any additions were made to the stock of graduates, and it will probably be 1980 before the educational system is producing as many graduates as it produced in 1963. *Within* the total, the most noticeable feature is the jump in the proportion of engineering graduates from 23 per cent in 1949 to 39 per cent in 1963.

Important aspects of any education system are the number of people enabled to reach its various levels and the sort of barriers to progress there are at each stage. Table 14 shows just how steep the educational 'pyramid' was before the Cultural Revolution. Not shown in the figures is the fact that all Senior Middle Schools and institutions of higher education were located in the cities. Thus very few got to the top, and the chances of doing so depended on where a student lived. Since the Cultural Revolution there has been a swing towards the development of rural institutions and, as a result, a probable increase in the percentage of children attending primary education. Visitors are usually informed that Primary School attendance is 100 per cent. This may be true of the more visited areas, but it is unlikely that more than 80 per cent to 85 per cent of the relevant age group receive significant primary training, and even now very few get the five-year, full-time primary education that is the norm in the cities.

The expansion of employment in jobs requiring skills   Let us now turn to our second indicator of the skilled labour supply: the number of persons employed in jobs or occupations requiring special skills. For this we must rely on Chinese classifications. The most important of these are the terms 'cadres', 'intellectuals', and 'administrative and technical personnel'. 'Cadres' include personnel working in Government or Party administration, and personnel with leadership or technical posts in economic units, health, education, scientific research or cultural work. The 'intellectuals' are a more restricted group, brought into prominence by Chou En-lai's famous speech, *On the Question of Intellectuals* (see below). The group includes people with higher or specialized secondary education, *and* those with jobs requiring such qualifications. In the mid-1950s this group was estimated to number about 100,000—about one person in 7,000 of the total population. Finally, the two main categories into which the 'cadres' are divided are the 'administratives' and 'technicals'.

Table 15: *Administrative and technical personnel, 1949-71*
(millions)

	1949	1952	1957	1959	1971
Administrative personnel	1.799	3.302	4.212	4.500	4.685
Technical personnel of which:	1.194	2.043	3.879	5.157	7.356
Engineers and Technicians	(0.126)	(0.212)	(0.800)	(1.000)	n.a.
Total	2.993	5.345	8.091	9.657	12.041

Source: J.P. Emerson (1973), p. 37.

The numbers of administrative and technical personnel are shown in Table 15. The expansion of these groups has followed the expansion of the economy: 8.65 per cent per annum growth during the First Five Year Plan, falling to 2.88 per cent per annum between 1957 and 1971. Within the total, technical personnel have increased particularly quickly, and an interesting feature of the later period is the very small growth of administrative personnel. This suggests that campaigns against the growth of the bureaucracy have had real success.

In the Soviet Union most members of the above groups have *formal* educational qualifications that give them an 'occupational title'. These titles—for example 'chemical engineer: petroleum technology'—are acquired on graduation, and constitute a person's 'ticket' for a job. Although the Chinese tried to adopt this system, the most striking fact about their skilled workforce is that few people in skilled jobs have appropriate titles, and that the average level of formal qualification is very low. For example in 1955, of the 3 million District level administrative staff, some were illiterate, less than 34 per cent had reached the Junior Middle School level (i.e. had had more than six years education), and only 4 per cent had received higher education. In industry half the skilled workers were reported illiterate in 1955, and a 1957 survey revealed that 64 per cent of all engineers and technicians were 'practicals', which means that their only qualification was experience acquired on the job. Among Chief Engineers (usually the number two men in an industrial enterprise), only 56 per cent were college graduates; and on the administrative side of industry the situation was equally poor—of 15,000 top level administrators surveyed in 1955, only 5.7 per cent were college graduates.[20]

Figures such as these prove that most personnel in higher positions acquire their skills *outside* the educational system, and explain why the supply of graduates from educational institutions is a very different thing from the supply of skills available to the economy. These surveys are up to twenty years old, but from the expansion of education and industry that has occurred since they were made, it is a matter of arithmetic that the discrepancy between the supply of trained staff and the total number of skilled jobs has not been reduced very much. During the past decade the situation must have worsened in some respects.

The educational system

Although we have summarized the numbers flowing through the education system, this does not reveal anything of the nature of their training or of its relevance to the economy. The Chinese educational system incorporates many different kinds of organizations and the training offered is as varied as these types. Schools and colleges, for example, are organized on full-time, part-time, and spare-time bases. There are schools run by Government, by local municipalities, and by thousands of factories, Communes and other organizations. In recent years there has also been a proliferation of education by correspondence.

The three main levels of education before the Cultural Revolution were as follows:

Name	Years of life spent at	Location
1. Junior School	7 to 12 years	(rural and urban)
2a. Junior Middle School and specialized technical Middle Schools	12 to 14 years	(urban)
2b. Senior Middle School	15 to 17 years	(urban)
3. Universities and other institutions of higher education	17 to 22 years	(urban)

Junior Schools concentrated on literacy, and education in the Middle Schools was also mainly academic. The specialized schools offered vocational training, normally to pupils not allowed to continue in the academic stream.

Recent educational reforms In 1966/67 the educational system was almost entirely shut down. Schools remained closed until 1970; higher education reopened gradually between 1971 and 1973. Enrolments in higher education in 1976 were well below the levels reached in the 1960s. Here we are exclusively concerned with the economic implications of this closure, and of the reforms that have taken place since reopening.

The main reforms have been the following. Entry to education has been made easier for the rural population and for the children of manual workers. At the university level, entrants must have worked for two years, and applicants to university are nominated by the units in which they are working. In many cases they return to these units after graduation. More attention is now paid to primary, rural, and spare-time forms of education. The length of courses has been shortened, so that the 6-3-3-5 year pattern (Junior, Junior Middle, Senior Middle, and Higher education) has been reduced to a 5-2-2-4 pattern. Courses and curricula have been made more relevant to pupils' future work. A particularly interesting innovation is the opening of July 21st Colleges. Named after Mao's July 21st statement on education, these colleges offer spare time, highly vocational education to adult workers. They are run by local bodies, 'trimmed of all frills', and provide opportunities for those who have missed the mainstream of formal education or who need courses to keep abreast of new technical developments. Like all other educational institutions July 21st Colleges operate 'open door' education, which means that contact between education and work is maximized.

These reforms represent Chinese responses to the tensions and difficulties facing the educational systems of many developing countries. Taken individually, an economic case could be made for most of them since their general thrust is to relate the educational system to economic necessity. For example, the shortening of courses and the encouragement of local financing mobilize resources for training that are probably beyond the reach of central Government. Other benefits of the reformed system include giving students a broad but practical training; emphasizing the realities of the employment situation; expanding rural educational opportunities; and, in the July 21st Colleges, ensuring that some form of education is available on a life-long basis. The latter, in particular, reflects a widely held philosophy that work and learning should be continuous, inter-related activities, and that concentration of resources on full-time formal education rarely represents their best use.

Unhappily, it must be realized that the price paid for these improvements has been high, and that it is questionable whether the benefits of this revolution have outweighed the costs. As pointed out, higher education enrolments are unlikely to reach their 1963 level until 1980. In other words, there has been a seventeen year gap in the growth of the formal system at this level. Secondly, the reforms have lowered some important aspects of educational quality—so much so that the head of Peking University was recently quoted as saying that the university was in danger of graduating illiterate students. It has also been argued that dogmatic insistence on 'practicality' creates a bias against theoretical work and the traditional academic curriculum which could make it impossible for the system to produce even the *minimum* number of properly trained specialists. For while it may be true that the *main* requirement of the economy is for people trained to relatively low levels, there will continue to be critical *minimum* requirements for academically trained chemists, engineers, surgeons, translators, agronomists, and so forth. To some extent the Chinese have handled this problem by providing specialized colleges attached to ministries and other organizations. Students have also been sent to study abroad. But there is a danger that inappropriate reforms may ultimately reach even these important (but unpublicized) escape hatches; and, in the long run, lack of theoretical work will undermine the quality of practical studies and make the Chinese incapable of exploring areas of learning crucial to their future. It was probably this problem that led Teng Hsiao-p'ing to argue that lagging scientific research and low quality of education constituted the 'greatest crisis' in contemporary China.[21] It is now clear that 'conservative' educational policies have been given powerful support by the new administration of Hua Kuo-feng.

The use of skilled manpower

Efficiency in producing skills will be nullified if the planners fail to make use of the people possessing them. Doing this involves both placing workers in appropriate jobs and motivating them to use their abilities to the full. Motivation is discussed in Chapter 6. On placing, the evidence shows that the system is erratic. The problem arises from the suspect political status of all skilled persons, especially the 'intellectuals'. Personnel in these categories have always been 'assigned' to their work, so that the responsibility for misplacement lies with the planners and managers. In the 1950s the deliberate misplacement of skilled persons became such a problem that in 1956 Chou En-lai felt called upon to make his speech *On the Question of Intellectuals.* Chou called for a completely new attitude to this question and reported that: 'Some intellectuals are assigned to one task today and another task tomorrow, but are never given the job for which they are qualified.'[22] After this speech revelations followed thick and fast. The Assistant Director of the State Planning Commission reported that of 98,000 engineers and technicians who graduated from higher education up to 1957, only 22 per cent were actually engaged in engineering work. And at the Peking College of Mining it was discovered that only 10 per cent of those who graduated between 1953 and 1956 had entered mining work. Not all the 'missing' graduates were necessarily working at low level jobs, but no one disputed that educational planning and manpower assignment were in a bad way.

No systematic surveys of this problem have been published since 1957, but during the Cultural Revolution thousands of skilled workers and staff were once more removed from their proper posts. The situation became so serious that in 1972 there was another rehabilitation campaign. During this, an investigation in the city of Swatow found that: 'principal leading cadres of the State-owned factories had been transferred to posts too remote from their original trades. This affected revolution and production . . . If cadres are transferred frequently . . . their enthusiasm for work will be affected, and their professional specialities cannot be brought into full play.'[23]

Since the 1972 campaign there has probably been an improvement in placement, and the problem of placing and motivating high level manpower was given high priority at the Eleventh Party Congress. Nonetheless, finding an effective way of ensuring that skilled people are used in the most effective way will remain a central problem for China's political and economic systems.

2
Organization and Planning

'It is very surprising to see a Nation so vastly numerous,
so naturally restless, so excessively selfish, and eager in its
Pursuit of Riches, kept within the Bounds of its Duty by a
small number of Mandarins at the Head of every Province.'

Thomas Astley, *A New General Collection*
of Voyages and Travels

Economic systems

Most of us take the organization of the economy we work in for
granted. We are accustomed to playing certain roles as consumers,
workers, tax payers, etc, but rarely stop to analyse the total network of
which we are a part. Even if we did, we would find it hard to reach
satisfactory conclusions.

The *constituents* of a Western economy are individual consumers,
firms producing goods and services, and various kinds of
Governmental institutions. The core *relationships* in such an economy
are those between producers and individual consumers; those between
producers who sell services to each other; and those between the
Government and everyone else. In practice, these relationships are the
outcome of lengthy historical processes and their precise nature is
obscure. If an economy's performance is noticeably poor, the 'system'
is often blamed. But even in economies about which much information
is available, credible demonstrations of what is wrong and of what
should be done are hard to find.

A number of people believe that the Chinese economy is easily
understood. I do not agree. It is true that in some respects China
projects an impression of simplicity and uniformity; but its actual
complexity is illustrated by the differences about it between scholars,
many of whom have spent years scrutinizing every kind of evidence.
The present chapter begins with a discussion of the basic characteristics
of the Chinese economy and the main organizations engaged in
planning; next, analyses the industrial enterprise and the People's
Commune (the most typical units of economic organization); and
finally, describes the nature of economic plans, the means used to
transmit them and to ensure that they are fulfilled, and current
planning problems. The planning of foreign trade is described
separately in Chapter 5.

Basic characteristics of the Chinese economic system

The three constituents referred to above — producers, consumers, and Government — are all found in the Chinese economy. The 'producers' are mainly industrial enterprises, People's Communes, and other collectively organized units. Compared to Western producers the distinctive features of these units are the nature of their ownership, and the importance in them of Government and political authorities. Both points are reflected in Table 16, which was published in China in 1975. This shows that the State owns nearly all industrial organizations with significant capital equipment. The table also describes a collective sector which employs over a third of all industrial workers and produces 14 per cent of total output (collective units are owned by their workers, not by the State).

Table 16: *The distribution of assets, employment, and economic activity by public and private sectors*
(percentage shares)

	State owned	Collectively owned	Private
Industry			
1. Fixed assets	97	3	0
2. Employees	63	36.2	0.8
3. Gross output	86	14	0
Agriculture			
1. Arable land and irrigation equipment	n.a.	90 approx.	n.a.
2. Tractors and draught animals	n.a.	80 approx.	n.a.
3. Output of foodgrains and crops for industrial use	n.a.	90+	n.a.
Commerce			
1. Retail sales	92.5	7.3	0.2

Source: *Red Flag* (Ch.), No. 4, 1975, pp. 5-6.

In agriculture approximately 90 per cent of cultivated land and irrigation equipment is collectively owned, mainly — as we shall see — by 'Teams', which often correspond to villages. Table 16 gives no figures for State-owned farms (which include those run by the People's Liberation Army) or for the private plots of land owned by the peasants. These two forms of ownership account for 10 per cent of land and irrigation equipment, and the private plots alone probably account for 5 per cent to 7 per cent of the land. A qualification to this statistic is that it has been presented to overemphasize the collective control of agricultural *output*. This has been done by omitting output of vegetables, fruit, pigs, and poultry; the private sector probably produces 30 per cent to 50 per cent of these — an effort quite disproportionate to the private share of agricultural assets.[1]

Organization and Planning

Table 16 suggests, but does not describe, the dominant economic role of Government and political authorities. This role is played partly by specialized administrative agencies — such as the economic ministries and their local offices — and partly by the normal organs of political power at the central and at various local levels. In some ways this mingling of administration and politics has parallels in the Soviet Union. In both economies, for example, an important economic document such as a Five Year Plan is drafted in the ministries, then debated and agreed at the highest political level. But there are also important differences. One of these is that the Chinese Communist Party is more active in the day-to-day administration of economic organizations than the Soviet Party has normally been. Another Chinese peculiarity is that since the 1960s the economy has been periodically affected by political activity organized *outside* Government or Party. The Cultural Revolution is a striking example of this.

We have now identified two important characteristics of China's economic organization: public ownership, and the pervasiveness of political control. Before describing China's economic institutions in more detail, we must remind ourselves that apart from being complex at any one point in time, the system has been through periods of rapid and violent upheaval. The most dramatic changes occurred between 1955 and 1962. During these years the Chinese attempted to bring the entire economy within the orbit of State control by collectivizing agriculture and nationalizing industry and commerce. This trend

Figure 2: *Administrative levels*

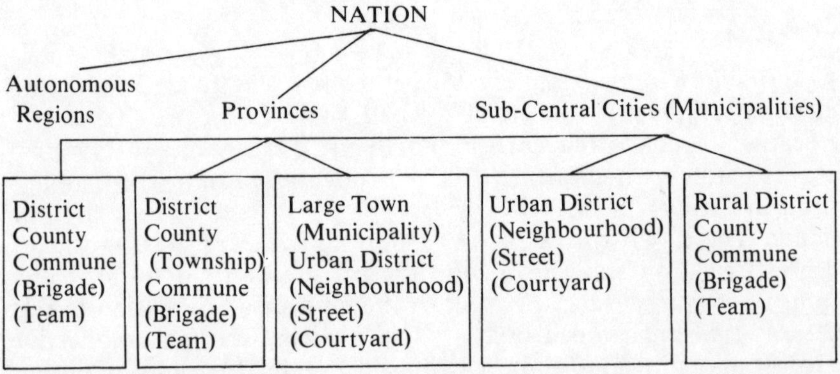

Note: There are 21 Provinces, 5 Autonomous Regions, 3 Municipalities at immediate sub-central level (Peking, Tientsin and Shanghai), approximately 2,200 Counties, and 50,000 Communes.

reached a climax in 1958 and was followed by a retreat. After 1962 the situation settled down. The Cultural Revolution had some implications for economic organization, but these were mostly shortlived. What is described below is the system as it has appeared to operate in the mid-1970s; this is broadly the system that emerged in the 1960s, after the Great Leap Forward, and after the Great Depression.

THE PLANNERS

Plans are made, legalized and supervised by institutions at various administrative levels. These are shown in Figures 2, 3 and 4. At the top are national institutions; below these are institutions organized in Provinces, Autonomous Regions, and the Sub-Central Cities. There are twenty-one Provinces, five Autonomous Regions, and three Sub-Central Cities.

The Province is a traditional unit of Chinese local government; below it are large towns, Rural and Urban Districts, Counties and People's Communes. Towns (Municipalities) also have various subordinate levels. Of these, Urban District administration and the Neighbourhood and Street Committees have been operating for many years now; recently in some towns a new unit — the Courtyard — was added. The Courtyard has only 100 to 200 persons in it.

There are three cities whose administration is at immediate Sub-Central level (i.e. at the same level as Provinces). They are Peking, Tientsin, and Shanghai. Large towns and the three Sub-Central Cities control a peripheral rural area that is organized in Rural Districts and Communes. In the case of Peking, for example, the rural area controlled by the city extends seventy miles North of the built-up area.

Figure 3 shows the administrative and political organizations involved in economic planning at Central and local levels.

At the apex of China's State structure is the National People's Congress. Under China's first Constitution (in force from 1954 to 1975) the Congress was supposed to meet annually, and every four years a new Congress was to be elected. Actually there was no meeting in 1963, or between 1964 and 1975. Membership of the Congress is by election and its meetings are important. It makes laws and approves documents, appointments, State Budgets, and national economic plans.

Immediately below the National People's Congress is the State Council. According to the current Constitution this body is empowered to formulate administrative measures; to issue decrees and laws; to exercise leadership over Ministries, Commissions, and local State bodies; to draft and implement National Economic Plans and the State

Figure 3: *Organs of the State administrative and political structure with economic responsibilities*

	Communist Party Central Committee (CPCC)	National People's Congress	State Council controlling Ministries and Commissions with economic responsibilities (see Figure 4)
National level	Politburo of the CPCC Standing Committee of the Politburo Party Congress		
Local levels	Party committees at each level down to rural brigade and urban neighbourhood	Revolutionary Committees at each level down to rural brigades and urban neighbourhoods	Offices of Ministries and Commissions of State Council Branches of the People's Bank of China
	Party committees in schools, enterprises and other units	Revolutionary Committees in schools, enterprises and other units	
	Provincial Party Congresses	Departments, Bureaux and offices of Revolutionary Committees with special economic responsibilities, e.g. heavy industry, grain, labour, etc. Industrial corporations reporting to local Bureaux	

Figure 4: *Organs of the State Council with economic responsibilities*

Commissions	Banks	Ministries
State Planning Commission	People's Bank of China	Agriculture and Forestry
State Capital Construction Commission	Bank of China	Building Construction
State Price Commission		Coal
		Commerce
		Communications
		Defence
		Economic Relations with Foreign Countries
		Finance
		Foreign Trade
		Light Industry
		Machine Building (Nos 1 to 7)
		Metallurgy
		Petroleum and Chemicals
		Railways
		Water Conservancy and Electric Power

Other special organizations under the State Council

Birth Control leading group
Government offices Administrative Bureau
Scientific and Educational leading group
State Bureau of Supplies
(State Statistical Bureau?)

Notes:
1. In the 1950s there was a State Economic Commission responsible for annual plans, while the Planning and Capital Construction Commissions dealt with longer-term matters. Subsequently the State Economic and State Planning Commissions were merged.
2. Some observers believe there still to be a State Statistical Bureau, but none of its personnel has been identified in recent years.

Budget; and to oversee all State administrative affairs.

Membership of the State Council includes the Premier, Vice-Premiers, and the Heads of the Ministries and Commissions under it. (Some Vice-Premiers are also Heads of Ministries.) The overall impression given by the Council and its subordinate organizations is one of great competence and professionalism. In 1975 no less than five of the twelve Vice-Premiers were men with considerable experience in economic matters. In contrast to the Soviet Union, the Council and the top ministerial positions are not filled with men whose background is in engineering; and the resilience and indispensable character of this leadership is indicated by the fact that in 1975 the Council included eleven members who had been rehabilitated since the Cultural Revolution.[2]

Below the State Council is a further group of organizations engaged in economic work. The most important of these are the State Planning Commission, the State Capital Construction Commission, and the People's Bank of China. These institutions are shown in Figure 4.

At local level the National People's Congress and the State Council are paralleled by People's Congresses and Revolutionary Committees (Figure 3). The Revolutionary Committees are permanent bodies which have offices and sections specializing in economic work. Other local bodies include the offices of the Central Ministries, the People's Bank, etc. The Corporations shown in Figure 4 are groups of enterprises in the same industry which are intermediaries between individual enterprises and planning bodies operating at the Municipal level.

An example of the structure of governmental authority as it works out in the case of the coal industry is shown in Figure 5. This illustrates that the nature of control varies according to the characteristics of the enterprise. Thus large enterprises, whose outputs are centrally allocated, are subject to powerful Central authority. Major *policy* decisions come down from the Centre through Revolutionary Committees at Provincial, Area, and Enterprise levels. Major *technical* and *management* decisions are transmitted from the Ministry through special agencies at Provincial and Area levels to the Chief Engineer in the enterprise. Smaller enterprises, whose outputs are consumed locally and not Centrally allocated, are controlled through different networks in which the main authority lies at sub-Central levels. One can see, therefore, that enterprises in this industry (which is fairly typical of heavy industry) may be subjected to some degree of control from no less than seven levels, i.e. Centre, Province, Area, Region, Municipality, County or Commune, the exact pattern depending on their location and importance.

The influence and authority of the most powerful political institution in China, the Communist Party, permeates economic

Figure 5: *The Industrial Planning System: The Coal Industry*

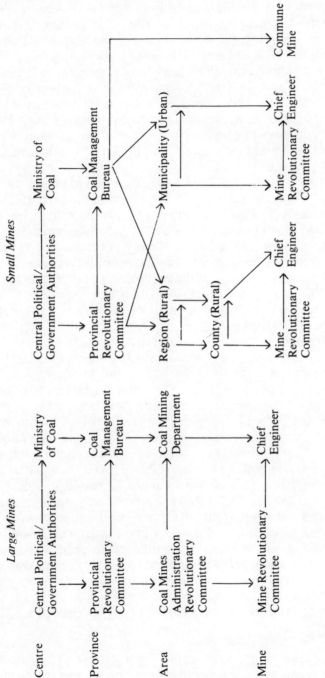

Notes:
1. Arrows represent the direction of authority.
2. The control of small mines at Region, County and Municipality levels involves the dual channels of Revolutionary Committees and Mine Departments responsible for policy and technical management respectively.

activity at all levels. The Party is reported to have had 28 million members in 1973. After the Eleventh Congress of August 1977 the Party central structure consisted of the Central Committee (333 members), the Politburo (26 members), and the Standing Committee of the Politburo (5 members). The last is the key group; it meets regularly in secret, and is involved in all important economic decisions.

Beneath the Central Party Committee is a network of local Committees and cells. These operate in all the basic organizations in China, such as hospitals, schools, industrial enterprises, People's Communes, and even in component parts of these. In general, Party organization runs parallel to the entire administrative structure.

The third constituent in China's power structure is the People's Liberation Army (PLA). The PLA has always played an economic role in China, and it became particularly important in the early 1960s when Mao supported Lin Piao's enlargement of its role. The PLA's importance was again emphasized when it was called in to control the chaos of the Cultural Revolution. Today, because the North-East China and Peking regions are both key strategic and economic regions, the PLA has a strong presence in the economy. The PLA also has a role as a troubleshooter — for example in handling emergency farming operations, transport problems, natural disasters, and industrial labour unrest — and it controls a high percentage of China's skilled manpower, transport, and communication equipment.

The total structure of power that controls China's economy should be thought of as networks of State, Party, and Military posts, which operate at local and national levels. The networks *interlock* in the sense that an individual can operate simultaneously in any part of them. The most important figures in China usually hold national and local posts *and* combine State, Party, and Military responsibilities. Thus Hua Kuo-feng is a Party, Military, and Governmental figure who, before rising to the top, was both a Provincial Party Secretary and the Central Minister for Security. This interlocking has increased in recent years. Nearly a third of the Provincial Party Secretaries, for example, are now army men, and the proportion of Central Committee members who hold concurrent local positions is about two-thirds. This complexity is one of the reasons why it is extremely difficult to unravel the patterns of authority and responsibility in Chinese economic administration.

INDUSTRIAL ENTERPRISES AND PEOPLE'S COMMUNES

Industrial enterprises

In cities the planners are responsible for a variety of organizations. These range from small, cooperatively organized groups engaged in

Figure 6: *The organization of an industrial enterprise*

	Committees	Individuals	Departments
Enterprise level	Party Committee Revolutionary Committee Trade Union Committee, etc.	Party Secretary Enterprise Director Deputy Director(s) and Chief Engineers	Office of the Revolutionary Committee Finance and accountancy Production and planning (design and innovation) Quality control Marketing and transport Organization Labour and wages Training Welfare Capital construction Raw materials Utilities Military Propaganda
Workshop level	Party Branch Revolutionary Committee Trade Union Research	Shop chief Specialist individuals as needed	
Section, sub-section, *team level*	Party small groups	Section/team leaders and supervisors	

production and distribution, to large, state-owned production and trading enterprises. Of all these, industrial enterprises are the most typical and important. Variations between enterprises are considerable. A small enterprise may employ only ten men and use the simplest forms of mechanization. Large enterprises — such as the steelworks at Anshan and Wuhan, the chemical works at Nanking, or the Loyang tractor complex — employ thousands of men, use modern equipment, and dominate the cities in which they are located. Despite these differences, industrial enterprises have important common characteristics. They are basic units of accounting, they have a legal identity, and patterns of internal authority and responsibility that are fairly similar.

The structure of authority The organization of a typical enterprise is illustrated in Figure 6. Below the highest level of control, authority coincides with the physical layout of the enterprise. These lower levels are the shop and the section or team. Supreme authority is vested in the enterprise Party Committee; below this is the Revolutionary Committee responsible for day-to-day management. Below the Revolutionary Committee are Committees such as the Trade Union Committee.

Revolutionary Committees usually have 15 to 20 elected members. Control over the Committee leadership is tight, since its composition has to be agreed with authorities above the enterprise. Moreover an enterprise's key men will usually be members of both the Party and Revolutionary Committees. The Committee is, however, capable of some representative functions as it draws its membership from all the major sections of the enterprise.

The most powerful men in an enterprise are the Party Secretary, the Director (and Deputy Directors), and the Chief Engineer. In a large enterprise, Deputy Directors will be in charge of specialist Departments, or of small groups of related Departments. Control of the Workshop and lower levels is usually given to a Deputy Director or Chief Engineer. At these lower levels the Party is represented by Party Committees and groups. Other leaders and specialists are appointed as required. Revolutionary Committees are also found at the Workshop level, but not below.

The functioning of Chinese industrial enterprises is similar to that of Western factories. There is a flow of authority from top to bottom in which the Deputy Director responsible for production is the crucial figure. This is the 'line'. The line uses, but is not subordinate to, advice from 'staff' in specialized Departments. The list of Departments in a Chinese factory largely parallels that found in a Western factory; in Figure 6 only the Departments for Military Affairs and Political

Propaganda stand out immediately as peculiar to the Chinese system. The organization illustrated is fairly complex, and would only be typical of enterprises with at least 1,000 workers. Smaller enterprises tend to have fewer senior staff and fewer Departments. In contrast, in the very largest enterprises the Workshop level might itself be so important that its organization would be as extensive as that of the entire enterprise illustrated here.

This pattern of organization is the result of a turbulent history of struggles. In the 1950s the Chinese copied many features of Soviet industrial management. Power was concentrated in the hands of the enterprise Director, and the major goal of the enterprise was the fulfilment of detailed, centrally-given targets for output. This system did not work well. It relied on the authority of individuals where the Chinese have a preference for groups; it fostered bureaucracies which became progressively divorced from practical needs; and its rigidities were costly in an economy where fluctuations were common and differences between enterprises and regions very great.

After the Great Leap Forward the authority of the Directors was taken by the Party Committees. Then during the Cultural Revolution the Revolutionary Committees appeared. At first these were groups of pro-Maoists drawn from the ranks of the Party, the workforce, the abolished Trade Unions, and the People's Liberation Army. They replaced the Party Committees as the supreme enterprise authority and dedicated themselves to the destruction of wasteful bureaucracy, special staff privileges, and all enterprise regulations felt to hinder the growth of productivity.

In the early 1970s the Party Committees reasserted their authority, but the Revolutionary Committees were retained in a subordinate administrative role. The Trade Unions were revived in 1973, since when they have continued to perform welfare and propaganda work.

The relevance of this history is that it reminds us of the fragility of enterprise organization and explains the frequent references in the Chinese press to the problem of 'factionalism'. Factionalism is mainly a legacy of the Cultural Revolution during which workers and staff of one faction would not speak to, or pass a tool or document to, members of another. Reports in 1975 and 1976 suggest that many workers, bewildered by competing demands for allegiance, still felt attached to the groups with whom they sided and fought in the Cultural Revolution. A recent report on the steel industry, for example, referred to 'leading cadres who are engaged in bourgeois factionalism. They fight for power and profit, and they are not united.' Another article spoke of the need to 'fight every kind of sabotage of the revolution and of production order.'[3] These reports show that beneath any simple charts we may draw are complicated, powerful currents, capable of breaking out and disrupting the flow of day-to-day operations.

Enterprise goals The goals of Chinese industrial enterprises are of two kinds: *quantitative* targets prescribed in plans, and *qualitative* indications of the spirit in which enterprise work is done. The *quantitative* targets are listed in Table 17.

Table 17: *Quantitative targets in industrial enterprise plans*

Physical	* 1.	Output of main commodities produced
	2.	Trial production of new commodities
	3.	Main technical and economic norms (e.g. units of electricity produced per unit of coal)
Financial	4.	Total value of output
	* 5.	Total profit
	6.	Total value of cost reduction
	7.	Rate of cost reduction
Labour	* 8.	Average size of workforce
	9.	Year-end size of workforce
	10.	Average wage
	*11.	Total wage bill
	12.	Productivity of labour

Note: * indicates targets that cannot be changed by the enterprise without permission.

Up to the end of 1957 all twelve targets shown in Table 17 were obligatory. But in practice fulfilment of such complicated plans proved impossible. One reason for this was that poor information and communications meant that plans were hardly ever consistent. In addition, equipment used by enterprises was so varied in age and quality that it was impossible to specify 'norms' of performance common to a whole industry. Most important of all, fluctuations due to harvests and political campaigns made plan changes during the year unavoidable.

The effect of these problems was that enterprises concentrated on some targets at the expense of others (usually physical output); connived to obtain 'easy' targets; concealed reserves of materials and labour; and even falsified statistical returns. Therefore, after 1957 enterprises were allowed more discretion. The twelve targets remained, but only four could not be adjusted without permission. For many enterprises these concessions were accompanied by a transfer of control from the Centre to the Province or Municipality. The flexibility introduced by all these changes would, it was hoped, remove the inefficiencies of the old system.

It has been mentioned earlier that the Party took control of enterprises in 1958, and that there were further political struggles in industry during the Cultural Revolution. These events were closely connected with the development of *qualitative* goals. *Qualitative* goals are concerned with the spirit in which plans are drawn up and implemented rather than with detailed statistics and bureaucratic rules. These goals were broadly defined in a document called the *Constitution of the Anshan Iron and Steel Company*. Reported to have been drawn up between 1959 and 1960, the *Constitution* was not published until several years later.[4] The *Constitution* emphasizes that enterprise leadership should be exercised by the Party; that planning should involve the widest possible participation; and that enterprise leaders should spend regular periods working on the shop floor. Other goals mentioned in the *Constitution* bear directly on the content of conventional planning. For example, enterprises are encouraged to expand output in ways that minimize demands on the State for new equipment; to reduce dependence on other enterprises for raw materials and semifinished products; and to set up special groups to intensify the search for cost-reducing techniques and other innovations.

These goals are not alternatives to conventional targets; they are complementary, and provide help in situations for which no conventional plans exist.

Finance   Figure 7 shows the main financial flows that pass through the industrial enterprise.

On the *inflow* side, the bulk of an enterprise's revenue consists of payments received for goods and services supplied. Enterprises also receive fixed and working capital of various kinds. Most of this capital is provided by National and Provincial budgets; channelled in many cases through local Bureaux and Industrial Corporations. Capital funds are also provided by the China Construction Bank. The duties of this organization are not entirely clear, but it is thought to dispense and control large capital expenditures. It is also a source of finance which may be drawn upon to balance out the sharp variations in financial needs associated with construction work. The Construction Bank is thus concerned with both non-repayable grants and short term loans repayable with interest. Strictly seasonal and 'emergency' finance is provided by the People's Bank for all enterprises and units.

The *outflow* side shown in Figure 6 is more complicated. First, there are enterprise costs. These include payments to other enterprises, the wage and salary bill, and payments to the Banks. The enterprise is *not* required to repay fixed capital. Instead, the State appropriates the net income of enterprises in the form of sales taxes and profit levies. Tax and profit rates vary by commodity. The tax rate for an industry is usually fixed at a level that will enable the *least efficient* to pay. Thus the least efficient enterprises will not make significant profits after tax has been paid; the most modern plants, on the other hand, will be

Figure 7: *Financial flow through an industrial enterprise*

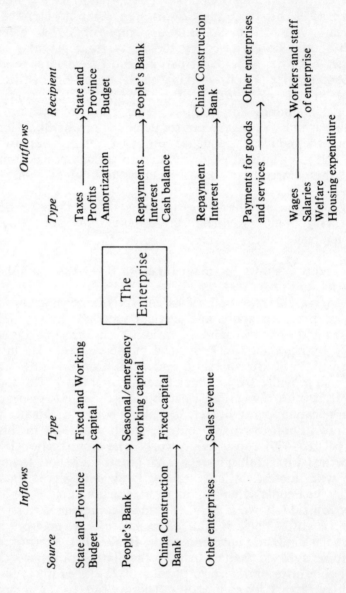

Inflows				*Outflows*	
Source	*Type*			*Type*	*Recipient*
State and Province Budget	Fixed and Working capital			Taxes Profits Amortization	State and Province Budget
People's Bank	Seasonal/emergency working capital			Repayments Interest Cash balance	People's Bank
China Construction Bank	Fixed capital	The Enterprise		Repayment Interest	China Construction Bank
Other enterprises	Sales revenue			Payments for goods and services	Other enterprises
				Wages Salaries Welfare Housing expenditure	Workers and staff of enterprise

Note: Some welfare and housing expenditure will benefit workers and staff indirectly.

expected to make large post-tax profits, which will then be taken by the State. It is also usual to allow enterprises to make 'surplus' profits, i.e. profits in excess of those stipulated in the official plan. These profits are divided between the central and local authorities, and, since some benefits from local spending may directly benefit the enterprise, this provides an incentive for enterprises to make profits.[5]

Although the system seems simple in principle, there are differences between the official accounts of it and what we know of enterprise practice from other sources. For example, official reports emphasize that *all* profits are handed over to either local or central authorities, yet we know that most enterprises have a margin of discretion over their revenues. This arises either because they *are* allowed to retain a small share of their profits if they do well, or because they can in practice spend on minor items of capital expenditure, on welfare facilities, or on other items *before* handing over profits. It may be that both loopholes operate. In any event, the evidence of the past twenty-six years is that spending in enterprises is more flexible and less controlled than one would expect from reading official regulations and textbooks, or from the reports of visitors.

Labour Enterprises are required to work closely with Provincial and Municipal Labour Bureaux. At one time these Bureaux were controlled by a Ministry of Labour in Peking. The Ministry was abolished during the Cultural Revolution and its work is now undertaken by officials in the State Planning Commission. The work of the Labour Bureaux includes investigating the local labour supply; ensuring that enterprises obtain their labour from approved sources; and checking that enterprises administer their labour in accordance with local and central labour regulations.[6]

Payment of wages and salaries in enterprises is in accordance with scales that reflect variations in the technical difficulty and unpleasantness of the job done, and variations in the skill and other qualities of individual workers. Workers' earnings are also influenced by bonuses, penalties, overtime, and other special payments.

In addition to cash, enterprises can provide their staff with other benefits. Some of these, such as canteen, medical and crèche facilities, are available equally to all. Others, including time off, holidays in special centres, and housing, are distributed unevenly. To some extent distribution is influenced by need and humanitarian factors, but, not surprisingly, we know that many enterprise managers manipulate the total range of incentives and rewards to ensure that their workers are compliant and work as efficiently as possible.

The People's Commune

The People's Commune is the name given to China's collective farms. Started in 1958, the Communes are the lowest level of government and thus have political and administrative as well as economic functions. *Communes* are made up of *Households*, which average about five persons; *Teams* of from fifteen to fifty Households; and *Brigades*, of eight to twelve Teams.

The relative importance of each of these levels, i.e. Household, Team, Brigade, and Commune, has varied. At first, ownership of land and other assets, and nearly all management power, were concentrated in the Commune. Later, in the Great Depression, power slipped down to the Team and in many areas even to the Household. In this period Teams and Households were responsible for meeting State demands and for planning day-to-day work. In the past fifteen years the system has stabilized in such a way that the Team has emerged as the unit on which the Commune pivots.[7]

These shifts have been accompanied by changes in the number and average size of Communes. In 1958 there were 24,000 Communes. In the mid-1960s there were 72,000. Currently there are about 50,000 units. These changes imply that the average size of Communes has varied between 7,000 and 20,000 persons. The *timing* of the changes suggests that Commune size varies with the changing importance of the different levels within the Commune. When power goes down to the lower levels, Communes split and shrink; when it rises, they amalgamate and grow.

The main objects in the collectivization of agriculture and the creation of the Communes were as follows:
(a) to obtain the benefits of large-scale organization—in particular to develop ways of organizing peasant households to undertake rural works which they would not do if they remained individual cultivators;
(b) to create a framework for the expansion of education, and for the dissemination of new techniques and new attitudes to farming practice;
(c) to establish a system by which the State could determine how land is used;
(d) to facilitate the acquisition by the State of whatever agricultural output was necessary to feed the urban population, supply industry, and increase exports.

The fundamental difficulty with the system has been that, if used to put excessive pressure on the peasants to increase and hand over more output, it lowers the incentive to work and encourages malpractices. These defeat the system's basic objectives. Also, centralized control of agriculture means that serious planning *errors* have widespread effects. This was vividly illustrated in 1958 when ill-advised water control work subsequently caused waterlogging, flooding and salinization from which it took years to recover.

Let us now consider the operation of the Commune in more detail. To avoid too much abstraction, most of the numerical data in the following account draws on information given to me in November 1974 when I visited Ch'un Hua Commune in Hunan Province with a party of scholars. Although Ch'un Hua was obviously a successful Commune, it owed much of its wealth to irrigation and to clever diversification into fruit, tree farming, and other activities; thus its character was quite different from that of the large, mechanized, frequently visited Communes found in the neighbourhood of cities.

The Team The average Team in Ch'un Hua has 37 Households. The Team owns land, draught animals, and small items of agricultural machinery. Leadership is vested in the Team leader and a small elected committee. All the members of the committee continue to work as regular Team members.

The Team's production plan consists of targets for the main and subsidiary crops. These are handed down by the Brigade, which receives them from the Commune, which itself receives draft plans and orders from Planning and Purchasing agencies in the Provincial capital. Plans for the major commodities—grain, cotton and oil-bearing crops—are made in terms both of the quantity required, and of the area of the land to be allocated to production. There is some scope for the Team to question the feasibility of targets assigned to it, but not much.

Within the limits set by the plan, the organization of the Team's resources is largely an internal matter. There are plans for sowing, weeding, harvesting, use of draught animals, manuring, etc. In many cases Teams have traditions that govern the allocation of duties to different Households and change these only slightly from year to year.

The current system of payment within the Team is a form of piecework. It operates as follows. Each agricultural task has an agreed quota of 'work points', say 200 points for weeding a given field. At the end of the day the work points earned by each peasant are recorded by the Team Accountant. Downward adjustments will be made if the work has not reached the proper standard. Work points are also awarded for special types of work such as attending meetings or working on State projects, and also for contributing nightsoil for collective use. At the end of the year the total work points earned by each peasant represent a claim on *part* of the Team's total income. This total income is calculated after the harvest. It consists of cash earned from sales during the year, and kind (mainly grain) still in store. For accounting purposes the value of grain and goods in store is calculated at official prices. When the total income is known it is allocated in the following steps:

(1)   Payment is made of the Team's share of the Agricultural Tax. (At Ch'un Hua the Commune's tax accounted for 9 per cent of grain output, and 5 per cent of the value of all forms of agricultural output.)

(2)   The Team's quota of compulsorily purchased grain is handed over and paid for by the State at 0.195 *yuan* per kg.

(3)   Working capital for the following year is set aside.

(4)   Funds for purchasing agricultural equipment are set aside.

(5)   Grain is added to store. (In a bad year grain will be drawn out of store.)

(6)   A contribution is made to the Welfare Fund.

(7)   The balance—usually 40 per cent to 50 per cent of total income—is available for personal income. If the value of this balance is, for example, 8,000 *yuan*, and the total work points earned by all Team members is 100,000, then the value of a work point for that year will be 8 cents. (In Ch'un Hua, the 1974 work point was actually worth 7 cents.)

According to accountancy handbooks, once these figures are known the final allocation to Households proceeds as follows:

During the year everyone will have received a 'basic' allowance of grain. (This is reported to be 137.5 kg of unhusked grain per annum.) In addition, peasants who work in the fields receive 'attendance grain' which on average is likely to bring the annual consumption of male working peasants up to around 300 kg—the precise amount depending on local variations in agricultural productivity. The total consumption of each Household (workers and non-workers) is recorded, grain consumed being priced at 0.196 *yuan* per kilogram. At the year-end reckoning this consumption, together with any cash advances received, will be *deducted* from the value of the work points earned by Household members.

Under this system, Households with few or weak workers sometimes find that they have not earned enough to pay for all the grain that they have consumed. In such cases supplies of 'basic grain' will continue, but the debt will be carried forward—possibly until a younger generation, who can earn enough to settle the account with the Team, has grown up. What we have here, therefore, is a social security arrangement in which the Team as a whole carries its weakest members when necessary.

Households which earn much more than is necessary to pay for their consumption and advances during the previous year are allowed to take some of their surplus income in grain, and the rest in cash. The reason for rationing the amount taken in grain is that grain taken in this way is priced at 0.196 *yuan* per kg, while the price of grain in some rural markets is reported to be 0.4 to 0.6 *yuan* per kg. Thus, unless stopped, Households would take far more grain than they needed and sell it privately. Actually many Households do resell some of the grain they are allowed, but by imposing limits on this the Government is able to purchase most of the grain that is left over after taxes, compulsory purchases, and rural rations are allowed for. When the Team sells this 'surplus' grain, it is paid one-third more than the price paid for grain acquired through compulsory purchase.[8]

The reader will note that under this method of distributing income peasants do not know in advance what they will earn from doing a particular job. One reason for this is that the value of the work points earned from a job will depend on the Team's total income, which in turn will depend on the collective effort and on the weather. Another reason is that peasants cannot know in advance how much of the Team's income will be allocated to personal income. The uncertainty due to weather is unavoidable. But in order to ensure that the peasants can calculate ahead, and do see a link between effort and reward, experience has shown that Teams must be small enough to ensure that individual effort is not diluted by idleness and lack of skill of others; and that allocation under heads 1 to 6 is not too large, or allowed to vary arbitrarily from one year to the next.[9]

The implications of this system can be appreciated only in relation to the operation of the peasants' private plots and to other private economic activities with which peasant incomes are supplemented. The plots account for up to 7 per cent of the cultivated area. They are used to grow vegetables, grain, and other staples such as sugar cane (in the South). Most of the plot's output is consumed by the peasants, fed to the pigs and poultry that are being privately raised, or sold in rural markets. The exact list of products that may be sold has varied. In general, restrictions are greater now than they were in the early 1960s, but from the evidence of informants we know that there are considerable regional variations in the rules governing this matter.

The value of work on the plots at the present time is hard to measure. It is believed that the plots account for 35 per cent of China's vegetable output, and in 1958 it was reported in some areas that private income accounted for 60 per cent to 70 per cent of total peasant incomes. It is doubtful whether the latter situation exists anywhere today, but there is no doubt that the plot offers substantial and relatively predictable rewards and that even in the mid-1970s, private economic activities probably accounted for 20 per cent of peasant labour time and earned about 30 per cent of their incomes. Thus, if the peasants are unhappy about treatment in the collective sector, it is not surprising that they switch their efforts to the plot and private occupations at the expense of the planned economy.

The Brigade At Ch'un Hua there are 14 Brigades, each made up of six or seven Teams. The role of the Brigade is rather shadowy. Led by a Revolutionary Committee, it acts as a planning intermediary and organizes rural enterprises considered beyond the scope of the Team. At Ch'un Hua, Brigade enterprises include rice husking, cotton ginning, and vegetable oil extraction. The Brigades charge the Teams for work done and, after a share of profits has been allocated for further investment, the balance is turned over to the Teams in proportion to their contribution of workers to run the Brigade activities. The workers all belong to Teams, and by working for the Brigade they earn work points that constitute a claim on the Team's income, as described in the previous section.

Apart from drawing on profits, the Brigade can obtain loans, and use all these financial resources for investment projects. These projects include the establishment of new and bigger enterprises, the acquisition of agricultural machinery, land improvement, or reclamation and water conservancy work which exceed the resources of the Teams. It has been reported that the allocation of help to Teams is often made on the principle of helping those that are relatively poor and backward.

The quality of the relationship between Brigades and Teams depends on two factors: one is the extent to which the Brigades make profits that are ploughed back into investment rather than being distributed to the Team to form part of its income; the other is the extent to which Brigades call on the Teams to provide labour for projects that do not have fairly immediate and tangible benefits. In short, if Brigades suck resources out of the Teams without providing tangible benefits in return, then tensions arise. If, on the other hand, Team-Brigade relations are mutually advantageous, then the system provides an ingenious framework for combining large- and small-scale activities.

The Commune The Commune is run by a Revolutionary Committee and a Party Committee. Its functions include overall responsibility for planning and the execution of large-scale projects. Like the Brigade it obtains income from profits earned in its enterprises. At Ch'un Hua, Commune enterprises include a machinery repair shop, a brick-making complex, and a unit for the provision of electrical services. Relations between Commune and lower levels parallel those between Brigade and Team, except that workers in Commune industry, like city workers, earn regular wages.

A Commune may be called upon to provide manpower and resources for Province- or Region-based projects. A famous example of this was the project to control the Haiho river in Hopei and Shantung Provinces. In this case the project headquarters:

allocated the number of people needed to 80 odd Counties. Each County organized a 'peasant-worker' regiment, recruiting its quota from its People's Communes, Production Bridges and Production Teams . . . this meant sending only two or three members from each Team to the worksite every year.

This system mobilized five million persons in a ten-year period. In the early stages the State provided payment to the workers on site; later the burden was borne by the Communes, Brigades, and Teams themselves.[10]

Thus the Commune is the highest level in one organization, yet an intermediate point in a hierarchy that stretches from State down to the Household. This hierarchy is organized to provide the incentives and sanctions necessary to secure the State's requirements from the agricultural economy. Up to now this has involved leaving considerable initiative at the level of the Team and Household. Thus, in spite of the revolution in agricultural organization, the family and the village remain important.

Since 1975 there has been a renewed effort to expand the role of the higher levels—especially that of the Brigade—by expanding their share of total income and assets. This campaign has been accompanied by pressure on 'sideline' and semi-private activities. The movement can only be interpreted as an effort to obtain greater control over agricultural resources, and it must reflect problems created by lack of agricultural growth—in particular the difficulty of persuading Teams to make investments in land reclamation and mechanization.

HOW ECONOMIC PLANS ARE MADE AND WHAT IS INCLUDED IN THEM

Frequency

The Chinese have long-, medium-, and short-term plans. *Long-term* plans embody thinking and aspirations about the general shape and size of the future economy. In 1952 the horizon for long-term plans was 1967, this being the limit of plans for Soviet economic aid by which the future at that time was determined. Subsequently Mao spoke of the 'several Five Year Plans' and of the 'hundred years or longer' needed to complete China's economic modernization. More recently, in January 1975, Chou En-lai's speech to the National People's Congress included statements that by 1980 China will have built 'an independent and relatively comprehensive industrial and economic system', and that 'by the end of the century there will be a comprehensive modernization of agriculture, industry, national defence, science and technology, so that our national economy will be in the front ranks of the world.' In the same speech Chou also reported that the State Council would be drawing up Ten Year, Five Year, and Annual economic plans,[11] and reports from China in the mid-1970s have confirmed that these three types of plan are all in existence. Long-term plans embrace either the whole economy or specific industries or sectors. No long-term industrial plan is known, but the most famous plan for a sector is the *Twelve Year Programme for the Development of Agriculture* published in January 1956. This plan was inspired and largely drafted by Mao and, since many Provinces have not fulfilled its targets, it is still often referred to today.[12]

In practice, the Five Year Plan is the principal *medium-term* plan. Two such plans have been published. The *First Five Year Plan* (for 1953 to 1957) was published in mid-1955. It was book-length in detail and largely fulfilled.[13] The *Second Five Year Plan* (for 1958 to 1962) was published twice in outline, but its targets and assumptions were overtaken by the Great Leap Forward and the Great Depression which followed. An unpublished *Third Five Year Plan* was reported for 1966-70, and Chou's 1980 targets were said to represent the end of the Fifth Plan.

For practical purposes the important plan is annual. In most enterprises this is divided into half-yearly, quarterly, monthly, and ten-day plans. Preparation of the annual plan begins in the autumn preceding the plan year, and final targets are sometimes not available until the following spring. By working on an annual basis the authorities are able to take account of the previous year's harvest and of changes in the international trading situation. Because China is still so dependent on the fluctuating performance of agriculture, this system is more satisfactory than one requiring public long-term commitments that can easily turn out to be unrealistic. However awkward for foreign observers, the current practice of not publicizing the details of plans has the advantage that under-fulfilment is not politically embarrassing.

Degrees of urgency

According to a secret document circulated in 1958 *(The Sixty Work Methods)* some plans have *three* variants—each of a different degree of ambitiousness. In order, starting from the least ambitious plan, these are:
(a) a 'published', Central plan that 'must' be accomplished;
(b) a secret plan that the Centre 'expects' to be accomplished;
(c) a further, secret plan, that the local authorities 'expect' to be accomplished.[14]

Whether this threefold system is still widespread is unclear. But if it is operated, even in modest form, it confirms that planning in China is a flexible affair. For if enterprises are to achieve the more ambitious plans, they *must* also be able to increase their supplies of raw materials and other resources. This implies that the economy must be capable of accommodating itself to a series of readjustments, rather than being tied to rigid targets.

Content

Almost all physical *commodities* produced in China enter into a plan of some sort. Important raw materials and commodities are planned by the Central authorities. In the case of agriculture, Central plans include foodgrains, vegetable oils, and crops that go to industry as raw materials. We have no full list of the industrial goods that are centrally allocated. Most observers think that the list includes all raw materials and capital goods—including transport equipment and tractors. Important consumer goods are also on the Central list.

Goods not centrally allocated either fall within the Provincial plan, or are controlled by localized agreements. Provincial plans include the less important commodities and, like Central plans, provide limits within which producing and purchasing organizations make contracts. Localized agreements are confined to commodities that would, under any system, be consumed near their point of production—for example, perishable agricultural products. Quite outside the plans are goods sold through small rural markets.

The *prices* at which centrally planned goods exchange are listed in official price books and change relatively infrequently. Unfortunately we have no detailed information about prices since the early 1950s, although we know that changes have taken place and we have some interesting fragments about individual commodities. The prices of provincially planned commodities are also controlled, but in a more flexible way. Locally controlled commodities have prices negotiated between the parties, i.e. they are designated in contracts between Communes and purchasing organizations. Most prices in rural markets are uncontrolled.[15] Overall responsibility for prices has been reported as being vested in a National Price Commission and special bureaux are responsible for local pricing.

The material balance table The controlling calculation in the national plan is a table of 'material balances'. The procedure for constructing this is as follows. First, an initial list of demand and supply for each centrally controlled commodity is drawn up for *each Province* and for the three Sub-Central Cities. At this stage the only demand considered is demand by enterprises that are at least partly under Central control. Plans are then adjusted and arrangements for exchanges between Provinces made so that demand and supply match. If the total demand for a particular commodity exceeds supply, the deficit may be imported, although officials always emphasize that this is a last resort.

This procedure is a version of Soviet practice. It was developed during the 1950s and, according to Mao, broke down completely during the Great Leap Forward. In 1959 he reported that:

The State Planning Commission and the Central Ministries have carried on for ten years. Suddenly, at a meeting at Peitaiho, they gave up. They called it planned directives which is equal to no planning. The so-called not taking care of planning means rejecting comprehensive balancing, with absolutely no calculation as to the amounts of coal, iron and communication required. The coal and iron cannot travel by themselves, they must be transported by carriages. This is what I did not foresee . . . I do not understand industrial planning.[16]

Planning by balances was gradually restored during the 1960s, but today the procedure is more flexible than it used to be. The Central table now provides broad limits for all kinds of transactions, and detailed plans are fixed at annual or semi-annual conferences, in which firm commitments are made. These commitments are then translated into Provincial and Municipal plans, and into plans for enterprises and Communes.

The system is less complex than it sounds because year-to-year changes are usually marginal. Thus, once the network of production and exchange has been set up, planning is largely a matter of small adjustments and appropriate expansion. The incremental character of planning explains why economic administration can exhibit great resilience during political upheavals. In a crisis, the previous year's arrangements are carried forward for a further period without change.

The use of ideological and political techniques of control

So far the plans discussed have been capable of precise numerical form- ulation. In its wider sense, Chinese planning involves the management of economic decisions and activities that cannot be predicted or defined so precisely. Planning is also concerned with the principles and with the human attitudes that determine economic behaviour, monitoring and control of which are considered inseparable from the control of the economy. Many of the principles inculcated into the population are statements by Mao; some are enshrined in the Constitution. An example of those principles is Mao's slogan: 'Take grain as the key link and ensure all-round development.' This sounds very general; nonetheless, its practical implications are spelt out in newspaper articles and interpreted by cadres and peasants all the time. Statements such as this, and the organization of pressures to implement them, are therefore as much a part of economic planning as a detailed plan target. To some extent this sort of control is an effort to avoid the inefficiencies that arise in any planned economy where—as Russian experience shows—determined people can always circumvent the rules and targets, however numerous these may be. It is also an effort to plan, in a country where backwardness, poor physical communications, and local differences all make formal administration difficult. In such an economy the moulding of unsupervised behaviour has to supplement and replace conventional planning.

The division of power between Central and local authorities

One of the most vexing problems besetting an understanding of Chinese planning is the locating of power and initiative. Opinions on this vary very much. According to the Constitution: 'the State applies the principle of . . . bringing the initiatives of both the central and local authorities into full play.' And according to the *Sixty Work Methods*: 'the immeasurable power is monopolized but the lesser power dispersed.' Other Chinese documents, and visitors' reports, are equally ambiguous. Some visitors claim that the main thrust is from local units and planning bodies; others argue that the system is highly centralized in terms of both power and initiative; a small number admit frankly that the situation is unclear.

If we move from statements of principle to actual behaviour, some definite facts emerge. If we try to define the planning role of the local authorities, for example, we have already seen that there are a number of commodities whose output and pricing are almost entirely a Provincial responsibility, and that the Provinces also play some part in the allocation and pricing of centrally controlled commodities. According to reports, material allocation meetings in particular are lively affairs at which the parties press their interests with vigour and ingenuity. Local bodies also play an important role as *coordinators,* for example in the organization of the labour force.

Although this much is clear, there are three areas within which central-local relations are more problematic. One of these is finance, which is discussed separately below. The others are the control of industrial enterprises, and the control of investment.

In the 1950's Central Ministries had direct control over all the important enterprises in the economy. In theory, Ministries were required to discuss the plans for their enterprises with local authorities, but in practice they were always pressed for time and were able to act largely without reference to the local consequences of their plans. The system thus worked to the detriment of locally controlled enterprises which had to yield to the prior claims of the big enterprises in everything. This planning was known as the 'dual track' method. It was never satisfactory and it disappeared between 1956 and 1958. By the end of 1958 it was reported that 80 per cent of all industrial enterprises had been handed over to local control, and local planners were also given powers to coordinate the centrally controlled sector.

In the mid-1960s it was estimated that centrally controlled enterprises accounted for about 10 per cent of the workforce and 30 per cent of industrial output. Recent visitors, however, report that even the largest enterprises are now under *some form* of joint, Central-local control. According to the most authoritative of these reports the situation appears to be that *all* enterprises are indeed formally subject to a degree of Provincial control, but that the plans of enterprises which are large, and which produce output that is centrally allocated, are determined by ministries at the Centre. Central control over the economy is also secured by control over investment and the allocation of skilled labour, important raw materials and capital equipment.

Control of investment is particularly important. There is indeed some discretion for enterprises, Communes, and local planning agencies to invest. But the evidence suggests that all major investment proposals are decided in Peking. Thus, wherever the precise initiative for planning the *existing capacity* of the economy lies, the nature and location of *future* development is a central decision.

The budget

China's budgetary and banking systems are designed to ensure that economic plans (made largely in physical terms) can be carried out. The job of these systems is to provide whatever finance is required by the production plan agreed for individual units in the economy. The fiscal and monetary authorities must also ensure that, overall, private expenditure for consumption goods equals the supply of goods at current prices. Year-to-year fluctuations in the economy and regional variations of many kinds make it necessary to handle these tasks in a flexible way.[17]

Almost everyone in China is involved in budgetary procedures of one kind or another. The smallest budgets are those made by individual units including industrial enterprises and Communes. The national budget, however, is composed of all the budgets made at the County, Municipality, Township, and Province levels of administration, plus the budgets of the Sub-Central cities.

The Central budget draws direct revenue from customs receipts, from the revenues of the transport system, and from centrally controlled industrial enterprises. In the past the Centre also raised money by loans from the public, but the last of these were paid off in 1968 and seem unlikely to be resorted to again. The Central budget draws indirect revenue through the Provincial budgets, which obtain income from many sources. These include the salt tax, the agricultural tax, the revenues of industrial enterprises, and industrial and commercial taxes. These taxes are collected by the Provinces and shared between the Province and the Centre. Certain minor taxes such as the vehicle, amusement, and slaughter taxes are collected and wholly retained at the Province level. There is no personal income tax in China.

Income drawn directly into the Central budget accounts only for 10 per cent of the total. The balance comes through the Provincial budgets. Within this balance, 40 per cent of income is from the profits of State enterprises under local management and a further 40 per cent from taxes on goods. These taxes are levied at varying rates and visitors' reports of these conflict somewhat. In general, rates are zero or low on necessities and capital goods. For example, pig iron, steel billets, fertilizers, machinery, cheap cloth, and coal briquettes are charged between 5 per cent and 20 per cent. Higher rates are charged for watches, bicycles, and luxury consumer goods, and at least 60 per cent is charged on cigarettes and grain alcohol. Direct tax on agricultural output is very low. Since profits also tend to vary in the same way as taxes, i.e. they are high on luxuries and low on necessities, the effect of the system is to produce a pattern of *prices* that enables the fiscal system to squeeze as much of its revenue as possible by high exactions on inessentials.[18]

From a Western point of view, perhaps the most unusual feature of the Chinese fiscal system is that although the Central budget balances income and expenditure in a very conservative way, Provincial budgets have surpluses and deficits. The effect of this is to transfer resources *between* Provinces.

The pattern of transfers between Provinces is imposed by the Government through its control of spending. The procedure is that each year Provinces draw up an estimate of the money they will need for administration, salaries, and social expenditure. They also make a 'bid' to spend on major investment projects including housing and urban construction. When the expenditure pattern is agreed, the Government fixes the Provincial contribution to the Central budget at a level that enables agreed expenditure to be paid for, and, if necessary, also pays out subsidies.

In practice, the biggest revenue burdens fall on the rich Provinces and cities, while the poorest areas receive net subsidies. A remarkable aspect of this redistribution is the immense subsidy that the city of Shanghai provides to the rest of the Chinese economy. During the First Five Year Plan, for example, Shanghai provided revenue sufficient to finance 20 per cent of total Government expenditure! This burden seems to be still growing, since, whereas in 1959 the city was reported to be remitting 76 per cent of its income to Peking, in 1972 the figure was reported as being 90 per cent. During this period the city's contribution in cash terms must have tripled.[19]

One point that is not clear is what happens to savings made at local levels which result in Provinces having a larger net income than had been forecast. For many years these unplanned surpluses had to be surrendered, but one report claims that since 1972 they have been retained by the Provinces.

Banking

One day China may become a moneyless Utopia. At present, money still plays a role in the economy, described officially as 'an indispensable medium in daily life'.[20] Like the fiscal system, the monetary system is 'passive', in the sense that the purpose of banking activity is to make sure that a pre-set plan for the output of the economy is fulfilled. Thus, whereas the authorities in a Western economy control the supply of money and allow the banks to allocate this among competing customers as they choose, in China financial support is given to enterprises only in so far as is necessary to ensure that their plans are fulfilled.[21]

The organization responsible for domestic banking services is the People's Bank of China. The Bank has 10,000 branches and many thousands of sub-offices; these are located in factories, shops, and other places of convenience to the public. At Province, Municipality, and County levels, the Bank has offices that work with local economic planning agencies.

The Bank receives deposits from State enterprises and other organizations, all of which are required to hold their balances and do monetary transactions through it. Private individuals also have accounts. These are secret, interest bearing, and may be transmitted to heirs.

The Bank has two main functions: the provision of credit to enterprises and agricultural units, and the mobilization of resources for investment. For industrial enterprises, the Bank provides the credit needed to meet seasonal or temporary cash problems. (Normal working capital is allocated directly by the State.) The maximum period for loans is one year and, in 1972, interest was charged at an annual rate of 5.04 per cent. Agriculture also benefits from short-term loans, which in 1972 were reported to be made at 4.32 per cent. However, whereas industry gets grants for capital spending from the State Budget as a 'gift', agricultural investment is partly financed by *loans* from the People's Bank. These are available for up to five years at 2.16 per cent interest per annum.

An important aspect of these loans is that, since they are given to facilitate plans, verification of proper use requires the Bank to become intimately acquainted with the activities of borrowers. This has made the Bank a key institution in the control of the economy. Planning agencies at the local level cannot continuously monitor financial performance, but, if necessary, the Bank does precisely this. Some remarkable manifestations of Bank power occurred during the Cultural Revolution. When Red Guards took over industrial enterprises they found that although they could implement all sorts of changes, in financial matters they were completely bound by the refusal of the Banks to violate regulations.

The other side of the Bank's work—mobilizing savings—brings it into daily contact with the public. The scarcity of capital in China requires the State to use every means to draw in resources for investment. As shown earlier, the Government's main sources of finance are the tax and profit levies on State enterprises; nonetheless, every cent of *voluntary* saving obtained from the public is important too. In the 1950s there were schemes for compulsory private savings, but today, although propaganda to increase savings is strong, private saving through the Bank is voluntary. The level of such saving therefore depends on the attractiveness of the Bank's terms and services. By current Western standards, interest rates (2.16 per cent for current and 3.24 per cent for deposit accounts) seem low. But alternative outlets for savings are few, and interest, like personal income, is tax free.

HOW PLANS ARE TRANSMITTED AND THEIR FULFILMENT ENSURED

Bureaucracy and politics

The basic procedures and institutions of planning have now been outlined. We need, finally, to know something of the methods by which plans are transmitted and monitored, and the sanctions and incentives used to make people fulfil them.

A great deal of planning is bureaucratic and legalistic in character, and this is reflected in the way plans are transmitted and monitored. For transmission either of information or of instructions, the planners use at least six different types of document. These range from those designated as 'laws' to those designated as 'suggestions'. Between are a mass of 'methods', 'regulations', and 'notifications' circulated by banks, ministries, and local agencies. Some documents are authoritative only in specific places, but are circulated more widely for information; others are national. Some are described as being in 'draft' or 'trial' form; others are 'fixed'. All the documents in this complex assortment are circulated through specified routes, numbered, filed, and acknowledged. A reverse flow of documents includes the work reports and statistical returns by which performance is evaluated.[22]

The rigidity of the rules surrounding this kind of paperwork is illustrated by widely publicized problems of access to documents. In the 1950s, for example, press reports discussed complaints of officials who were denied access to documents because they were not Party members. More recently informants have told us that, because promotions have been frozen for many years, a point was reached in the early 1970s where a cadre ranked, say, eighteenth in the 24 grade system, would actually be doing higher, grade 12 or 13 work, but would find it impossible to work properly because he would still be allowed access only to the documentation classified as appropriate for the lower grade.

Planners' paperwork is supplemented by telephone calls, by personal visits, and by meetings. The development of the telephone in the late 1950s transformed opportunities for communication, although informants report that some statistics are regarded as so confidential that they are spoken of in code! Oksenberg has identified no less than seven major types of meetings. The Chinese names for these include 'work conferences', 'specialist meetings', 'transmission meetings', 'exchange experience meetings', and 'report back meetings'. Such meetings may be held at the national level, or at any lower level down to that of the smallest unit. They are used to exhort, explain, inform, obtain feedback, and to work out the practical methods of implementing specific policies.

To some extent meetings, telephone conversations, and paperwork go together. But on occasion, meetings and telephone calls are used to transmit information and orders considered too sensitive for written form.

A device that plays an important role in enabling the planners to obtain factual information is the 'investigation'. Routine reports and statistics provide some information for higher levels, but they may not tell the whole story, or they may be falsified. If trouble is suspected, an 'investigation' is ordered. These are usually, but not always, open. The most famous secret investigations of recent years were those undertaken by Wang Kwang-mei, the wife of Liu Shao-ch'i. Wang visited the countryside incognito where, aided by Public Security officers, she uncovered corruption and illegal activities. In one case, her investigation culminated in the violent death of a local villain on a high voltage electric wire.[23]

A recent example of an open investigation occurred in Kwangsi Province in February 1974. This was prompted by a letter written by a female worker and sent to the Party Branch of an agricultural machinery repair works. This complained that over five years the management had increased its staff from 6 to 39. This was contrary to official policy, which is to minimize 'non-productive' staff. The letter eventually found its way to the Party authorities at the County level, who sent down an 'investigation team'. The team's report confirmed the allegations which were described as 'totally in line with the facts'. The report, together with the original letter, was then published in *The Kwangsi Daily*.[24]

This incident illustrates three points: it shows that the control of economic units is not simply a matter of verifying the fulfilment of quantitative targets; it brings out the role of the Party (which bypassed the normal channels, initiated and undertook the investigation); and it provides an example of how a model case is publicized in the media to warn and instruct other units. The Chinese press is full of incidents of this kind, all revealing the same mixture of politics and administration.

On occasion, political intervention in the economy is at a much higher level, and takes rather indirect forms. For example, if the Prime Minister appears at a forum of specialists and urges family planning, or if the Party Chairman writes to a Commune to congratulate it on its development of public pig farming, officials all over China take note and modify their work accordingly.

One of the most interesting and lengthy interventions of this kind was the journey round China of Chen Yung-kuei. Chen became famous as the leader of the Tachai Brigade in a Commune in North-West China. This Brigade transformed the productivity of its land by ingenious and back-breaking terracing, and by water-control work. Chen has now left Tachai and is a member of the Central Committee of the Party. During 1973 and 1974 he travelled throughout China, and a typical visit was the one he made to Hupei Province in December 1973. Chen spent five days in Hupei, during which time 'he gave many important instructions' (instructions that would have had the authority of Mao and the Central Committee); he addressed a congress of senior Party officials; he made an important speech to regional and County Party secretaries; and he also found time to visit China's second most important steel plant at Wuhan, 'to inspect and give guidance'.

In addition to briefing the leadership, one of Chen's speeches was relayed to four million listeners by radio, and *The Hupei Daily* carried articles and reports of the meetings. The main purpose of Chen's tours seems to have been to emphasize the implementation of the principle of 'more work more pay' and to warn local leaders of the dangers of pressing the peasants too hard. He may also have been transmitting secret policy briefs from the Central Committee.[25]

Economic incentives

In so far as the economy is controlled by bureaucratic and political action, the penalties for disobedience are criticism, demotion, and penalties specified in written regulations. In addition, the planners can to a certain extent rely on sensations of guilt or shame experienced by those whose unplanned actions conflict with the collective, socialist good. These are powerful weapons. Criticism, for example, usually takes place at 'struggle' meetings where ritualized hysteria is unleashed and physical violence may occur. In one such case, 'the Brigade Party Branch First Secretary was continuously struggled against by members of the work team (who operated in shifts) for more than three days. The end came only when the Secretary collapsed from exhaustion . . . '[26] Demotion, too, even without violence of any kind, can have traumatic personal consequences. Other sanctions include consignment to State farms in remote parts of China. Despite the availability of these weapons, the leadership still makes use of economic incentives — incentives that make obedience to plans materially beneficial.[27]

Under capitalism, economic incentives work through the price system. As demand for goods and services changes, so do their relative prices and thereby the rewards for producing them. Earlier, I emphasized that Chinese plans are set mainly in physical terms. Does this leave any role for prices, profits, or variations in personal income?

On prices, some visitors accept the view (frequently asserted by officials) that they have no role whatever. But it is more accurate to say that the importance of prices varies from time to time and from sector to sector — subject to Mao's general principle, 'with us, plans are primary and prices are secondary.'[28]

The sector where prices are very important is agriculture. Since the Great Depression, prices have been used both to increase the general level of incomes in the agricultural sector, and to encourage the production of particular agricultural commodities. Incomes have been increased by raising the prices paid to peasants for commodities they sell and by lowering the cost of the consumer goods, agricultural machinery, tools, fertilizers, etc. which they buy. Reports in the 1970s suggest that while purchasing prices for peasants' produce had risen 60 per cent since 1952, prices for industrial goods purchased by the peasants had risen only 20 per cent. A more detailed illustration of this is a recent account of the work of a People's Commune in Hopei Province which reported that while the average price of three types of fertilizer between 1961 and 1971-73 fell 25 per cent and prices of Walking Tractors and East is Red 28hp tractors declined by 52 per cent and 50 per cent, there was a 29 per cent rise in the purchase price of wheat over thirteen years and an even larger increase for cotton producers.[29]

Prices are also very important in rural markets where the peasants buy and sell a variety of agricultural and handicraft products. As a recent article put it: 'The great majority of our country's commodities' relative prices are fixed by the State, but relative prices in rural markets are largely determined by demand and supply.'[30]

In industry prices change infrequently and there is nothing equivalent to the rural markets. Steel prices, for example, are reported to have been unchanged for twenty years and nearly all statements to visitors emphasize that prices do not influence enterprises in choosing what to produce, and that profits do not influence planners in deciding which projects to invest in. This is broadly credible. There is no legitimate link between enterprise profits and wages and salaries (as there is in the Soviet Union) so that the personal incentive to maximize profits is missing. Nonetheless, enterprises do have some *ability* to improve profitability, and there have been complaints against managers who 'pursue profit rather than plans and the collective good'. These criticisms suggest that, in practice, there may be advantages in being profitable. It may, for example, enable an enterprise to spend more on staff welfare or other non-monetary benefits, and it may encourage further investment in the enterprise. In the latter case, enterprise staff and workers will acquire the many advantages of 'bigness', i.e. higher wage standards, more welfare benefits, and more prestige.

This leaves the problem of ascertaining how far variations in incomes are used as incentives. This topic is discussed in Chapter 6. But it should be stressed at once that they are important. Article Nine of the 1975 Constitution reminds us that: 'The State applies the socialist principle: "he who does not work, neither shall he eat" and "from each according to his ability, to each according to his work". '

Payment systems thoughout the economy reflect this approach. Income variations are substantial and are reflected in consumption. The more you earn, the more you can buy. And good work performance is likely to produce benefits other than cash.

The one major qualification to this is that, unlike capitalists and most other socialists, the Chinese do not use relative incomes to encourage movement *between* jobs. The labour force is allocated to its place of work largely irrespective of individual preferences, and allocation is enforced by control of food and rations. Wages and salaries reflect the difficulty of the job, and how well it is done, *after* the worker is placed in it. [31]

CONCLUSION: CURRENT PROBLEMS

The issue dominating the planning system in the mid-1970s has been the struggle by the Centre to regain control over as much of the economy as possible. As has been demonstrated, strong forces pull the Chinese towards decentralization: the variations that make local cooperation and judgement indispensable, and the danger that dependence on detailed orders from Peking suppresses incentives to work hard and intelligently. These forces led to major changes in China's organization in the late 1950s. The Great Depression of the early 1960s also pushed the economy towards decentralization; for when conditions became really difficult, the Centre had little alternative but to rely on the Provinces, which themselves handed over to Communes, Teams, and even Households.

In some ways the 'costs' of decentralization in the 1960s were not great. In industry, central direction is most important when deciding on the scale and location of major new plants. In such decisions, the interest of the localities and the Centre conflict. Localities each want a share of new initiatives, and therefore favour numerous small-scale projects; while from the national perspective, a small number of large-scale plants may be appropriate. During the 1960s, the economy was still completing and absorbing the Soviet projects started between 1953 and 1959 and there were few resources for new developments.

By the late 1960s this had changed. The economy had recovered to the point where big investment decisions were needed again, and there was growing anxiety over corruption and over the expansion of regional economic power to which decentralization seemed to have led. On corruption, Mao commented in 1964: 'today a Branch secretary can be bribed for a few packs of cigarettes, and there's no telling what one could achieve by marrying one's daughter off to such a person.'[32] Corruption was therefore a target of the Cultural Revolution, which was also aimed straight at local leaders who wanted to create 'independent kingdoms'. Many of the crimes committed by those disgraced in the Cultural Revolution were economic, and they included concealment of Provincial statistics from the Centre, refusal to ship grain to other Provinces and, in one case, plans to violate the State monopoly of foreign trade.[33]

Campaigns to reassert central control of the economy have continued since the Cultural Revolution. Chou En-lai discussed the subject at the Party Congress of September 1973, and the theme of centralization also appeared in the campaign to criticize Lin Piao and Confucius in 1973-75. In this campaign the ancient opponents of Confucius were praised for encouraging farming, for enforcing State control of the economy, and for establishing 'an autocratic system of centralized power'. It is not easy to judge in detail how China's new leaders will move, but the signs so far suggest that the establishment of careful, centralized planning systems will continue to be a major policy objective.

3
Agriculture

'When the Mountains are rocky, the Chinese loosen the
Stones, and make little Walls of them to support the
Terraces; then they level the good Soil, and sow it with
Grain.'

Thomas Astley, *A New General Collection
of Voyages and Travels*

The development of agriculture and the balance between food and
population are China's fundamental economic problems. They are old
ones. The classical histories praise emperors for devotion to agriculture
and much of China's modern history is the story of the unfolding
struggle to feed a peasant population, which has been growing steadily
but has had limited opportunities to migrate abroad or to find a viable
life in the cities.

Today, although agriculture accounts for only a quarter of the
National Product, it is still the main determinant of the standard of
living and the principal occupation of at least 70 per cent of the
population.

Agriculture also determines the progress of industry because
industry needs both agricultural raw materials and food for its
workforce. The failure of agriculture to supply these halted and later
reversed the industrial progress of the 1950s. After 1960 new emphasis
was placed on agriculture, and the slogan 'Agriculture is the
foundation of the economy' has remained a central Chinese economic
policy ever since.

In addition to the direct links between agriculture and industry, there
is an indirect link due to the relationship between agriculture and
foreign trade. Many of China's exports are either agricultural raw
materials or consumer goods based on them. A flourishing agriculture
therefore boosts exports. It also reduces the need to spend foreign
exchange on imports of grain and cotton, thereby enlarging the
capacity of the economy to import machinery and commodities for
industry. Thus, if agriculture performs well, both the level and
composition of trade favour industrial progress. The converse is true if
agriculture is weak.

The first half of this chapter describes the agricultural scene in
China: the regions, the crops, recent trends of agricultural output, and

Table 18: *The agricultural regions of China*

Name	Provinces	Rainfall (mm)	Growing season (months)	Per cent of land cultivated	Crops	Comment
Spring wheat region	N. Hopei, Shensi, Shansi, Kansu, S. Liaoning, Ninghsia, Inner Mongolia	350 (variable)	$6\frac{1}{2}$	18	main crop wheat + millet, potatoes, kaoliang, barley, peas	Sparsely populated
Winter wheat-millet region	Shansi, Shensi, Kansu	430	$7\text{-}7\frac{1}{2}$	22	wheat, millet, cotton, kaoliang	Loess country. Most fertile areas are the valleys of the rivers Fen and Wei
Winter wheat, rice, kaoliang region	Honan, Hopei	600	8	68	wheat, kaoliang, cotton, millet, corn, soya beans	The North China Plain. Considerable rice now grown especially in Honan and some double cropping
Yangtze rice-wheat region	Hupei, Anhwei, Kiangsu	1000	10	35	rice, wheat, cotton, mulberry trees and silk farms	Very rich with many important non-food crops. Increasing multiple cropping
Rice-tea region	Hunan, Kiangsi, Chekiang, Fukien	1500	10-11	18+	rice, tea, rapeseed, mulberry trees	Rich; hilly terrain keeps cultivated area low
Szechuan rice region	Szechuan	1000	11-12	$33\frac{1}{3}$	rice, wheat, corn, rapeseed, sugar cane	Traditionally a big exporter of grain to other regions
Double-cropping rice region	Kwangtung, Kwangsi, Fukien, Kiangsi	1750	12	13	rice, sweet potatoes, sugar cane, fruits	Cultivated land, very productive but many hills and intense population pressure
South-West rice region	Yunnan, Kweichow	1150	12	7	rice, corn, peas, beans, rapeseed	One of the fastest growing regions for grain production since 1949
Soya bean-kaoliang region	Heilungkiang Kirin, Liaoning	500-800	5	16 approx.	wheat, kaoliang, soya beans	An area where new land has been brought into cultivation and rice now grown

the adequacy of these in relation to China's needs and the world situation. The second half of the chapter analyses the ways in which the Chinese are transforming agriculture with new techniques and modern investment.

THE AGRICULTURAL REGIONS

The agricultural scene in China is extremely varied. The main axis of change is a climatic one that runs from North to South. As one moves down this, differences are found in temperature and rainfall, the length of the growing season, the availability of surface water, and in crops and cropping patterns.

Cultivated land is scarce in China. According to an official estimate, the cultivated area is about 10 per cent of the total area of land.[1] An additional 5 per cent of the land area could possibly be brought into cultivation, but most of this is situated in sparsely populated and inaccessible regions of North China, Sinkiang, and Tibet. The main concentrations of cultivated land are in East China, the Manchurian Plain, and in parts of the South and South-Western Provinces.

In general, the productivity of cultivated land rises as one approaches the Eastern seaboard. This variation in the productivity of land is reflected in the distribution of population. So much so that one Chinese geographer calculated that if a line is drawn between the cities of Aigun in the North-East and Tengchung in the South-West, China divides into two regions; one contains 64 per cent of the land area and 4 per cent of the population, and the other, 36 per cent of the area and 96 per cent of the population. Thus, running across the North-South climatic axis, there is an East-West axis of cultivability. These two axes provide the framework of China's agricultural regions.

Within this framework agronomists have identified twelve major agricultural regions. Nine of these are summarized in Table 18. Looking at this, we see that in the North the *growing season* is as short as six and a half months, and *rainfall* as little as 350 mm per annum; while in the South, the growing season can last all year, and rainfall can be as high as 1,750 mm. In some respects these figures understate the relative natural advantages of different areas. In the North China Plain, for example, the problem of water arises not only from the small *size* of the annual fall, but from its *variability*. It is generally thought that if rainfall varies by more than 20 per cent from year to year, stable harvests are impossible. In parts of the North China Plain the variability is 25 per cent to 30 per cent and lack of spring rains has been a frequent cause of crop failure in this densely populated region.

Table 18 shows that, in terms of *crops*, the simplest way to analyse

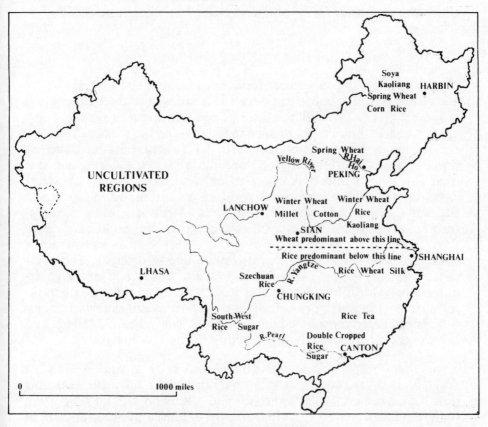

The agricultural regions of China

China's agriculture is to think of the North as a wheat area, the South as a rice area, and the Yangtze valley and Central China as a region that grows both. The table gives only the briefest summary of the crops grown. If the full number of these were taken into account, we should find complicated variations in the patterns of successional planting and interplanting. These patterns are important because changes in the extent to which it is possible to interweave several crops, or obtain multiple harvests of one crop in the agricultural year, are keys to agriculture's productivity. In the North, for example, there are areas where additional wheat and cotton crops are being grown and, despite the cold, there is increasing exploitation of the possibility of growing rice. In the South, where temperature and water availability are so favourable, further development of double and triple cropped rice and many more intensive forms of interplanting have been introduced.

CROPS

Grains　So far, the only staple food crops mentioned have been wheat and rice. The Chinese also grow corn and barley, and three other grain crops, relatively unfamiliar in Europe but important in China. These are the 'coarse' grains—kaoliang and millet—and the sweet potato.

Kaoliang is grown mainly in North China where its resistance to drought makes it a valuable crop since rainfall is low and irregular. It is used for human and livestock feeding, and the long, tough stalks characteristic of its commonest varieties are an important source of fuel and building materials in rural areas.[2] Millet is another drought-resistant crop which, because of its short growing period of three to five months, is not only a main crop but is also sown as an emergency source of food if the main crop is failing due to drought. The sweet potato can be grown in North and South China and although its nutritional value is low, it is an easy and safe crop whose yield (in terms of weight) is very high per unit of land. The virtues of the sweet potato were particularly appreciated during the difficult years of 1960-62, and it is still the subject of widespread popularization campaigns.

Vegetables　Staple foods are supplemented by a wide variety of vegetables, sugar, cotton, and oil bearing crops. Intensive vegetable growing makes a contribution to the Chinese diet out of all proportion to the land allocated to it. As in the Soviet Union, a substantial share of the peasants' private plots is used to grow vegetables, which are cultivated with minute care and lavish application of organic fertilizer. Every scrap of vacant land in and around the cities also has its quota of cabbages, beans, peas, cucumbers, egg plants, peppers, onions, and so on. These plots usually belong to industrial enterprises, schools, and other organizations that grow vegetables for use in their canteens.

Agricultural Communes situated close to cities also specialize in vegetable growing. The evidence suggests that mechanized irrigation, polypropylene covering in the North, and large applications of chemical fertilizer now produce yields upwards of 75 tons per hectare.[3] Thus, compared to other crops, vegetables benefit both from intensive *private* activity and from disproportionate shares of modern fertilizing and irrigation aids supplied in the *public* sector.

Sugar　Sugar is grown in beet and cane form and is a very important crop in the Southern Provinces—especially Kwangtung and Szechuan.

Oils China is a major producer of vegetable oils of which there are eleven important edible varieties. These include oils obtained from soya beans, peanuts, rapeseed, and cottonseed. The most important industrial oils are extracted from the tung tree, castor, perilla, and hemp seeds. An important characteristic of peanuts and soya beans is that they are used as foods as well as being a source of oil. The dominant crop of this group is the soya bean. The Japanese developed Manchurian soya bean potential with great vigour in the 1930s and at one time China accounted for four-fifths of world soya bean output.

Output and yields

Grain Grain in China is defined to include all the major crops such as rice, wheat, corn, millet, and kaoliang. It also includes various beans and peas, potatoes, and soya beans. Grains are measured on an unmilled basis and potatoes are converted to a 'grain equivalent' by dividing their weight by a factor of 4 or, more recently, by a factor of 5. Since the crops included in grain output have different agronomic and nutritional characteristics, changes in the *composition* of output can be as significant as changes in its *level*.

Grain output is one of the most vital and controversial statistics in the Chinese economy. From 1958 to 1971 no official data were issued, and few can accept the official figures for other years without reservation.

The grain data that have appeared since 1971 have been widely accepted; perhaps too widely, since the Chinese have been secretive about important changes in grain accounting conventions, and in 1976 reported to the Food and Agriculture Organization that they could not supply information for the world food programme because China lacked a systematic crop reporting system.[4]

One way of appraising China's grain performance is to interpret the official data on total output. A second way is to make use of data reported at Provincial levels. A third approach is to estimate the output of grain from information about long-run trends in the growth of the 'inputs' that produce it, i.e. new land, capital, and manpower.

The series shown in Table 19 includes estimates calculated on the basis of local data collected by Professor K. R. Walker, and (for recent years) official Chinese data. The only figures which readers may encounter that differ significantly from these are those produced by US Government Departments. Until 1975 these sources tended to put the level of output in the 1960s and 1970s at 20-30 million metric tons lower than those shown here, and to exclude soya beans from their

Table 19: *The output of grain, 1930s-1976*
(million metric tons)

	1930s	1949	1952	1957	1958	1960	1965	1970	1971	1972	1973	1974	1975	1976
a)	170-80	111	161	191	209	153	204	243	250	240	250	275	276	280
b)		111	161	191	206	156	194	243	246	240	266	275	284	285

Notes:
1. Data include soya beans and potatoes. Potatoes are 'converted' to grain at the ratio of 5 to 1.
2. a) is author's series used throughout; b) is new CIA series (Summer 1977) produced too late for complete incorporation in the text.

Sources: Data and discussion are available in T.H. Shen, *Agricultural Resources of China*. Kang Chao, *Agricultural production in Communist China 1949-1965*. US Department of Agriculture, *The Agricultural Situation in the People's Republic of China and Other Communist Asian Countries: Review of 1973 and Outlook for 1974* (USDA *Review and Outlook*); the same, *1974-75, 1975-76*, and *1976-77*. I have also used a revised series supplied by Prof. K.R. Walker, which includes soya beans and adjusts the official data by standardizing the potato:grain ratio. CIA, *China's Agricultural Performance in 1975* (Washington, 1976); see also Neville Maxwell, 'Recent Chinese grain figures', *The China Quarterly*, No 68 (1976), pp. 817-18.

definition of grain. In Moscow current Soviet estimates continue to insist that official Chinese data overstate actual output by at least 10 per cent.

Table 20: *Growth rates of grain output, selected periods, 1930s-1974 (per cent per annum)*

Period	Significance	Annual rate of growth
1930s-74	Long-run trend	1.1
1952-57	*First Five Year Plan*	3.48
1952-58	Period of fastest growth	4.44
1952-74	Long-run post-war trend	2.01
1958-74	Post Great Leap trend	1.73
1949-74	Officially claimed long-run trend	3.7

Source: Table 19.

Note:
The 'long-run post-war trend' is the least squares linear trend calculated for the years 1952-74 included in Table 19, but excluding the exceptional downturn in 1960 ($R^2 = 0.90$). This measure gives a more accurate indication of the trend than the compound growth between the two years 1952 and 1974 which is 2.46. The provisional data for 1975 and 1976 also suggest that 2.46 per cent is too high as an indicator of the long-run trend. (See Table 19.)

The series in Table 19 starts with a figure for the 1930s. This is an important benchmark because it indicates that the apparent growth of grain output between 1949 and 1952 was actually a recovery from a level of output abnormally depressed by war. This point must be borne in mind when examining official claims for the growth of food or grain output.

If we look at the growth of grain in particular sub-periods (Table 20), we observe that the fastest growth of 4.44 per cent per annum occurred between 1952 and 1958. After this, output declined from 209 million metric tons in 1958 to 153 million metric tons in 1960. There was a recovery in the 1960s and modest growth between the mid-1960s and mid-1970s.

Table 21: *Structure of grain output, 1952, 1957, 1974 (percentage shares)*

	Rice	Wheat	Soya beans	Potatoes	Miscellaneous grains	Total
1952	42	11	6	10	32	100
1957	45	12	5	9	28	100
1974	43	11	3-5?	10	33	100

Sources: Tables 19 and 23.

Table 21 shows the relative importance of the different grains in 1952, 1957, and 1974. The 1950s figures are official while the 1974 figures are conjecture based on a variety of sources. Rice is seen as China's dominant crop. Its share of output has increased marginally. The share of soya beans is not clear. In the mid-1960s it fell to about 3 per cent. Recent American estimates claim that in the 1970s output grew very rapidly, but the evidence for this is weak. In 1973 China became a net importer of vegetable oils and imported soya beans from the United States, France, and Brazil; and in 1974 and 1975 the Chinese were unable to fulfil contracts for the export of soya beans to Japan. We also know from residents' reports that in Peking soya bean based foods disappear for weeks on end. (They are always rationed.) All of which suggests that supply may be very constrained, and that the share of soya beans in total grain output may well be below that suggested by some of these American estimates.

Finally, there is the question of grain yields. The estimates of average yield in the 1950s set out in Table 22 are firmly based on official data. For the 1960s and 1970s there are no comparable figures, although the Chinese news media have reported many examples of local yields. The latter, however, are rarely typical. We know this because, if they *were* representative, total output of grain would have to be far higher than it

Table 22: *China's long-run grain performance compared with that in other Asian countries*

A Growth rate per annum (per cent)	Asia (including China)	China
	1948/52-70	*1952-74*
grain output	3.0	2.0-2.46
area sown to grain	1.5	0.71

B Yields (tons per hectare)

	Rice		Wheat	
	1952	*1970s*	*1952*	*1970s*
China	2.3	3.1	0.7	1.0
	1948/1952	*1974/1975*		
India	1.1	1.7	0.7	1.3
South Korea	3.6	5.2	1.5	2.1

Notes:
1. The definition of 'grains' in Asian data excludes sweet potatoes but includes all other fine and coarse grains. Chinese data in Table A include sweet potatoes and soya beans. In Table B, Chinese data exclude soya beans but include sweet potatoes.
2. Increases in the areas sown to grain reflect both new land brought into cultivation *and* increases in the number of crops taken per annum. In China's case, the expansion of sown area is almost entirely a result of increasing the number of crops. Lack of potential for opening new land explains China's poor showing on this indicator.

Sources: As Tables 19, 20, 23. Asian data from Food and Agriculture Organization, *Production Yearbook* (Rome, various years).

is. The estimates for 1973 are not as reliable as those for the 1950s. Underlying these estimates is the view that since 1957, the grain-sown area has increased marginally; thus growth of yields and growth of output are almost the same thing (Table 23).

Table 23: *An estimate of cultivated area, sown area, and multiple cropping index, 1952, 1957, 1973*

	1952	1956	1957	1973	Rate of growth per annum
Cultivated area (million hectares)	110	112	112	107	−0.13
Multiple cropping index	134	142	140	160	
Sown area (million hectares)	147	159	157	171	0.72
Sown area allocated to grains (million hectares)	124	136	134	144	0.71
Grain sown area as percentage of total sown area	84	86	85	84	

Notes:
1. The *multiple cropping index* equals 100 if one crop is grown per year on the whole cultivated area. The *sown area* is calculated by multiplying the *cultivated area* by the multiple cropping index. Thus, if the cultivated area produces two crops, the multiple cropping index would be 200, and the sown area is double the cultivated area.
2. These data represent judgements about the 1973 situation, not estimates based on detailed Chinese figures. The 1956 data are included since they represent the peak effort to maximize the area sown to grain — an effort that produced a grain sown area that could not be maintained.

Source: Estimates supplied by K.R. Walker, based in part on data supplied to the author and Walker in Peking in 1974. These figures differ in some respects from the estimates in USDA, *Review and Outlook 1975-1976,* p. 62.

The large gap between this estimate of current average yields (which must be broadly correct) and the local figures met with in the press or on visits to China, does not necessarily mean that the local data are fabrications. Natural variations between regions are large and we tend to hear of the richer regions. Also, mechanization and chemical fertilizers *can* raise yields to the reported levels. Thus we should think of high claims as representing feasible, long-run targets for particular regions, rather than as descriptions of typical cases. For example, grain yields in Southern Kiangsu above six tons per hectare level (more than double the national average) are plausible in view of the special advantages of this region. High claims for irrigated and mechanized areas in the North China Plain are equally credible. Against high claims must be placed the Chinese report of 1976 that only nine Provinces and Municipalities in China had reached the targets set in Mao's agricultural plan for 1956-67.[5]

The grain crops account for 80 per cent of the calorie intake in the average Chinese diet. Nonetheless, varied and often critical roles in

China's economy are played by other food crops. The most important of these are vegetables, fruit, and crops that provide edible oil.

Vegetables and fruit No official data on vegetable and fruit production have ever been published. Pre-war analysts estimated that 1.1 per cent of the cultivated area was used for vegetable growing and that annual output in the 1930s was about 20 million metric tons. In recent years many cities have encouraged the development of vegetable growing on their outskirts; and since vegetable growing yields high incomes to the growers, whether they use private or public land, it is possible that up to 1.5 per cent of the cultivated area is now used for this purpose—approximately 1.47 million hectares. How much could be produced on this area? Pre-war yields were about 24 tons per hectare, but it is probable that average yields are now up to 50 tons per hectare. This would give an annual output of 74 million metric tons; a figure nearly four times the pre-war level.[6] Similar growth in fruit production is also possible. China produces many varieties of pears, apples, peaches, melons, oranges, persimmons, etc. Fruits are an important export in fresh and canned form, and total output could now be as high as 10 million metric tons per annum.

Oil crops Estimates of the output of the main oil-bearing crops are shown in Table 24. This shows the rising importance of peanuts and reports the conflicting estimates of the soya bean situation.

Table 24: *Output of important oil-bearing crops, 1952-76*
(million metric tons)

	1952	1957	1970	1974	1975	1976
Peanuts	0.44	0.42	2.65	2.7	2.8	2.9
Rapeseed	0.93	0.89	0.93	1.16	1.4	1.38
Soya beans						
(official and USDA)	9.52	10.05	6.9	9.5	10	9.5
(official and CIA)	9.5	10.1	7	17	n.a.	n.a.

Sources: N.R. Chen, *Chinese Economic Statistics,* pp. 338-39; USDA, *Review and Outlook 1973-1974,* p. 4; the same, *1974-1975,* p. 6; the same, *1975-1976,* p. 7; the same, *1976-1977,* p. 6; CIA, *China: Agricultural Performance in 1975,* p. 9.

Cotton China's most important non-food crop is cotton. Domestic raw cotton output influences activity in the cotton industry, and has implications for living standards and foreign trade. Pre-war output touched a peak of 1 million metric tons and plans made after 1949 included ambitious proposals to increase output and eliminate imports. Table 25 shows that output did grow in the 1950s, but that since then pressure to produce more food has kept cotton output at levels below those desired by the planners. Since 1973, output has fallen in three successive years.

Table 25: *Output of raw cotton, 1952-76*
(million metric tons)

	1952	1957	1961	1965	1971	1973	1974	1975	1976
Total	1.3	1.64	0.89	1.65	2.22	2.55	2.5	2.4	2.35

Growth rate per cent	1952-57	1952-76	1957-76
per annum	4.76	2.5	1.91

Source: USDA, *Review and Outlook 1976-1977*, p.7.

Forestry The largest gap in our knowledge of China's agriculture is forestry. This is unfortunate. Forestry influences industrial construction and fuel supplies. It also has an impact on agriculture because it assists land reclamation and can create localized climatic changes that improve the yield of crops. Visitors to China see thousands of recently planted trees and many Communes have tree nurseries. This activity reflects a response to Chairman Mao's slogan, 'Cover the countryside with trees!' These developments started from a weak base in the 1950s but, if they continue at a rapid pace, their impact will be substantial.

Sugar, tea, jute, tobacco Data in Table 26 are based on official published sources and on information given to me by an official in Peking in 1974; they show that output of these crops grew more rapidly than grain. In the case of sugar, an intensive effort has had to be made to replace the Taiwanese crop, which before 1947 accounted for two-

Table 26: *Output of sugar, tea, jute, and tobacco, 1949-73*
(million metric tons)

	1949	1952	1957	1973	Rate of growth 1952-73 (per cent)
Sugar	0.199	0.451	0.864	1.19	4.73
Tea	0.041	0.0825	0.1115	0.29	6.17
Jute	0.032	0.191	0.295	0.35	2.93
Tobacco	0.043	0.2215	0.256	0.56+	4.52

Note: Sugar data converted to raw sugar.

Sources: *Ten Great Years*, pp. 124-26; N.R. Chen, *Chinese Economic Statistics*, pp. 100, 188-89, 338-39; 1973 figures supplied to the author by Chinese officials in 1974; New China News Agency, April 26, 1974. Rest of data are an FAO estimate; an estimate which I believe to be conservative. See Sino-British Trade Council, *Newsletter*, August 1974.

thirds of China's total supplies. In spite of these efforts China is still importing sugar. The growth of tea, on the other hand, reflects the importance of this crop as an export.

Table 27: *Livestock, 1949-74*

	1949	1952	1957	1972	1974
Large draught animals (total)	59,775	76,173	83,457	95,042	n.a.
Sheep and goats	42,347	61,778	98,582	148,215	n.a.
Hogs	57,752	89,765	145,895	259,884	261,000
Aquatic products (catch) (million metric tons)	0.448	1.666	3.120	8.2	n.a.

Sources: N.R. Chen, *Chinese Economic Statistics,* p. 340; USDA, *Review and Outlook 1975-1976,* pp. 8-9; CIA, *Handbook of Economic Indicators* (1976), p. 11; Aquatic products (comprising salt and freshwater fishing) as Table 26.

Livestock and fish Progress in livestock was uneven in the 1950s owing to periodic slaughtering and lack of interest by the peasants in the collectivization drives. There has been an improvement in recent years largely in response to the fairly strong incentive provided (see Table 27). The growth of fisheries appears to have been exceptionally good in recent years; this is particularly so in the freshwater sector (see Table 27). The FAO estimates that China is the world's largest fishing nation, and visitors to China have accumulated a great deal of qualitative evidence of the intensity of the drive to produce fish in freshwater ponds, lakes and reservoirs. This drive is logical since the yield of protein per hectare obtained from fish farming can be higher than that obtained by any alternative use of agricultural space.

Summary

Grain is the most important part of China's agricultural output and between 1952 and 1975 its output grew at 2 per cent to 2.46 per cent per annum. Output of vegetables, fruit, fish and livestock (Tables 26 and 27) has probably grown faster. This is suggested both by data for individual products and by the Chinese claims for the growth of total agricultural output. The weakest parts of agriculture's performance have been production of raw cotton, and possibly of soya beans. The modest growth of grain and these two weak crops have led to China's becoming a substantial importer of agricultural commodities.

THE ADEQUACY OF AGRICULTURE'S PERFORMANCE

Four relationships can provide us with a framework for assessing the adequacy of agriculture's performance. These are the relationships between:

(1) population and food;
(2) agriculture and industrial development;
(3) agriculture and foreign trade;
(4) China's agriculture and the world agricultural situation.

Population and food

Chinese spokesmen claim that the food supply is growing at more than double the rate of growth of population. For example, at the Fourth National People's Congress in 1975, Chou En-lai stated that since 1949 grain output had increased by 140 per cent, and population by 60 per cent. This implied annual growth rates of 3.56 per cent and 1.9 per cent respectively. But, as we have seen, if we take 1952 as the base year, the long-run growth of grain output is only in the range of 2 per cent-2.46 per cent per annum. The facts of population growth are less certain, but as discussed in Chapter 1, the trend is about 2 per cent. Thus the margin between trends in population and food is probably minute. Grain appears to have grown ahead of population, but only just. Moreover, it is possible that the relatively high growth of grain output between 1952 and 1958 included an unrepeatable element of post-war recovery.

There is a further difficulty with official claims. Accurate appraisal of the grain situation requires that the figures for demand and supply be broken down by regions and Provinces. China is an enormous country in which transportation is scarce. It is therefore essential that a balance between grain and population be kept, not only at the national, but at lower levels. This is not to say that every minute geographical subdivision must be self-sufficient in food. There are bound to be local variations in agricultural conditions and it is appropriate that areas suited to the growing of non-food crops should specialize. But as the Chinese have emphasized, whole regions cannot be allowed to have large and growing food deficits.

Lack of local information makes it hard to appraise agriculture's recent performance in this respect. In the 1950s progress was definitely uneven. Professor K.R. Walker has estimated that in four out of six major Provinces in North China, grain output per head of the population *declined* during the First Five Year Plan (1953-57). In the 1960s and 1970s the new emphasis on agriculture has been accompanied by efforts to achieve regional and Provincial self-sufficiency. Under Mao's slogan 'Eliminate the transportation of grain from South to North', resources have been applied to raising output in deficit Provinces—especially the North China Plain Provinces of Honan, Hopei and Shantung. There is some evidence that regional imbalance has diminished, and it is claimed that, exclusive of Peking and Tientsin, the region comprising Honan, Hopei and Shantung is self-sufficient in an average year. Thus, if this spatial factor is taken into account, the recent performance of grain production is better than might be judged from looking solely at the moderate growth of total output.

The evaluation of other food crops is harder because the data are so weak. From what is known, however, it can at least be argued that increases in output of fruit, vegetables, fish, and livestock have generally exceeded that of grain. If this is correct, secondary foodstuffs will have improved the food supply by providing additional calories and also by supplying the vitamins and minerals necessary for a more balanced diet.

Agriculture and industry

Agriculture's impact on industry operates through variations in its ability to supply raw materials and urban food, and also through its impact on foreign trade.

There can be no doubt that the growth of agriculture has been less than necessary to sustain the pace of industrial development desired by the Government. The difference between the 1950s and later years is that in the 1950s the tensions between agriculture and industry were not properly anticipated. Since then the problem has been recognized much more clearly and the dependence of urban growth on agriculture has now become a widely quoted 'law' of socialist development.

The history of cotton output and its impact on the textile industry is a particularly striking part of this story. During the 1930s China's imports were as much as 8 per cent of her raw cotton requirements. These imports partly reflected the need for cotton of special characteristics, and partly shortfall of domestic output. During the 1950s cotton imports were stopped; so when the domestic supply of raw cotton grew more slowly than anticipated, the result was widespread excess capacity in the textile factories. In the 1960s imports of cotton were renewed, and in 1974 these reached 348,000 tons—more than four times the highest pre-war figure and equal to 13 per cent of total requirements. In spite of these cotton imports, the stationary level of cotton cloth output indicates that domestic cotton supplies are still causing substantial excess capacity in the textile industry.

Agriculture and foreign trade

Foreign trade has been particularly influenced by the vicissitudes of grain. Grain imports started in response to a crisis in the food supply in 1961. They were inescapable, but regarded as temporary. This is revealed by Mao's comment to the economic planners in 1964: 'We must struggle for a number of years to achieve a cessation of grain imports—using the foreign exchange saved to purchase more technical equipment and materials.'[7] Yet in 1973 and 1974, despite record harvests, imports of grain were also at record levels. To some extent imports can be explained by China's internal transport problems; it is easier to supply eastern cities with foreign grain by sea than by domestic transport from the interior.[8] There is also the difference in wheat and rice prices which enables the Chinese to get more calories by selling rice and buying wheat in the international market. But these factors cannot explain the long-term *overall scale* of imports; and the recent Chinese emphasis on the need for self-sufficiency in food, and the dip in imports in 1975, show that the elimination of foreign grain is regarded as an urgent task.

China and the world agricultural situation

China's relationship to world agriculture raises two questions: how does its agricultural performance compare with that of other low income countries (especially those in Asia)? And will China's development generate demands that the world economy cannot meet?

In comparing China with other countries, one has to appreciate that, for a pre-modern agriculture, China has already achieved exceptionally high yields. In the 1930s China's yields for almost every major grain were higher than the world average, and from Table 22 it will be seen that her yields in the 1950s were superior to those elsewhere in Asia both for rice and for all grains taken together.

If we compare China's recent performance with that of other Asian countries, we find that China's growth of grain output of 2-2.46 per cent per annum is below the 3 per cent average achieved in Asia as a whole. But the importance of this should not be exaggerated since not only must one bear in mind that China's growth started from a more advanced point, but if we look at the longer historical perspective, we find that the major trends of output, consumption, and trade in grain in China and Asia move clearly together. For between the 1920s and the 1970s grain *output* per head in both has remained stable, while rising living standards have led to an increase in *consumption* per head; an improvement achieved by converting both China and Asia as a whole from the status of net exporters to net importers of grain.[9]

There is one feature of the Chinese performance since 1949, however, that *is* both unusual and impressive. In the average Asian economy, about half of the increased grain output was achieved by increasing the sown area (i.e. by increasing both new land brought into cultivation *and* the number of crops per unit of land). In China, at most a third of its growth can be accounted for in this way, and the increase attributable *solely* to new land is minute. This disparity arises because, even by Asian standards, China is relatively short of land. And the implication is that to increase output China has to rely almost exclusively on increases in *yields*.

Turning to the second question—the demands that might be made by Chinese agriculture on the rest of the world—we find that in the past these have taken two forms: demand for grain and demand for fertilizer. Of the two, fertilizer is now less of a problem, although until recently China had a predominant position in world fertilizer trade. Between 1957 and 1973 China imported over four million tons of fertilizer per annum. And in 1971 China was by far the world's largest importer of nitrogenous fertilizers, importing three times as much as India, the second largest importer. A further complication in the fertilizer situation has been the mutual dependence of China and Japan: Japan providing up to 70 per cent of China's supplies, and China's share of Japanese exports being as high as 80 per cent. The dangers inherent in this became apparent in 1973 when Japan refused to satisfy China's demands for fertilizer and, despite a special visit to Tokyo by the chief of the China National Import and Export Corporation, finally supplied less than 80 per cent of requirements. These problems are likely to prove transitional. By the end of the decade China's domestic capacity for fertilizer production should be adequate to meet all domestic demands—although imports of fertilizer raw materials, such as brimstone, phosphate, and ash rock, are likely to remain substantial.[10]

The future of grain imports is less certain. Although they fell back in 1975, grain imports have begun to move upward again and have on average remained obstinately high. A major obstacle to accurate forecasting is that China's *absolute* levels of consumption and production are so high that minor errors in estimates of long-run trends of output and consumption result in large differences in estimates of China's potential demand for foreign grain. For example, in 1973/74, 151 million metric tons of grain were traded on world markets. China's total output in 1973 was about 200 million metric tons (measured in *milled* grain). Thus a 10 per cent shortfall in China would have been equal to 13 per cent of world traded grain in that year. Current projections of the world food situation are that the food deficit of the developing countries *as a whole* will continue to grow, and that the imports of developing countries in 1985 will be double their 1975 level. It is this potentially alarming situation that is prompting the Chinese to redouble their efforts to reduce grain imports. But to succeed in a policy of food self-sufficiency, China will have to break decisively away from the general Asian pattern of production, consumption, and trade in food. This will be difficult, since this pattern reflects the shortage of land that gives the region a natural *disadvantage* in food production compared to other regions of the world, a shortage that in China is extreme, even by Asian standards.

AGRICULTURAL MODERNIZATION

In the past twenty-five years the Chinese countryside has experienced dramatic changes in organization, and an acceleration of the technical modernization that began in the pre-war period. The main types of technical change that are taking place, and their contribution to growth, will now be considered. Some of these changes have taken the form of learning new techniques for agricultural work and of reorganizing the resources of labour, land, and capital that existed in agriculture before 1949. Agricultural progress, however, has also depended on new investment that has been undertaken; indeed, a major reason for collectivization was to increase such investment. Unfortunately it is very difficult to measure the *total* investment effort that has been made, because so much of this takes forms that do not involve machinery, fuel and other easily measurable resources, and because there are no comprehensive statistics on the amount of labour used for capital construction work such as water conservancy, land reclamation, road building, housing, construction, etc. Because of these problems, it is easy to underestimate agricultural investment, and to concentrate—as official data do—on the more easily measurable investment activities in industry. An important Western investigation which attempted to allow for these biases estimated that investment in agriculture accounted for 31.8 per cent of total fixed investment in 1952, and despite the rapid growth of investment in industry, still accounted for 23.5 per cent in 1957. However it must be remembered that the figures are *gross* (i.e. they include the investment needed to replace worn out capital) and that if only *net* new investment were considered the bias towards industry would appear much greater; and further, that in relation to agriculture's share of output in 1957 (42 per cent) and to its share of employment (about 80 per cent), a 23.5 per cent share of investment is not large. Thus although it would be incorrect to describe Chinese investment in agriculture as negligible up to 1957, these estimates do confirm that lack of investment was probably a major explanation for the crisis that developed in agriculture in the late 1950s.[11]

As a result of the rearrangement of economic priorities in 1960, investment in agriculture expanded rapidly. One indication of this is the estimate that between 1957 and 1970 capital construction in agriculture grew at 9.64 per cent per year, compared to a rate of growth of capital construction in all other sectors of 5.76 per cent per year. For the same period it has been estimated that the share of agriculture in construction and installation work (which itself accounts for more than half of total investment) rose from 8.6 per cent to 22.6 per cent. What the figures have meant in terms of specific agricultural modernization will be seen in the rest of this chapter.[12]

One crucial feature of this modernization programme as it developed in the 1960s was the adoption of the policy of concentrating the application of new equipment, chemical fertilizer, and the total investment effort, into areas capable of achieving 'High and Stable Yields'. This was a logical policy in the sense that this concentration probably meant that the returns to the investment were higher than would have been the case had it been spread evenly and thinly over the whole of China. In the mid-1960s the High and Stable Yield Areas were estimated to account for 25 per cent of the cultivated area; an official figure published in 1975 suggests that this figure has risen to $33\frac{1}{3}$ per cent, and the current plan is to raise the share to 50 per cent by 1980.[13] Some idea of the degree to which this policy led to uneven distribution of resources is given by the estimate that in the 1960s these areas absorbed 80 per cent of the supply of chemical fertilizer.[14] But while the economic logic of the policy was powerful, it had one very important by-product: it increased inequality between different areas. This occurred because the places which were the obvious choices to be made High and Stable Yield Areas were *initially* relatively well endowed both with natural resources and with access to urban technology, markets, and transport. The policy thus confirmed the advantageous position of favoured areas. To the best of our knowledge, the only mitigation of this inequality has been achieved by special Government measures to aid particularly poor areas, and by a policy of encouraging Communes to allocate resources *within* the Communes in a way that brings the backward Teams and Brigades up to the level of the more advanced.[15]

Land

China's shortage of cultivable land has already been mentioned. Estimates based on recent Chinese statements indicate that only 10-11 per cent of the total surface area (about 100-107 million hectares) is cultivated, and that the expansion of the cities has actually caused the cultivated area to *decline* since the 1950s (see Table 23). The data show that recent increases in the area sown to crops are *entirely* due to increases in the number of crops taken per unit of land. This may seem hard to reconcile with evidence of surges of effort to bring new land into cultivation—often by moving the cultivated area up the hillsides in terraces. There have been some well publicized successes in this at Tachai, in Sinkiang, and in the Gobi desert. But much of this work only offsets losses near to towns, and often mainly results in improvement of the *quality* and manageability of the land, rather than in genuine additions to the cultivated area. Moreover, extreme efforts to make new fields and terraces are often followed by their abandonment, a fact that visitors to China can observe for themselves.

The development of collectivized agriculture in the 1950s had some positive effects on the size of the cultivated area. This was because the amalgamation of private farms eliminated paths and boundaries, which according to pre-war observers used up to 10 per cent of the cultivable area. In the early stages of the Communes, awkwardly placed homes and graves were also destroyed in an effort to bring more land into use. Today, however, although land utilization has improved, grave mounds can still be seen in the fields, and official data confirm that gains of all kinds have been offset by the losses that occur as agricultural land disappears under the expansion of the built-up areas. These trends are unlikely to be reversed in the future.

Water

The improvement of agriculture requires simultaneous advance on many fronts. Electrification, water control, chemical fertilizer application, mechanization, seed selection, etc., have only limited value if each is employed in isolation. Productivity increases are the result of their interaction and complementary use. Thus, electricity powers the irrigation that allows use of new crop varieties whose yields depend on fertilizer, and so on. In spite of this qualification, I would argue that improvements in water control are the most important single development in Chinese agriculture in the past twenty-five years.[16]

The main problems of water control in China are:
(1) the unequal distribution of surface water between North and South;
(2) the vulnerability of the North China Plain to drought and waterlogging caused by erratic rainfall and lack of drainage channels;
(3) the need to develop controlled supplies of water to increase wheat yields in the North and double cropping of rice in the South;
(4) special problems associated with the behaviour of major rivers—especially the Yellow, the Huai, and the Haiho systems.

A measure of China's inequality of water distribution is that North China has 51 per cent of the cultivated area and 7 per cent of the surface water flow, while the Yangtze Valley and South China have 33 per cent of the cultivated area and 76 per cent of the surface flow.[17]

During the First Five Year Plan water conservation was the only major item in the State Budget for agriculture. With Soviet advice, some major schemes were undertaken, including the disastrous project at San Men gorge. The aim of the San Men project was to control and harness for electrical generation a crucial segment of the Yellow river. But the Soviet experts miscalculated the size of the silting problem created by the dam. As a result, while the scheme (now over thirty years old) has led to improved control of the river, only a small fraction of the plan for power generation has ever been realized.[18]

Water conservation was also a central feature of the Great Leap Forward. Indeed, the Leap was originally conceived as a way of revolutionizing the organization of labour for water conservation purposes. But although projects were initiated all over China, many of these were misconceived and incorrectly executed. The effects on flood control were appalling and a salinization problem was created in North China from which recovery took many years.

Despite the problems and errors of the 1950s, the Government has persisted, and substantial progress in large and small scale programmes of water control has been made. The United States Department of Agriculture estimate that the irrigated area in 1975 was approximately 46 per cent of the cultivated area, and recent Chinese data report that additions to the irrigated area have been made at a rate of 1.6 million hectares a year. At this rate, however, it will take more than thirty years to irrigate the entire country.[19]

The special water problems of the North China Plain have been tackled by combining major controls of the big rivers with subsidiary schemes that use the water resources and electricity produced by the big rivers according to local needs and initiatives. The region has also long been known to have rich supplies of artesian water, and in recent years an enormous underground sea has been discovered in an area that includes the Provinces of Kiangsu, Honan, Anhwei, and Shantung. The investment in water control and agriculture in this region appears to be linked to wider plans to develop the North China Plain—especially the segment bounded by Peking, Tientsin, Tangshan, and the Pohai gulf—into a key economic region, one that is self-sufficient in food and in basic industries. Comprehensive data on this are not available, but it is remarkable that, time and again, the model Communes analysed in the Chinese press are located in this limited area, and reportedly owe their advances to improvements in water control.

Electricity and mechanization

The drive for electrification and mechanization started in 1959. The decade of development from 1949 had shown that without substantial technical modernization, continuous reorganization of agriculture was futile. In 1959 Mao summed up his own perception of the situation as follows:

The fundamental way out for agriculture lies in mechanization. Ten years will be needed to achieve this. There will be minor solutions in four years, intermediate ones in seven, and major solutions in ten.[20]

As usual, the time scale was too short; but the policy has stuck, and this slogan can be seen fixed to the walls in Communes and agricultural machinery plants all over China.

China's population and workforce are so large in relation to the limited area of cultivable land that one might ask whether rural mechanization is necessary. Would it not be more rational to allocate *all* modern investment to industry and use the rural population for labour-intensive forms of agriculture? Briefly, the case against this is that: (1) there are agricultural tasks that cannot be done efficiently by unaided labour—however much is available; (2) important improvements in cropping lead to *seasonal* labour shortages; and (3) labour released from certain tasks can—if organized and motivated—find productive alternative work in agriculture, particularly in land improvement and rural construction.

Electrification Electricity is probably the most comprehensive indicator of the progress of technical modernization. Table 28 shows that the rural *share* of electricity consumption has increased twenty-fold since 1957. The early 1960s was the period of most rapid growth, but, even since 1965, rural consumption has greatly increased its share

Table 28: *Electric power consumption in rural areas, 1952–75*

	1952	1958	1965	1973	1974	1975
Supply to rural areas (million Kwh)	43	142	3,200	12,800	15,360	20,256 (est.)
Share of total supply (per cent)	0.6	0.5	7.6	12.7	14.2	16.2 (est.)

Sources: R. M. Field, JEC (1975), pp. 165–167; *A Glance at China's Economy*, p. 11; New China News Agency, October 10, 1975; *Peking Review*, 1975, No. 41, pp. 14–15; Chao Kang, *Agricultural Production in Communist China 1949–1965*, p. 139.

of national output and in 1975 it was reported that 70 per cent of the Communes had an electricity supply.[21] Much of the rural supply is provided by 60,000 small hydro stations whose construction is often linked to new water control systems.

It is probable that at least 70 per cent of rural electricity is used for driving irrigation equipment, the balance being divided between machinery for processing rural products, rural industry, and lighting.

Mechanization While electrification has been a nationwide phenomenon, the mechanization of basic farming operations has been restricted to particular areas. Mechanization is most easily applied to relatively level land and is most effective in the cultivation of crops such as wheat and soya beans. It is thus ideal for Manchuria, for parts of the North China Plain, and for Sinkiang. These regions combine the appropriate type of agriculture with the availability of fuel resources.

The exact extent of mechanization is unknown. Official statements suggest that not more than 10 per cent of China's arable area is ploughed with tractors; lower percentages are sown and reaped. The most intensive mechanization is in Sinkiang, where agriculture is in the hands of the People's Liberation Army who are technically well equipped for this. Reports from Sinkiang claim that 54 per cent of the cultivated area is ploughed by tractor, and that 42 per cent of the area is sown by tractor-drawn equipment.

The significance of mechanization in North and North-West China is that not only does it enable basic earth-breaking and sowing operations to be performed more efficiently, but that by reducing the time needed for harvesting, preparation, and planting, it enables the region to add winter wheat to its crop cycle. It also lessens the problems created by the erratic North China rainfall.

In the South, rice cultivation is less amenable to mechanization, but it can increase the feasibility of double cropping and is directly applicable to ancillary operations in rice production such as husking and milling.

Tractors The main types of tractors produced in China are listed below; most of them are based on Soviet designs.[22]
(1) East is Red 75 HP and 54 HP tractors. These are used for cultivation of large areas.
(2) Red Banner 100 HP. Used for earth moving and field construction.
(3) East is Red 42 HP and 28 HP, which are smaller, faster versions of East is Red 75 HP and 54 HP models.
(4) Bumper 35 HP. A lightweight tractor for paddy fields.
(5) Worker-Peasant 7 HP. A hand controlled, garden tractor.

In recent years, in response to demand from Brigades and Teams (whose financial resources are limited by comparison with the Commune), the Chinese have concentrated on the production of smaller tractors. All larger tractors are unimportant in South China, but the Worker-Peasant is used for terraced fields and vegetable cultivation. An added attraction of all tractors is that they have power off-take points that enable them to drive a variety of other small machines. The utilization of tractors and agricultural machinery in China is extremely intensive.

Table 29: *Powered irrigation equipment and tractors, 1956-75*

	1956	1965	1970	1975
Powered irrigation equipment (1000 HP units)	170	1150	n.a.	6440
Conventional tractors (15 HP units)	0	23,000	70,000	140,000
Garden tractors (15 HP units)	0	875	9,000	40,000
Total stock of garden tractors (7 HP units)	0	2,194	44,138	319,395

Note: Tractor output is standardized in 15 HP units. Thus a 60 HP tractor counts as 4 units.
Sources: CIA, *Handbook of Economic Indicators* (1976), pp. 13, 20; *Foreign Broadcast Information Service,* June 30, 1976.

Details of the growth of tractor output are shown in Table 29. Large as this may appear, it must be kept in perspective. Reading China's foreign language publications might lead one to think that mechanized farming is common in China. Actually, one can travel for hundreds of miles without seeing a single mechanized operation. Comparative figures bear out this impression. For example, the number of tractors per hectare in China is about $2\frac{1}{2}$ per cent of that in the United States, and until recently China's annual tractor production has been lower than India's.

In the case of garden tractors, it is the contrast with Japan that is striking. In Japan four-fifths of all agricultural households have a garden tractor; in China only one household in 400 has one, and even if the staggering recent growth of garden tractor output is sustained, it will take at least a generation for China to reach Japanese levels of availability.

Fertilizers

China's domestic fertilizer industry has grown rapidly since the early 1960s. The policy of increasing fertilizer application to increase crop yields has not been questioned for fifteen years, and to maintain a

growth of fertilizer supply of over 17 per cent per annum in the 1960s
and 1970s the Chinese sometimes resorted to importing on a large
scale. Table 30 shows growth of fertilizer supplies since 1952, broken
down by origin and by type of fertilizer.

Table 30: *The supply of chemical fertilizer by type and source, 1952-75*
(million metric tons, nutrient weight)

	1952	1957	1965	1970	1974	1975
Domestic production						
Nitrogen	0.19	0.68	4.15	7.81	15.81	17.72
Phosphorus	—	0.12	3.45	5.90	8.62	9.66
Potassium	—	—	—	0.29	0.45	0.50
Imports	0.20	1.34	3.20	7.41	3.00	3.10
Total supply	0.39	2.14	10.80	21.41	27.88	30.98
Imported share of total						
supply (per cent)	51	63	30	35	11	10

Notes:
1. The data are measured in nutrient values rather than gross weight, i.e. ammonium sulphate is converted by a factor of 0.2, super-phosphates by 0.187, etc.
2. Imports have been almost entirely nitrogenous fertilizers.

Sources: R.M. Field, JEC (1975), p. 166; CIA, *Handbook of Economic Indicators* (1976), p. 27; *Current Scene,* Vol. xiv, No. 10, October 1976, p. 2.

The cultivated area has remained fairly stable since 1952, so that
almost all the increase in fertilizer represents increased intensity of
application. The effect of this has been to raise China's rate of
application to 68 kg per hectare in 1975. Table 31 shows how China's
performance compares with other countries.

Table 31: *Chemical fertilizer application in China and other countries, current and
future levels*
(kilograms of nutrient per hectare)

	1973	1975	1980 (estimate)
China	57	68	80
India	17		
Japan	425		
World average	53		

Note: Estimate for 1980 based on capacity of chemical fertilizer plants planned and under construction.
Sources: Chao Kang, 'Production and application of chemical fertilizers in China', *The China Quarterly,* No. 64 (1975), p. 724; Table 30.

It is clear that China's decisive progress in fertilizer application is a
major reason for China's above average success in raising crop yields.
Moreover, one must bear in mind that China's application of *organic*
fertilizers is very high. Organic fertilizers include animal manure, night

soil, oil cakes, pond mud, ashes, 'green' manure crops, and straw. The assiduous collection and application of these have always been an admired characteristic of China's agriculture, and specialists estimate that they add at least 40 kg of nutrient per hectare of land.[23] Thus China's total application of fertilizer is probably now over 100 kg per hectare.

The late 1970s are likely to see further advances in fertilizer production. Urea plants imported from abroad should enable China to maintain a growth rate of fertilizer output of 8-9 per cent per annum up to 1980. By this time domestic production of all types of chemical fertilizer could be over 40 million metric tons. If output does reach this level, the application of all forms of nutrients per hectare (with a modest level of imports) could reach 120 kg.

Development of new varieties, changing crop patterns and agricultural research

China's seed varieties and cropping patterns are the product of millennia of experiment, and, in recent centuries, two important changes have occurred. One is the discovery and dissemination of rice strains that mature in relatively short periods, thereby enabling more than one crop to be grown per year. The other is the introduction of tuber crops (e.g. sweet potatoes) that have a very high yield per unit of land. These developments have enabled agriculture to support the accelerated growth of population that began in the eighteenth century.

Contemporary agronomists in China largely continue these traditions. In seed selection, they are now searching for rice varieties that respond to fertilizers and irrigation, and which are suitable for multiple cropping. They are also putting efforts into the improvement of wheat by developing varieties with high yields, short growing periods, and resistance to rust and lodging. Other activities include research on a wide range of other crops, on vegetables, on animal husbandry, and on fish farming.

The main centres for this work are the institutes under the direction of the Chinese Academy of Agricultural Sciences. There are also many smaller research groups and organizations going right down to the Commune level and below. Unfortunately we do not have the information needed to evaluate all this work properly. Professional visitors from abroad are impressed by the efforts to disseminate new techniques at the Commune level, but visits to the larger research establishments have produced mixed responses. Some visitors report that useful work is being done, but others have expressed disquiet at the lack of fundamental research, and are alarmed at the long-term implications of the collapse of postgraduate education. Thus, although evidence from other Asian countries suggests that China must have considerable *potential* for increasing productivity through research and its application, miracles are not possibie, and the slow growth of total grain output shows that they have not occurred. In this context, it must be remembered that, while good results may be obtained on trial plots, dissemination is often difficult. The time span that can be involved is illustrated by the fact that rice yields obtained on trial plots in the 1920s in Taiwan did not become general for nearly forty years—in spite of extension programmes for agriculture that are generally judged to have been unusually successful.

One factor very much in China's favour at the present time is the availability of foreign research work. The Russians had nothing much to give the Chinese in this field, but China's new links with Japan and other Asian countries offer the prospect of cooperative efforts that could be of great benefit to the Chinese. The Japanese in particular have plenty of relevant expertise, notably in the development of rice production in cold regions, and it has been reported that they have already given China assistance in the fields of grain, soya beans, and fish farming.[24]

Conclusions

The main elements of China's agricultural modernization have now been described. The description is not exhaustive; it could not be, since almost every aspect of the economic and political system affects agriculture. In the long run agricultural progress in China will depend on more than the availability of physical resources and on the types of technical progress described above. It will depend also on incentives, on the spread of education and communications, and on the emergence of a scientific outlook among hundreds of millions of peasants. A traditional agricultural proverb has it that 'to learn to be a farmer one does not need to study, one needs only to copy one's neighbour.' Conservatism such as this is the natural response of illiterate peasants at the margin of subsistence; for them modern techniques are a mystery, and an error potentially ruinous. Unfortunately, these attitudes were probably reinforced in the 1950s by the imposition of ill-considered technical changes—especially those of The Great Leap Forward.

During the 1970s exceptional efforts have been made to adapt education to agriculture and to change attitudes to technical progress. The publishing houses are producing millions of books, pamphlets, and magazines with materials on agronomy; Communes, Brigades, and Teams all have small groups working on the application of new techniques. In spite of this, there may well be a gap between intention and performance. Reforms have lowered some educational standards—a point recently pressed by Teng Hsiao-p'ing—and although direct information from the rural scene is scarce, some informants have reported that literacy standards in the villages are declining, and that the new educational system is failing to produce the core of relatively literate peasants needed to provide technical leadership. In a very long perspective, this may prove a transitional problem, but its consequences for the present must be serious.

4
Industry

'The Chinese are great Proficients in Arts; though they
have not yet brought them to that Perfection which is seen
in Europe.'

Thomas Astley, *A New General Collection
of Voyages and Travels*

The Chinese have consistently emphasized the central role of industry
in the transformation of their country; nonetheless, in adapting
policies to circumstances, they have had to be flexible about this in a
number of ways. In its early stages the Chinese industrial strategy was
to achieve a rapid build-up of the type of industries necessary to ensure
a powerful defence capability and the potential for self-sustaining
industrial growth in the future. In 1953 the *People's Daily* summed up
this policy in the following way:

What is the foundation for developing production? Simply, the expansion of
industry and agriculture; and, of the two, industry comes first, in particular,
heavy industry. Only if there is development of heavy industry . . . can China
be guaranteed complete economic independence and security of national
defence . . . and only in this way will the livelihood of the people continually
improve.[1]

At the time this was written, most of agriculture and much of
industry were privately owned. The Chinese, therefore, not only saw
the manipulation of publicly owned industry as a means of *producing*
output, but also as a means by which hostile elements in society and the
economy could be *controlled*.

After 1956 industry's role began to change. More stress was placed
on its ability to assist agriculture; and smaller-scale, locally planned
enterprises were favoured at the expense of large-scale, centrally
controlled industry. Emphasis was also placed on building up industry
on the Eastern seaboard and in the pre-war cities, in contrast to the
earlier policy of concentrating exclusively on newly established, inland
locations.

In recent years there has been a more even balance between regions,
between types of industry, and between agriculture and industry, but
industry—especially modern industry—remains at the heart of China's

modern economic development. Making profits in industry is still the means by which the State acquires most of the resources it needs for government spending and investment and, because it supplies commodities that are indispensable to defence and agriculture, the sector retains a pivotal political and economic position.

RESOURCES FOR INDUSTRY

Investment

The most striking evidence of the Chinese commitment to industrialization is the investment devoted to it. According to the best Western estimates, in 1952 China devoted between 10 per cent and 11 per cent of her Domestic Product to investment; of this, industry and transport accounted for a third. By 1957 investment had risen to between 18 per cent and 21 per cent of the Domestic Product, and investment in industry and transport had increased two-and-a-half-fold to account for nearly half of the total. These estimates include *all* forms of investment (i.e. public, private, urban and rural). If investment in the State Budget is looked at alone, the pattern of the Government's priorities is even more obvious; for, in the First Five Year Plan, industry and transport were allocated 77.4 per cent of all State investment in capital construction.

The course of events since 1957 is less clear. The most authoritative estimate is that by 1970 China had increased the share of Domestic Product being invested to 24.5 per cent; within the total, the share of industry and transport is unlikely to have fallen much below the level of 1957. In absolute terms, therefore, between 1957 and 1975 annual investment in industry and transport probably tripled.[2]

Labour and productivity

The other two resources flowing into industry have been labour, and the complex package of effort that increases productivity. The latter includes personal effort, skill acquisition, and any increase in efficiency achieved by industrial reorganization.

There is nothing notable about China's *supply of labour* as such, since, even now, industrial employment forms only a small part of total employment. The effort to increase *labour productivity*, however, has been striking. Usually in developing economies labour productivity in the early stages of industrialization increases very slowly, if at all. (This reflects the low average quality of workers and management.) But in China, increased labour productivity is estimated to have

accounted for 40 per cent to 50 per cent of the industrial growth that
occurred between 1952 and the mid-1970s.[3] This contrasts sharply with
the performance of the Soviet Union, where, during Stalin's First Five
Year Plan, labour productivity fell.

THE PACE OF INDUSTRIAL GROWTH

China's industrial progress has been rapid but uneven. This unevenness
can be seen in year-to-year changes, as well as in differences between
the four clearly defined stages of industrial growth shown in Tables 32-
34. These tables describe what happened to total industrial production,
and to its main subdivisions—producer goods and consumer goods—
from 1949. The data are the best Western reconstructions of Chinese
data. Where direct comparisons are possible, the reconstructions
suggest a rate of progress slightly below Chinese claims, but there is no
difference in the general pattern of change.

Between 1949 and 1952 all branches of industry grew extraordinarily
rapidly. This was because plant was brought back into production,
improved, and worked more intensively. Between 1952 and 1960 (a
period that includes both the First Five Year Plan and The Great Leap
Forward), industrial production grew at double its long-term rate, and
the new foundations of China's industrialization were laid. During this
period there was a dramatic divergence between the pace of producer
and consumer goods which advanced at 25.3 per cent and 8.35 per cent
per annum respectively.

Between 1960 and 1965 the picture became complicated. In 1961
total output fell by over 40 per cent. This was followed by a recovery,
and the 1960 level of output was finally regained during 1965. During
this trauma, producer goods fared particularly badly; their output fell
further, and stayed down longer than that of consumer goods. The
latter made a swift recovery and, over the five year period, actually
performed better than at any time apart from the exceptional years
following 1949. Since 1965 total industrial output has been growing at
almost 9 per cent per annum, with producer goods growing slightly
more rapidly than consumer goods. It is interesting to note that output
grew more rapidly between 1965 and 1970—the period which included
the Cultural Revolution—than in the five years since 1970.

Table 34 enables us to compare this industrial progress with the
growth of agriculture. Taking grain as representative of agriculture, we
find that industry grew more than four times as fast as agriculture.
Table 34 shows that the gap between industry and agriculture was
particularly large between 1949 and 1960; this could not be sustained
and both sectors collapsed into a steep decline after 1960. Since 1965

Table 32: *Indexes of industrial output, 1949-75 (1960 = 100)*

	Total industrial output	Producer goods	Consumer goods
1949	11	6	25
1950	15	9	32
1951	21	13	42
1952	26	16	53
1953	33	22	64
1954	38	26	72
1955	40	28	71
1956	48	35	82
1957	54	42	88
1958	79	70	103
1959	96	89	115
1960	100	100	100
1961	59	54	70
1962	62	58	73
1963	74	67	96
1964	89	77	118
1965	108	89	161
1966	126	105	180
1967	110	87	171
1968	121	96	188
1969	144	122	204
1970	170	146	238
1971	185	167	237
1972	202	181	258
1973	226	202	291
1974	235	211	299
1975	259	237	317

Note: This index is the product of many years' work by R.M. Field and his staff in Washington. This version includes factory industry and handicraft activity. The index for factory industry has been calculated using information on physical output for 42 commodities grouped in eleven branches of industry (electric power, coal, petroleum, ferrous metals, machine building, chemical processing, building materials, timber, paper, textiles and food processing). The 'group' indexes were constructed using prices as weights for individual commodities and then combined in a composite index in which the groups themselves were weighted using value added shares. The index excludes defence industries narrowly defined.

This index is generally reliable for the 1950s. For the 1960s and 1970s there is the problem that the growth of small-scale and rural industry has required that the index take account of output of variable quality. This is particularly a problem in the fertilizer, ferrous metals, machinery, and consumer goods industries. If 'superior' and 'inferior' output are simply added, the result may be misleading, since it may suggest more growth than has actually occurred. Unfortunately, it is difficult to find a sound basis for 'discounting' inferior outputs. Other problems with the index for recent years arise from failure to take account of quality *improvement* in the modern factory sector and the danger of overstatement of growth due to the mispricing of new commodities. Happily, some of these biases cancel each other out.

Sources: R.M. Field, JEC (1975), pp. 149, 165-167; CIA, *Handbook of Economic Indicators* (1976), p. 1.

Table 33: *The growth of industry, selected periods, 1959-75*
(per cent per annum)

	1949-52	1952-60	1952-75	1960-65	1965-70	1970-75
Total industrial output	33.89	18.29	10.51	1.58	9.50	8.79
Producer goods	40.71	25.30	12.43	−2.20	10.41	10.17
Consumer goods	28.92	8.35	8.09	9.93	8.13	5.90
Difference between consumer and producer goods	11.79	16.95	4.34	−12.13	2.28	4.27

Source: Table 32.

the gap between the growth rates of the two sectors has been
relatively small.

   A look at the whole picture reveals the following pattern: between
1952 and 1960, heavy industry oriented growth, followed in 1961 and
1962 by a crisis and, finally, by a readjustment to slower growth with
the progress of agriculture and the two sectors of industry more in
harmony. It remains to be seen whether this last phase—which extends
to the present—represents a balance that can be sustained.

Output of individual commodities

Tables 35-36 show the output of seven important commodities. These
figures provide a more detailed and tangible picture of China's
industrialization than the general indexes discussed above. The figures
confirm that a remarkable break occurred in 1960. If we compare the

Table 34: *The growth of industry and agriculture, selected periods, 1949-74*
(per cent per annum)

	1949-52	1952-60	1952-74	1960-65	1965-70	1970-74
Industrial output	33.89	18.29	10.52	1.58	9.5	8.43

	1949-52	1952-58	1952-74	1958-65	1965-70	1970-74
Agricultural output (grain)	13.2	4.44	2.01-2.46	−0.35	3.56	3.14
Difference between agriculture and industry	20.69	13.85	8.06	1.93	5.94	5.29

Note: The sub-periods for agriculture and industry have been selected to illustrate the most
important phases of growth of each.
Source: Tables 32 and 19.

Table 35: The output of seven industrial products, selected years, 1949-75

	Electric power million kwh	index	Machine tools units	index	Crude steel million m. tons	index	Chemical fertilizer million m. tons	index	Freight cars units	index	Crude oil million m. tons	index	Cotton cloth million linear m.	index
1949	4,308	9	1,582	4	0.158	1	0.027	1	3,155	14	0.121	2	1,889	39
1952	7,261	15	13,734	34	1.349	7	0.194	8	5,792	25	0.436	8	3,829	78
1957	19,340	41	28,297	71	5.350	29	0.803	32	7,300	32	1.458	27	5,050	103
1960	47,000	100	40,000	100	18.700	100	2.523	100	2,300	100	5.500	100	4,900	100
1961	31,000	66	30,000	75	8.000	43	1.850	73	3,000	13	5.300	96	3,300	67
1962	30,000	64	25,000	63	8.000	43	2.780	110	4,000	17	5.800	105	3,500	71
1965	42,000	89	45,000	113	12.500	67	7.600	301	6,600	29	10.800	196	6,400	131
1970	72,000	153	70,000	175	17.800	95	14.000	555	12,000	52	28.200	513	7,500	153
1973	101,000	215	80,000	200	25.500	136	24.760	983	16,000	70	54.800	991	7,600	155
1974	108,000	230	80,000	200	23.800	127	24.880	986	16,800	73	65.800	1187	7,600	155
1975	124,960	266	90,000	225	26.000	139	27.900	1106	18,500	80	74.500	1355	7,600	155

Note: The rounded figures coming after 1960 are an indication that their margin of error is larger than that for 1949-57.

Sources: R. M. Field, JEC (1975), pp. 165-67; CIA, *Handbook of Economic Indicators* (1976), p. 1.

pre- and post-1960 trends, we find that the average rate of growth of
the seven commodities fell from over 25 per cent to 7.49 per cent per
annum. The contrast between the 1950s and the crisis and recovery of
1960 to 1965 is even more dramatic.

Table 36: *The rate of growth of seven industrial products, selected periods, 1952-75
(per cent per annum)*

	1952-60	*1960-75*	*1960-65*	*1965-70*	*1970-75*
Electric power	26.30	6.74	−2.30	11.38	11.66
Machine tools	14.30	5.56	2.47	9.24	5.15
Crude steel (a)	38.91	2.22	−7.70	7.33	7.87
(b)	(22.02)	(4.09)	(−0.73)	(6.05)	(7.04)
Chemical fertilizers	37.80	17.38	24.66	13.00	14.79
Freight cars	18.81	−1.44	21.93	12.70	9.04
Crude oil	37.28	18.97	14.41	21.60	21.45
Cotton cloth	3.13	2.97	5.55	3.22	0.27
Average	25.22	7.49	2.17	11.21	10.03
Standard deviation	13.79	8.22	15.08	5.72	6.84

Notes: Steel output(a) is for all plants. Output(b) is large plants only.
Source: Table 35.

Another feature of the figures is the changing relationship *between*
commodities. If we compare the long-run trends before and after 1960,
we find that in the latter period individual commodities moved in closer
harmony. (The *Standard Deviation* from the average rate of growth
declined from 13.79 to 8.22.) However, this period needs itself to be
considered in segments. For between 1960 and 1965, inter-commodity
differences actually widened. Thereafter the differences narrowed to
less than half their 1950s size. Thus it seems that when industry is *either*
violently expanding *or* violently contracting, differences between
commodities accentuate; in periods of steadier progress, movements of
the different commodities are more harmonious.

Tables 35-36 contain three other important features. First, there is
the slow but relatively constant growth of *cotton cloth* output. In the
1950s cotton cloth grew at less than one-eighth of the average rate of
growth of this group of commodities; during the decline of industry in
the 1960s, however, it was the only industry to improve on its earlier
performance. The second feature is the deteriorating performance of
steel. In the 1950s steel was the fastest growing commodity; since 1960
it has dropped to sixth place among the seven commodities and its rate
of growth has scarcely exceeded that of population. Finally we should
note that the most striking industrial performers in the past fifteen
years have been *chemical fertilizers* and *crude oil*. This reflects the
ruthless allocation of industrial resources to ensure that industry

provided support for agriculture, and became independent of Soviet oil as rapidly as possible.

MINERAL, METAL AND FUEL RESOURCES FOR INDUSTRY

The adequacy of China's mineral, fuel, and metal resources is not properly known, and present evidence on this matter contains some puzzling features.[4] Many people imagine that China is a vast storehouse of raw materials. A Chinese source, for example, made the unqualified claim that 'China possesses rich mineral resources in its vast territory and coastal sea'; and K.P. Wang, an official of the United States Bureau of Mines, has recently written that 'China is one of the world's rich mineral areas, fully capable of supporting a modern, first rank industrial economy.'

There is substance in these statements; yet they must be reconciled with the fact that in the 1970s, exclusive of mineral fuels, China has been importing more minerals and metals than she has been exporting. In 1975 this deficit cost China $1.850 billion,* and by 1980 it is thought that this figure could increase to $2.450 billion.

To grasp this more precisely, we need to know the current levels of production of individual commodities and the adequacy of these in relation to needs. We also need information about the likely size and character of reserves; these being particularly hard to come by. This lack of information reflects both the unevenness of survey work and understandable secrecy on the part of the Chinese. Contrary to popular belief, serious surveys of China's resources were undertaken before 1949. Foreign involvement in China was partly a result of interest in natural resources; and coal and iron ore in particular were the objects of careful enquiry by the Japanese and other foreign prospectors. Since 1949 official reports have described the continuous expansion of survey work, much of it organized at local levels of government. The results of this work are reported in occasional statements by Chinese politicians and in local statements. Much surveying is very professional, but there also appear to have been difficulties in reconciling the enthusiasm of the masses with the scientific standards taken for granted in the rest of the world. During the Great Leap Forward, for example, it was claimed that as a result of mass surveying, identified reserves of natural resources increased severalfold; but the precise character of newly found reserves was not ascertained or described with precision. Figures such as those produced in 1958 often bedevil the foreign

*Here and throughout this book, sums quoted are in US dollars; and 'billion' means one thousand million.

Industry

Table 37: *China's resources of minerals, metals, and fuels*

Commodity	Deposits/Reserves Size	Quality	Adequacy of current output*	Comment
Metals				
Aluminium	Considerable-huge	poor	—	substantial importer from France, Canada, Japan and elsewhere
Antimony	Largest in the world	excellent	+	can easily satisfy own demand and export
Bismuth	Huge	good	B	small exporter
Chromite	Small	unknown	—	seriously deficient, has to import
Copper	Modest	poor	—	produces only 30 per cent to 50 per cent of requirements; accounts for three-fifths of non-ferrous metal imports
Gold	Modest	variable	B	at present a very small-scale producer by world standards
Iron ore ⎫	Huge	poor	—	importer (see text)
Pig iron ⎬				
Steel scrap ⎭				
Finished steel			—	importer (see text)
Lead	Modest	unknown	—	net importer
Manganese	Huge	good	B	small exporter, mainly to Japan
Mercury	Huge	excellent	B	small exporter
Molybdenum	Huge	excellent	+	exporter, mainly to Eastern Europe
Nickel	Small	unknown	—	heavily dependent on imports which account for one-fifth of all non-ferrous metal imports
Tin	Large	fair	+	important exporter, particularly to United States
Tungsten	Largest in world	good	+	important exporter
Zinc	Modest	unknown	—	net importer

Non-metallic minerals				
Asbestos	Large	fair	B	minor exporter
Barite	Huge	good	+	exporter
Fluorspar	Huge	good	+	world's largest producer; two-thirds of output exported
Graphite	Large	poor	B	very small amount available for export
Magnosite	Huge	good	B	small exporter
Phosphates	Medium	unknown	B	small importer
Pyrite	Modest	unknown	B	self-sufficient
Salt	Huge	good	+	world's second largest producer; 10 per cent exported
Sulphur	Large	fair	—	net importer
Talc	Huge	good	+	half of output exported, mainly to Japan
Mineral fuels				
Coal	Huge	variable	B	small exporter; but overall situation very tight—especially coking coals
Petroleum (crude)	Huge (see text)	poor	+	marginal exporter at present
Natural gas	Small	unknown	B	
Hydroelectricity	Huge		B	

*+ = current production surplus to domestic requirements.
 – = imports necessary.
 B = approximate *balance* between domestic supply and requirements.

Sources: This table is based mainly on material in K.P. Wang and John Ashton, JEC (1967), pp. 167-95, 297-315; CIA, *China's Minerals and Metals Position in the World Markets* (Washington, 1976); Peter D. Weintraub, 'China's minerals and metals'. *US-China Business Review*, Nov.-Dec. 1974, pp. 38-53.

analyst, and lead to the circulation of data that are mutually irreconcilable and useless for purposes of international comparison.

Table 37 presents a brief survey of the current position of the main metals, minerals, and fuels. The unevenness of China's resources is immediately revealed. Energy apart, the commodities fall into four groups. The first includes tin, antimony, molybdenum, tungsten, fluorspar, and talc; China is a major producer and exporter of these. Next, there is a group in which China, on present evidence, is deficient in both production and reserves; this group includes copper, chromite, nickel, and zinc. In the third group are iron ore and aluminium; resources of both are large, but production is bedevilled by problems arising from the low *quality* of Chinese deposits. The fourth group includes all those resources in which China is at least reasonably well endowed, produces sufficient for her own needs and, in some cases, also produces a surplus for export; at present, oil still falls into this category, although in future it is expected to move into the group of commodities of which China is both a major producer and exporter.

ENERGY

China is the world's fourth largest consumer of energy.[5] In per capita terms China's consumption of energy during the early 1970s was approximately 400 kg of 'coal equivalent' per head. This is one-fifth of the world average, but considerably higher than the consumption found in many other economies normally classed as 'developing'. In India, even before the oil price rises, consumption per head was less than 200 kg.

Table 38 shows China's output of the four main sources of primary energy. In Table 39 these data are converted to rates of growth, and supplemented with data on the *total* energy supply. Table 40 shows how relative importance of different sources of energy changed between 1952 and 1975. Taken together, the information in these tables enables us to draw conclusions about the general role of energy in China's industrialization, and about the changing importance of individual energy sources.

From Table 39 it is clear that over the long run the expansion of *total* energy supplies has been marginally slower than that of total industrial production (10.17 per cent per annum as compared to 10.50 per cent per annum). Up to 1963 these supplies included both domestic output *and* substantial imports of oil from the Soviet Union. If we now turn to a comparison of trends before and after 1960, a strong contrast appears. In the earlier period, energy supplies were growing at a pace distinctly ahead of industrial output; in the latter period, the rate of

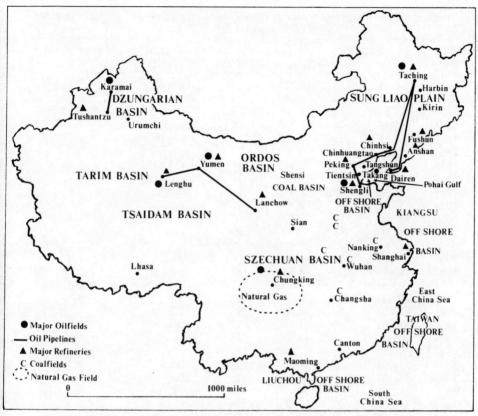

Distribution of China's oil, natural gas, and coal industries

growth of energy supplies fell by three-quarters to a rate below that of industrial output. These figures suggest that energy problems were a major cause of the decline of the industrial growth rate in the 1960s.

The explanation of all this lies in the fortunes of the individual sectors, and the crux is coal. Although China is currently the world's third largest producer of coal, growth of domestic coal supplies fell from 19.69 per cent per annum before 1960, to 2.85 per cent per annum in 1960-75. Even during the last ten years of this latter period, the rate of growth was only 6.9 per cent per annum. Thus, had the Chinese not been able to bring crude oil on stream as rapidly as they have, the coal crisis might well have halted China's industrialization. The dramatic impact of oil on the energy situation is illustrated in Table 40. This shows that oil's contribution to total energy supplies increased from insignificant levels in the early 1950s to over one-fifth in 1975. Natural gas, from negligible beginnings, had also come to supply one-tenth of the total. As a consequence, coal, which used to account for nearly all

Industry

Table 38: *Output of primary energy, 1949-75: absolute quantities and index numbers (1960 =100)*

	Coal Output	Coal Index	Crude oil Output	Crude oil Index	Natural Gas Output	Hydroelectricity Output
1949	32.43	12	0.121	2	Negligible	Negligible
1950	42.92	15	0.200	4	Negligible	Negligible
1951	53.09	19	0.305	6	Negligible	Negligible
1952	66.49	24	0.436	8	Negligible	0.2
1953	69.68	25	0.622	11	Negligible	n.a.
1954	83.66	30	0.789	14	Negligible	n.a.
1955	98.30	35	0.966	18	Negligible	n.a.
1956	110.36	39	1.163	21	Negligible	n.a.
1957	130.73	43	1.458	27	0.61	0.6
1958	230.00	82	2.300	42	n.a.	n.a.
1959	300.00	107	3.700	67	n.a.	n.a.
1960	280.00	100	5.500	100	n.a.	1
1961	170.00	61	5.300	96	n.a.	n.a.
1962	180.00	64	5.800	105	n.a.	n.a.
1963	190.00	68	6.400	116	n.a.	n.a.
1964	204.00	73	8.700	158	n.a.	n.a.
1965	220.00	79	10.800	196	9.2	1
1966	248.00	89	13.900	253	n.a.	n.a.
1967	190.00	68	13.900	253	n.a.	n.a.
1968	205.00	73	15.200	276	n.a.	n.a.
1969	258.00	92	20.300	369	n.a.	n.a.
1970	310.00	111	28.200	513	20.7	2
1971	335.00	120	36.700	667	n.a.	n.a.
1972	356.00	127	43.000	784	n.a.	n.a.
1973	377.00	135	54.800	996	n.a.	n.a.
1974	389.00	139	65.800	1196	n.a.	3
1975	427.00	153	74.500	1355	34.6-60	4

Note: Coal and crude oil are in million metric tons; natural gas is in billion cubic metres; hydroelectric power is measured in million metric tons of coal equivalent.

Sources: R.M. Field and B.A. Williams, JEC (1975), pp. 166, 228; CIA, *Handbook of Economic Indicators* (1976), p. 22; *Foreign Broadcast Information Service,* June 30, 1976.

Table 39: *Rate of growth of primary energy sources, selected periods, 1952-75 (per cent per annum)*

	1952-60	1960-75	1952-75
Domestic coal output	19.69	2.85	8.42
Domestic crude oil output	37.28	18.97	25.05
Total energy supply including net trade	20.54	5.01	10.17
Industrial output	18.29	6.55	10.51

Note: Total energy supplies are calculated using coal equivalents for oil, gas and hydro.

Sources: Based on Table 38: CIA, *Handbook of Economic Indicators* (1976), p. 27.

Table 40: *Supply of primary energy, percentage shares, 1952 and 1975*

	Coal	Crude oil	Natural gas	Hydroelectricity	Total
1952	98	2	neg.	neg.	100
1975	68	21	10	1	100

Note: Some authorities believe that the share of natural gas is higher than indicated here, e.g. A.A. Meyerhoff, 'Development in China 1949-1968', *American Association of Petroleum Geologists' Bulletin,* Vol. 54, No. 8.

Source: CIA, *Handbook of Economic Indicators* (1976), p. 27.

of China's primary energy, now accounts for only two-thirds of it. This share remains substantial, and China's dependence on coal is still three to five times the level found in most other economies; the slow growth of coal output, therefore, remains one of the most serious obstacles to sustained economic growth in China.

COAL

Reserves

China may have the world's largest coal reserves. 'Probable' reserves were reported as being 1.5 trillion (i.e. million million) metric tons in 1957. In 1958 this figure was raised to 9 trillion, but no serious substantiation for this claim has ever been put forward. 'Proven' resources are much smaller; probably between 80 and 100 billion tons, of which at least 90 per cent are bituminous, and 35 per cent are coking coal. The size of these reserves means that, even on the most pessimistic assumptions about Chinese coal technology, reserves are adequate for many decades of industrial growth. There are, however, problems of quality and of location. The quality of Chinese coal is variable and there is evidence, for example, that it is difficult and expensive to obtain mixes of treated coals appropriate for the metallurgical industry. For many years coal treatment plants do not seem to have had their share of investment and the capacity of such plants is equal to only 25 per cent of current coal output.

The location problem is reflected in the distribution of both production and reserves. The remote and underdeveloped regions of Western China account for 57 per cent of reserves, but only 10 per cent of current output. Moreover, even within Eastern China, the distribution of reserves and output is unsatisfactory. Both are concentrated in the North-East, so that to supply coal to the industrial cities of South and Central China involves substantial transport facilities. The Chinese have reported that, between 1952 and 1956, coal transported between regions increased two-and-a-half-fold and that by

1956 coal was accounting for 40 per cent of *all* rail freight. In 1957 a city such as Shanghai was being supplied by no less than 32 different mines of which the most distant were three thousand kilometres away![6] Apart from questions of cost, the fact that coal is essential to the power and metallurgical industries means that these industries are extremely sensitive either to genuine congestion or to deliberate disruption of the railway and transport systems.

Coal development since 1949

Coal was one of the few industries that had been substantially developed in pre-Communist China. Before 1949 the highest level of production of 66 million metric tons was achieved in 1942. After that year output fell and did not recover the 1942 level until 1952—the eve of the First Five Year Plan.

During the First Five Year Plan considerable efforts were made in mining. The industry took nearly 12 per cent of State investment in industry, and output grew by 14.34 per cent per annum. Productivity growth was also considerable during the Plan; output per man-day for underground workers rose from 1.081 metric tons to 1.542 metric tons. There was plenty of scope for this improvement. In 1952 over 20 per cent of output was produced wholly by manual methods, and the entire industry had only 191 mechanical coal cutters, 44 electric shovels, and less than 5,000 drills of all types. During the 1950s much new equipment was installed and the Long Wall method of mining was introduced. Much of this development was assisted by the Russians, and most of it took the form of construction of large-scale, modern mines.

Towards the end of the Plan, the scale and location of new mining efforts were increasingly debated. Critics argued that what was needed was an increase in small-scale mines, the output from which could be consumed locally, thereby easing the transport bottleneck. This thinking was reflected in the Second Five Year Plan, which included the target that by 1962 the number of Provinces self-sufficient in coal should rise from seven to seventeen.[7] Due to the Great Leap Forward, however, small-scale mining got completely out of control. Over 110,000 pits were opened, and by 1960 'native' mines were producing over 80 million metric tons of coal. At the same time existing mines were pushed to the limit, with the result that total output rose dramatically. The value of this output, however, was problematical; much of it was of low quality, and the imbalance between coal mining and coal processing deteriorated further.

During the 1960s construction of new mines halted for a while. When it resumed, more emphasis was placed on developing coal in

East, Central-South, and North-West China. This made sense in terms of the location of reserves, but was not entirely consistent with the continued growth of heavy industry in North-East China.

Reports from China during the 1970s leave no doubt that coal continues to find it difficult to meet the demands made upon it. Total energy supply cannot for long grow at a rate substantially slower than that of industrial production as a whole, and since coal still accounts for two-thirds of China's energy supplies, the industry must improve its performance if ambitious industrialization plans for the future are to have any prospect of fulfilment. At one time it was possible to provide additional coal for industry by squeezing the amount of coal used for domestic purposes; however, domestic share of coal is now only 25 per cent of output, and it seems unlikely that it can be squeezed further without causing acute hardship, especially in the cities of North China where the winter temperatures are very low. There are also limits to the savings that can be made by switching coal-fired power stations to oil, or dual firing systems; or by substituting diesel for coal-fuelled rail locomotives.[8]

In autumn 1975 the leadership called a special conference which was described as 'the largest gathering of the coal industry since the founding of the People's Republic of China'. This conference can only be interpreted as a sign of the deep concern about the coal situation which exists in China. Speeches at the conference called for 'unprecedentedly high' growth of both output and productivity. In practice, increases of output higher than those achieved in the 1950s are inconceivable; even moderate progress will depend on careful planning, on a certain level of foreign imports of equipment, and on sensible wage policies towards the miners. Coal production actually performed relatively well in 1975, but the earthquake of July 1976 damaged China's largest mine, as well as affecting a key rail terminal for the movement of coal.[9]

OIL AND NATURAL GAS

The dimensions of China's oil performance are very important. The industry supplements the weakness in coal, and China's potential as an oil exporter is of international as well as of domestic concern.[10] It is, therefore, unfortunate that oil data are among the weakest industrial data we have. Statements by officials, and press reports of the oil industry's progress, usually take the form of fragmentary data and of percentage increases of various kinds. From such data, US Government analysts have estimated the series quoted in Table 38; but the series is liable to need revision and can only be regarded as an approximate guide. In 1976 it is estimated that oil output was 84.19 million tons, giving China tenth place in the world ranking.[11]

In the same year natural gas production was between 38 and 67 billion cubic metres. The higher figure would give China fifth place in the world ranking.

Before 1949 China produced little oil. One estimate is that total consumption between 1900 and 1950 amounted to only 30 million tons. Of this, less than 10 per cent was produced domestically. In 1949 domestic output of oil was a minute 0.121 million tons, but from that year onwards output grew remarkably. Even so, imports remained important. They reached a peak of 3 million metric tons in 1959, in which year they accounted for 45 per cent of total supplies.

Table 41: *Oil output in sub-periods, 1949-76*

	Per cent per annum growth	Increase in annual average output compared to previous period (million metric tons)
1949-55	41.37	n.a.
1955-60	41.60	2.33
1960-65	14.45	4.58
1965-70	21.16	10.90
1970-75	21.45	36.68
1976	13.00	9.69

Sources: Table 38; *Peking Review*, 1977, No. 3, p. 7.

Table 41 shows that, although the growth rate of oil has been declining, it is still high; what this rate of growth has meant in terms of absolute quantities of oil produced is indicated in the right hand column of the table. This shows that in the 1950s output was growing at over 40 per cent per annum, but the absolute increases of output were small. In the 1960s and 1970s, however, the total tonnage increases have become enormous. A further decade of growth, even at rates as low as 10 to 12 per cent per annum, means that output in China will reach about 350 million metric tons of oil by 1985. At this level, China's share of world output would rise from about 2 to 9 per cent.

The location of output

China's oil output is spread over a vast area. There are five major basins in the far West: Tarim, Dzungarian, Turfan, Tsaidam and Prenan-shan; in the middle are the Ordos, Szechuan, Kwangsi, and Kweichow basins; and in the East are the Kiangsu, North China, and Sung Liao basins. Offshore fields are Liu Chou, Taiwan, Pohai and Kiangsu. The feature of natural gas, in contrast to oil, is that it is concentrated in one place — Szechuan — which is estimated to provide

87 per cent of current natural gas output.

Various conjectures and estimates have been made of the contribution of the main oilfields to total production, and it is generally agreed that the three most important fields are Taching, Shengli, and Takang. These are all in the North or North-East regions of China, and Takang extends into the Gulf of Pohai. These three fields were discovered in 1959, 1962, and 1964 respectively, and they have been intensively developed because they are reasonably close to industrial consumers and to ports for the development of exports. Taching is China's most famous oilfield and its development eliminated China's dependence on foreign oil. In 1975 Taching's share of China's oil output was estimated to be 33 per cent. In the same year Shengli and Takang together accounted for another 22 per cent of output.

Transportation is a major factor in China's oil development. Some substantial pipelines have been built, notably the 1,152 kilometre pipeline connecting Taching with the port of Chinhuangtao, and the pipelines taking oil from the western fields of Karamai and Yumen to refining facilities at Tushantzu and Lanchow. Various other lines are under construction including a 1,000 kilometre line from Tibet to Tsinghai Province. The production of these pipelines creates enormous demand on the steel industry, and considerable quantities have had to be imported. Road and rail are also used to transport oil, and China has more than thirty tankers. The largest of these tankers are 100,000 tons draft, and most of China's growing tanker fleet is registered under flags of convenience in Somalia, Panama, and Hong Kong. China's limited port facilities are still a constraint on oil transport and are likely to remain so for several years. Only one Chinese port has got facilities for loading 100,000 ton tankers, the new Lu-ta facilities in Manchuria. No port can handle really large supertankers.

Onshore reserves

There are no recent official Chinese estimates of the size of oil reserves. International practice classifies reserves as 'proved', 'probable' and 'potential'. These terms have precise technical meanings, but refer broadly to the degree of certainty of a particular estimate. In 1966 a Chinese source referred to 'proved and probable' onshore reserves of 1,000 million metric tons, and to 'potential' reserves of 6,000 million metric tons. Subsequently, an American specialist, Meyerhoff, and other non-Chinese analysts, made their own evaluations. The best of these are based on data supplied by the Soviet Union and Taiwan, and on geological information collected by satellites and other means. Meyerhoff's latest estimate is that proved, probable and recoverable reserves may be between 2,800 and 5,700 million metric tons, while a Japanese source, published in 1975, suggested that the figure should be 7,500 million metric tons, of which 4,500 were described as 'exploitable'.

One technique for estimating the likely level of 'proved' reserves is to assume that the Chinese keep output growing at a rate that keeps reserves and output in a fixed proportion, i.e. the state of ultimate depletion is always kept a fixed number of years ahead. The world reserve: output ratio is over 30, and has been held at this level for many years. If the Chinese were maintaining a ratio of only 20, then present oil reserves must be at least 1,600 million metric tons, and must be expected to rise to at least 3,000 million metric tons by 1980. These figures do not include shale deposits or natural gas. The latter are substantial. Western published estimates put total reserves at 500-800 billion cubic metres.

Offshore reserves

Offshore deposits have been identified in the Pohai Gulf, the Taiwan Straits, and around the Paracel Islands in the South China Sea. The size of these reserves is unknown, but they could well be up to 7,000 million tons. Western experts have stated that 'The continental shelf between Taiwan and Japan may be one of the most prolific oil reservoirs in the world.' Chinese claims have been equally enthusiastic, and equally lacking in detail. A conservative estimate would be that offshore reserves equal onshore ones, and that by the late 1970s China may account for 5-10 per cent of the world's proved reserves of oil.

Exploration

In the long run the pace and technical quality of exploration determine the development of production. In the 1950s Soviet and East European specialists surveyed large regions of China using the most up-to-date techniques. This cooperation ceased after 1960, but the great discoveries of Taching, Shengli, and Takang were all based on careful Soviet work. According to recent Chinese claims, the level of exploration activity (measured by million feet drilled) may equal 10 to 15 per cent of world activity. Unfortunately these claims have not been accompanied by firm information about finds, and it remains to be established whether onshore exploration activity is establishing new, proved reserves at a rate adequate to compensate for the very rapid growth of output.

Offshore exploration has so far concentrated on the Gulf of Pohai.

This is shallow, and unlike the two other offshore regions, not subject to legal disputes. Pohai exploration uses Chinese and Japanese equipment and is reported to be moving into progressively deeper water. In 1976 the Chinese purchased two American designed jack-up rigs with a capability of drilling 25,000 feet in up to 300 feet of water. Thus, although this is an area of activity where foreign technical assistance and equipment pose difficult questions for the Chinese, it is clear that within certain parameters they do not hesitate to use it.

Refining

Estimates of China's refining capacity vary, but it is agreed that it falls short of total output. The gap between output and refining capacity is widening, and is now about 15 million tons. The export of crude oil has eased this imbalance somewhat, but there is evidence that ever since the upsurge of oil output from new fields began in the 1960s, finding storage for crude oil has been a problem. The main refineries and oil-based chemical plants are in the cities of Fushun (Liaoning Province), Taching, Lanchow, Shanghai, and Peking. In 1975, capacity of these and all other refineries was estimated to be 61.4 million tons; this should be compared to output of 74.5 million tons in the same year. Small-scale refining is thought to be insignificant.

The role of oil in the economy

Current consumption of oil is 80 to 90 kg per head. This is minute by Western standards, and not much higher than is found in a comparable developing country such as India.

The main consumers are transport and industry, which together are estimated to account for 72 per cent of total oil consumption. Oil is also of growing importance in agriculture, and this sector's share of total consumption may now be up to 17 per cent. The balance (11 per cent) is available for military and household purposes. Looking to the future, pressure on the oil industry is likely to be intense. The planners will require the oil industry to carry an increasing share of domestic energy supplies *and* to provide exports. We can obtain some idea of the magnitude of future demand. Between 1965 and 1974 oil grew at 2.4 times the rate of growth of industrial output; thus if the planners are looking for even a modest 6 per cent to 8 per cent per annum growth of industry to 1980, the growth rate of oil would have to be at least 19 per cent per annum, and higher if exports are to be significant. Most experts consider that these rates are impossible, and recent Chinese statements suggest that growth at 10-12 per cent is the most likely.

ELECTRICITY

The production of electricity has grown by 13 per cent per annum since 1952. The course of *output* has naturally reflected variations in industrial activity although the development of new *capacity* has been smooth—reflecting the high priority given to this industry in China's economic strategy.[12] Electricity is produced by thermal and hydro means; resources for both are enormous. At present hydroelectricity accounts for a fifth of the total output, but a recent estimate is that unexploited hydro resources could provide capacity of 300,000 megawatts; this represents an output 30,000 times greater than the present level, and resources second only to those in the Soviet Union. The author of this estimate has also predicted that China may eventually build the world's largest power station on a hairpin bend of the Brahmaputra river in eastern Tibet. An additional virtue of these hydro resources is that they are mainly located in South-West China—an area deficient in oil and coal.

Most of China's early development of hydroelectricity took the form of large-scale power stations. These are now supplemented by 60,000 small stations of 20 to 50 kilowatt capacity. Small hydro stations often use hydro resources created by flood control and irrigation schemes. Recent Chinese reports note that since 1965 the expansion of electricity generating capacity in the form of small-scale stations has proceeded twice as rapidly as that of large scale, and that small-scale stations now account for a third of all hydroelectricity capacity. (See Table 47.)

IRON AND STEEL

Historical development

Steel is an essential ingredient of industrial growth, and the potential scale of China's industrial sector ensures that this is an industry for which the ambition of self-sufficiency is logical.[13] The foundations of China's steel industry were laid by the Japanese. Modern pig iron smelting began as early as 1919, and the Japanese eventually built nine blast furnaces in the Manchurian city of Anshan. Pre-war steel output was never higher than one million tons and a good deal of Japanese iron and steel plant was either damaged in the war or removed by the Russians.

Between 1949 and 1952 increases of output were the result of the rehabilitation and improvement of old plant. These continued during the First Five Year Plan, during which most growth was a result of Soviet assisted developments at Anshan. At the same time two important new steel centres were established: one at Paotou in Inner Mongolia, and the other at Wuhan, in Hupei Province, Central China.

The development of the steel industry between 1949 and 1957 was judged by most observers to have been impressive—although doubts about the location of the Wuhan and Paotou plants were voiced by Russian specialists. In view of this, it was extraordinary that the industry should be given a major role in the Great Leap Forward. The main idea of the Leap in iron and steel production was to make use of small, localized deposits of raw materials, and of 'surplus' local labour, to produce low quality metal by *traditional* metallurgical techniques. This movement (known as the 'backyard furnace' campaign) failed because the technical problems of producing usable metal in this way were greater than had been foreseen. It was also found that the labour absorbed was actually needed for agricultural production. However, after the backyard furnaces disappeared there emerged a new, significant movement to develop small-scale plant using modern rather than traditional techniques. This reached a peak in 1960, and small-scale plants have remained a feature of the industry ever since.

During the 1960s the loss of Soviet assistance was crippling. Savage retrenchment reduced steel output from over 18 million tons in 1960 to about 8 million in 1961 and 1962. The 1960 level of output was not reached again until 1971. Thus there was an eleven year interval in the industry's progress. Throughout the 1960s progress in the steel industry took the form of completing partially finished projects, of consolidating and improving quality, and of increasing the varieties of steel produced. One major development since 1960 has been the emergence of Shanghai as a major steel producer and as a source of technical innovation in the industry.

The main steel centres at the present time are listed in Table 42, together with an estimate of their outputs in 1957 and 1973. Anshan is still China's main steel city, although Shanghai's steel output has been growing three times as fast as Anshan's, so that by 1973 its output of 4.2 million tons made it the second ranking steel producer in China.

During the 1970s foreign equipment and expertise resumed their role in the industry. Imports of foreign steel plant were renewed in 1965, and since that year contracts amounting to $1.1 billion have been made. Within this total, $957 million are accounted for by contracts with German and Japanese consortia to supply steel making and finishing plant for Wuhan. These contracts include provision for over 500 German and Japanese technicians to work in China, and for the training of 200 Chinese technicians in Japan.

The most striking fact of steel output in the early 1970s is that, although crude steel output reached new peaks in 1972 and 1973, in

Table 42: *Crude steel output at various plants, 1957 and 1973*

Place	Output (million tons)		Share of total output (per cent)	
	1957	1973	1957	1973
Anshan	2.9	5.9	54	23
Shanghai	0.5	4.2	9	16
Wuhan	0	1.8	n.a.	7
Paotou	0	1.6	n.a.	6
Shihchingshan (Peking)	0	1.6	n.a.	6
Other modern plant	2	7.2	37	28
Small scale plant	negl.	3.2	0	13
Total	5.4	25.5	100	100

Source: A. H. Usack Jr and James D. Egan, JEC (1975), p. 285.

1974 it fell by 1.7 million tons; and that in recent years the industry's growth rate has been below that for industry as a whole (Tables 36 and 33). At the same time China has become an importer of finished steel, scrap, and iron ore, and the goal of self-sufficiency seems remote. To understand this, we must consider the raw material situation and the problem of the balance between different parts of the industry.

Table 43: *Output of pig iron, crude steel, and finished steel, 1949, 1975*

	Pig iron		Crude steel		Finished steel	
	million tons	index	million tons	index	million tons	index
1949	0.252	1	0.158	1	0.123	1
1952	1.929	7	1.349	7	1.11	10
1957	5.936	22	5.35	29	4.29	38
1960	27.50	100	18.67	100	11.30	100
1962	8.80	32	8.0	43	6.0	53
1965	13.80	50	12.5	67	9.4	83
1970	22.00	80	17.8	95	13.4	119
1974	31.40	114	23.8	127	17.8	158
1975	33.80	123	26.0	139	19.5	173

Sources: Table 42; CIA, *Handbook of Economic Indicators* (1976), p. 22.

Raw materials

The quality and location of a country's raw materials play a major role in determining the best way for its iron and steel industry to develop. China's problem is that she is short of high quality iron ore, of coking coal, of scrap, and of the cobalt, chrome, and nickel needed for alloying processes. These difficulties have been compounded by the mislocation of the Paotou plant in Inner Mongolia, where local raw materials have proved inadequate. There are two solutions to these problems: either the Chinese can become major importers of high quality raw materials, or they can make appropriate investments in mining and in the plants needed to process their own low quality raw materials. Up to the present, the Chinese have pursued neither of these courses with thoroughness. As a result they are having to use raw materials of declining quality. This lowers productivity and, since increasing quantities of iron and coal are needed per unit of metal, additional strain is placed on the transport and handling systems. Combined with labour unrest, these factors explain the low increases of output and the rising dependence on imports.

Inter-industry balance

Steel making consists of four main stages: (1) raw material acquisition and handling; (2) production of pig iron; (3) production of crude steel; (4) production of finished steel. The plants at Anshan, Wuhan and Paotou are 'integrated', i.e. they include all four stages. As described, China's main weakness is in (1), but there are problems in (4) as well. Blast furnaces for pig iron (2) are relatively modern, but have a maximum capacity of only one million tons and do not therefore compare with the scale of plants now being developed in other parts of the world, or of those likely to become common in the late 1970s and 1980s. The crude steel stage is the strongest link in the industry. Open hearth furnaces account for 60 to 70 per cent of output; basic oxygen furnaces for 15 to 25 per cent; and side blown converters for 5 to 10 per cent. This pattern reflects the Soviet influence; while the low share of the more modern, basic oxygen furnace, reflects lack of development in the 1960s.

Steel finishing capacity is still too small in relation to crude steel output. This is why imports of finished steel have been growing at 17 per cent per annum since the mid-1960s, and why recent contracts for plant imports have been mainly for finishing facilities.

Future prospects

The future of the Chinese economy is inextricably related to steel. If the leadership fails to evolve and implement a sound strategy, the industry will either retard the rest of the economy or become progressively dependent on foreign raw materials, as well as on imports of finished steel. In any event, foreign techniques and equipment will continue to be important. If well used, they will enable the Chinese to enlarge the steel industry in such a way as to give it a balanced structure, and eventually, the capability of making better use of China's raw materials.

MACHINE BUILDING

China's First Five Year Plan stated that 'the machine building industry is the key to the technological transformation of our national economy.' This is no exaggeration. Machine building includes production of machine tools, construction, transport, agricultural and powered equipment of all varieties, electronics, light industrial equipment, and miscellaneous machinery of all kinds.[14] The pivotal character of the industry arises from the way in which it draws its own supplies from the basic materials and metallurgical industries, and provides every other sector of the economy with the means of enlarging its size, and of improving the range and quality of its output. Machine building is also important because of its demands on the supply of skilled human resources, and because of its close relationship to defence production.

During the 1950s the industry's performance was exceptional. Between 1952 and 1960, machinery output grew at 30.29 per cent per annum — 60 per cent higher than the average for all industry. This reflected enormous domestic investment supplemented by Soviet assistance. The size of this effort is reflected in the fact that 63 of the 156 major projects in the First Five Year Plan were in the machine building industry. After 1960 the industry's advance slackened; nonetheless, between 1960 and 1975 the industry maintained a rate of growth of 7.04 per cent per annum — still slightly above the average for all industry.

Another contrast between pre- and post-1960 is the composition of the industry's output. In the 1950s machinery output was largely allocated to building up heavy industry and defence. After 1960 the industry was directed towards the support of agriculture. This was done by establishing new agricultural machinery plants, and also by converting thousands of existing machinery enterprises to the production of powered irrigation equipment and a wide range of other agricultural machinery. This contrast is demonstrated in Table 44 in which the rapid growth of output of tractors and of powered irrigation equipment in the 1960s may be contrasted with the relatively slow growth of the machine tool sector.

The role of foreign technology

The exceptional growth of machine building in the 1950s reflected the demand for machinery created by the First Five Year Plan. Of this demand, only 55 per cent could be met by Chinese plants; the balance had to be imported.[15] Thus at this time foreign machinery played a dual role; it filled the gap between domestic demand and supply, and it

Table 44: *Output of Machinery, 1949-75*

	Electrical generating equipment (kilowatts)	Machine tools (units)	Textile spindles (units)	Sewing machines (000 units)	Powered irrigation equipment (000 HP)	Tractors: large and garden (15 HP units)	Radios (000 units)	Military procurement (index)
1949/50	10,181	1,582	n.a.	0	0	0	0	n.a.
1952	29,678	13,734	383,128	257 (1953)	0	0	25 (1953)	n.a.
1957	312,000	28,297	484,000	278	52	0	390	100
1960	n.a.	40,000	n.a.	676	1,610	23,800	1,500	n.a.
1965	780,000	45,000	1,400,000	1,571	1,150	23,875	1,000	n.a.
1970	n.a.	70,000	n.a.	2,400	n.a.	79,000	n.a.	264
1975	5,460,000	90,000	n.a.	3,894 (1973)	7,000	180,000	11,000	n.a.
Rate of growth 1957-75 (per cent p.a.)	17.24	6.64	n.a.	17.94	31.31	14.44	20.39	6.26

Note: Sewing machines growth rate is 1957-73; Tractors growth rate is 1957-70; Military procurements growth rate is 1960-75.

Sources: CIA, *Production of Machinery and Equipment in the People's Republic of China* (Washington, 1975), passim; JEC, *Allocation of Resources in the Soviet Union and China — 1975* (Washington, 1975), p. 45; New China News Agency, March 25, 1976; CIA, *Handbook of Economic Indicators* (1976), pp. 20-21.

also built up the machine building industry to enable China to achieve self-sufficiency in the future. The main foreign supplier in these years was the Soviet Union. Over 30 per cent of Soviet exports to China during the First Five Year Plan were machinery, and technical assistance was also supplied on a very large scale. For example, of the 51,500 machine tools produced during the Plan, 43,500 required Soviet blueprints. This phase of dependence reached a peak in 1959, after which imported machinery and the Soviet role faded away. Although China now produces 95 per cent of the machine tools supplied to the economy, there has recently been a revival of machinery imports (see Chapter 5).

Special features of machine building

There are three features of the machine building industry that justify further comment. First, China's machine building enterprises are exceptionally integrated. That is, they consist of a large number of plants which, between them, produce everything from raw materials and basic steel to relatively minor and specialized components. The Chinese call such plants 'omnicompetent'. Thus, not only is the industry as a whole now fairly self-sufficient, but so are its largest enterprises. These enterprises are for the most part the Soviet projects of the 1950s enlarged, and a second characteristic of several of them is that they dominate their own sectors. This is particularly true of the Changchun automobile enterprise, the Loyang tractor enterprise, the Shenyang transformer and cable enterprise, and the Wuhan heavy machinery enterprise. These not only make most of the output for their particular industries; they also serve as training centres and suppliers of equipment and techniques to smaller enterprises in the same industry. A typical case is the Loyang tractor enterprise. This was a Soviet project that came on stream in 1960; it now consists of 120 associated enterprises employing 23,000 people; its capacity in 1973 was over 70 per cent larger than its original, designed capacity. In 1960 the enterprise accounted for 80 per cent of China's output of large tractors; in 1973 it still accounted for the majority of China's tractor output.

The third feature of machine building is its dependence on steel. Machine building absorbs a quarter of all steel output and is thus closely affected by setbacks or progress in steel development. A particular problem is that machine building requires a large variety of *special steels*. In the 1950s, 30 to 50 per cent of the steel required for some machines could not be produced in China, and for this reason about a third of machine buiding's sheet steel had to be imported during the First Five Year Plan. Much progress has been made since then, for although the pace of steel growth has been modest, the ability to produce special steels has multiplied remarkably. This probably reflects defence considerations more than any other, since defence machinery is particularly demanding in terms of the varieties of steel required.

TRANSPORT

China's transportation system is extremely varied. It has modern and traditional components (motor powered and human powered respectively), and the modern sector in turn may be subdivided into road, rail, water, and air forms of transport. Most of our data is for the modern sector, but the traditional sector, consisting of carts, bicycles, trailers, non-motorized boats, etc., is very large, and very important. In terms of freight carried, the traditional sector is probably still as large as the modern sector, and in recent years may have grown as rapidly.

Rail

Table 45 contains a variety of information indicating the pace and nature of developments in modern transport. Rail transport is by far the most important form of modern transport; it accounted for 78 per cent of freight in the late 1950s, and its share has been even larger in the 1970s.

Table 45 shows that the growth of new track has not been particularly rapid and was particularly slow in the 1960s. In the 1970s, however, although the growth of new track remained modest, the effectiveness of the rail network was significantly strengthened by the development in South-West China of a spectacular network of major lines linking the mountainous Provinces of Szechuan, Yunnan, and Kweichow. By this, railway tracks have now been extended into every Province except Tibet.

Rail traffic has been growing three times as fast as new track. This has been accomplished by improving the power of locomotives, by increasing the length of trains and the size of freight cars, and by using all forms of rolling stock very intensively. Indeed, the Chinese railway system is probably the most intensively used in the world.

Road

In the 1950s roadbuilding was determined largely by military and political considerations, notable examples being new networks on the

Table 45: Indicators of transport development, 1949/50-75

	Output of main line locomotives	Output of freight cars	Output of motor trucks	Total rail track (kilometres)	Road network (kilometres)	Inland waterways network (kilometres)	Rail traffic (billion ton-kilometres)	Motor truck traffic (billion ton-kilometres)	Motor vessel traffic (billion ton-kilometres)
1949/50	0	3,155	0	22,512	99,600	73,615	39.41	0.38	2.9
1952	20	5,792	0	24,518	126,675	95,025	60.16	0.77	10.61
1957	167	7,300	7,500	29,862	254,624	144,101	134.59	3.94	34.39
1960	602	23,000	15,000	33,000	500,000	168,000	228	n.a.	n.a.
1965	50	6,600	30,000	35,000	550,000	n.a.	199	n.a.	n.a.
1970	435	12,000	70,000	40,000	650,000	n.a.	298	10.5	n.a.
1973	495	16,000	110,000	n.a.	726,912	n.a.	403	13.5	n.a.
1974	505	16,800	121,000	n.a.	n.a.	n.a.	420	14.1	n.a.
1975	530	18,500	145,000	84,000	750,000	n.a.	458	15.6	152 (est.)

Sources: Philip W. Vetterling and James J. Wagy, 'China: the transportation sector 1950-1971', JEC (1972), pp. 147-49; R.M. Field, JEC (1975), pp. 165-67; 'Daily expanding transportation' in *A Glance at China's Economy*, Foreign Languages Press (Peking, 1974), pp. 31-35; *Peking Review*, 1975, No. 50, p. 29; *Current Scene*, October 1976, p. 20; CIA *Handbook of Economic Indicators* (1976), pp. 20-21, 29-31; *Current Scene*, November 1976, p. 20.

Indian border and the great highway to Tibet. However, supplies of modern trucks were small at this time, so that the economic significance of new roads was slight. Since 1960 there has been a programme to build small local roads to serve agriculture, and it is likely that the economic effects of this have been important. In 1976 it was reported that 83 per cent of the People's Communes were accessible by road and, in total, roads are now reported to exceed 750,000 km, of which one-eighth are surfaced by tar.[16] Roadbuilding has been accompanied by an expansion of domestic truck output and by a programme through which over 300,000 new and secondhand trucks have been imported, mainly from France and Japan. In spite of these improvements, civilian road traffic remains relatively underdeveloped. China has less tarmacked mileage than the State of Michigan, USA, and the economic significance of road transport is small, even by comparison with other poor Asian countries.

Water

China's arterial waterways are the Pearl River in the South, the Yangtze River in the Centre, and the Sungari River in the North. Of these, the Yangtze is by far the most important. It penetrates across China to connect Shanghai, China's largest industrial city and port, with Wuhan and Nanking in Central China, and Chungking in the West. Table 45 quotes estimates that reflect the growth of modern water transport and there has probably been at least an equal growth of traditional water transport.

Civil aviation

Between 1950 and 1974 China's civil aviation network increased fivefold to a total of 68,300 km.[17] This network is made up of 85 domestic routes that are served by 230 flights a week. Although restricted to small, specialized passenger services, air transport is becoming particularly important in linking the mountainous South-West and North-West regions to the Eastern Seaboard; it is also used for transporting high value freight, emergency supplies, and for agricultural and forestry work. We have no detailed data on passenger and freight loads, but aviation has certainly shared in the general transportation improvement of the 1970s. Since 1972 total seating capacity in civil aviation, for example, has grown by 50 per cent, to over 25,000 seats.

TEXTILES

Cotton

Textiles was the largest industry in pre-Communist China. In 1956 it was still the largest industrial employer and this may still be true today.[18] The industry plays the same important role in China that it does in other developing economies; it supplies the most important manufactured goods consumed by the population at large, and is an important exporter. In China's case, by the mid-1970s textile exports accounted for a third of all foreign exchange earnings. The basic data on the cotton sector are shown in Table 46. Compared to other products, cotton cloth output has grown very slowly. The long-run, average rate of growth has been only slightly above 3 per cent, and in the 1970s growth has virtually ceased. Since exports have had to grow rapidly, this means that domestic consumption has increased only marginally during the past twenty years.

Slow growth and the stagnation in the 1970s are a result of the inability of agriculture to supply raw cotton. The history of domestic cotton supplies is shown in Table 46; a particular feature of this is the dramatic fall in cotton output in 1961 and 1962, which was a result of peasants switching land from cotton to food production. This fall was reflected in production of cotton cloth and, to a lesser extent, in cotton exports. To be precise, raw cotton and cotton cloth output fell 35 per cent and 33 per cent respectively, while the value of exports fell only 11 per cent. These figures reflect the policy of keeping up cotton exports to repay Soviet loans at the expense of the Chinese consumer. The situation has not improved dramatically since the mid-1960s. Strong economic incentives and other pressures have been applied to encourage the Communes to grow cotton, but there is evidence that for many years peasants were reluctant to develop cotton at the expense of food production since, in time of crisis, food was the safer crop. The Chinese supplement domestic cotton with imports — only part of which reflect the need to import types of cotton not available in China. However, although imports became very substantial in the mid-1970s, they were insufficient to reverse the deteriorating domestic situation. As a result, there is now considerable excess capacity in the spinning and weaving sectors of the textile industry, and domestic consumers continue to be squeezed to enable exports to earn foreign exchange.

Man-made fibres

Man-made fibre plants first appeared in China between 1957 and 1961; they produced glass fibre, nylon, and capron fibres. The cotton crisis

Table 46: *The cotton industry, 1949-75*

	Output of raw cotton (million metric tons)	Net imports of raw cotton (million metric tons)	Total supply of cotton (million metric tons)	Total installed spindles (millions)	Output of cotton cloth (million linear metres)	Value of textile manufactured exports ($ million)
1949	0.44	0.052	0.49	5	1,889	n.a.
1952	1	0.077	1.377	5.6	3,829	30
1957	1.64	0.016	1.656	7.62	5,050	247
1960	0.91	0.022	0.932	9.5	4,900	554
1961	0.89	0.03	0.92	9.6	3,300	479
1962	1	0.014	1.014	10	3,500	481
1965	1.9	0.168	2.068	11.8	6,400	485
1970	2	0.066	2.066	13.9	7,500	495
1973	2.5	0.407	2.91	18	7,600	1,200
1974	2.5	0.339	2.839	n.a.	7,600	1,300
1975	2.3	0.95	3.25	n.a.	7,600	1,315

Sources: N.R. Chen, *Chinese Economic Statistics*, pp. 338-39, 408; N.R. Chen, JEC (1975), p. 647; A.L. Erisman, JEC (1975), pp. 328-29, 344; Kayser Sung, 'The development of Mainland China's textile industry with special reference to the changing pattern of its foreign trade', *Textile Asia* (Hong Kong), January, 1976; Rockwood Q.P. Chin, 'The validity of Mainland China's cotton textile statistics', *The Southern Economic Journal*, January, 1968; Mah Feng-hwa, *The Foreign Trade of Mainland China* (Edinburgh, 1972), pp. 198-200; CIA *Handbook of Economic Indicators* (1976), p. 1; A.H. Usack and R.E. Batsavage, JEC (1972), p. 353; CIA, *International Trade Handbook* (1975), p. 12; the same (1976), p. 14; Alexander Eckstein, *Communist China's Economic Growth and Foreign Trade* (New York, 1966), pp. 114-15; USDA, *Agricultural Statistics of the People's Republic of China 1935-1969* (Washington, 1972).

of the early 1960s stimulated further interest in this field and since the mid-1960s development has been considerable. The emergence of the oil industry has greatly increased China's potential for man-made fibre output and during the 1970s a number of major deals for plant and equipment were signed with foreign firms — mainly Japanese. The present level of man-made fibre output of all kinds is thought to be 55,000 million lbs. — 2 per cent of the combined cotton and man-made fibre output. By 1980 output could increase tenfold, by which time it will account for 7 per cent of total fabric output.[19]

Silk and wool

China is in the process of regaining from Japan her place as the world's leading producer of silk. Much silk is still produced in Central and South China, and in recent years the industry has also developed in Manchuria. Silk exports have earned over $300 million per annum in recent years, and the industry has been making considerable progress in design and in marketing.

Woollens still occupy only a small place in the textile industry, but the manufacturing side of the industry is growing. New woollen mills have been established close to the sources of raw material in the North-Western Provinces of Shensi, Inner Mongolia, Kansu, and Tsinghai. Important factories have also been established in Peking and Shanghai where the technical level of the industry is at its most sophisticated. At present, China exports mainly her rarer wools such as cashmere, but if agriculture plays its role and develops wool production vigorously, the industry has considerable potential for growth and export.

SMALL-SCALE AND RURAL INDUSTRY

The heart of China's industrialization is the growth of large-scale, modern industry mainly controlled by Central Ministries. We may call this Sector A. Around this sector is a vast periphery of enterprises known variously as 'local', 'small-scale', 'rural', or 'indigenous'. We may call this Sector B. The essential characteristic of Sector B is that it is controlled by Counties, Communes, Brigades, or by some level of Municipal government — with the County as the most typical level. Apart from the level of control, Sector B enterprises are also frequently small-scale, and use relatively primitive technologies; although this is by no means always the case, since some Sector B enterprises employ over a thousand people. With regard both to scale and technology, moreover, the situation is dynamic in the sense that enterprises in Sector B are expected to grow and to develop, and thus eventually to merge into Sector A.

Sector B enterprises exist in cities and towns of all sizes, and in rural areas. Rather confusingly, much 'rural' industry is located in the County Townships which may have populations of· up to 20,000 inhabitants. These townships are the normal location for cement, chemical fertilizer, agricultural machinery, iron and steel, and similar relatively large-scale plants. At Commune and Brigade level are found brickworks, electrical and machinery repair shops, and food processing plants.

In the urban areas Sector B includes both small workshops which employ housewives producing very simple consumer or producer goods, and relátively large-scale units that are closely connected (through subcontracting) to the modern sector.

The development of Sector B has been uneven. Between 1949 and 1956 growth was restricted and very traditional forms of production in rural and urban areas went into decline. In 1956 and 1957 private activity largely ceased and individual producers and small-scale workshops were organized into collectives. In this form the sector received some encouragement from Mao and during the Great Leap Forward expansion was dramatic. Thousands of defunct traditional activities were revived and new ones were started, so that at the Commune level alone at least 200,000 small-scale units were operating by 1960. In 1961 and 1962 Mao ordered a severe retrenchment of small scale enterprises; but since 1966, scattered official statistics suggest, and most observers agree, that growth of the small-scale sector has again been rapid.[20]

The case for Sector B

The advantages of developing Sector B are economic, social, and political. Mao and Chinese commentators have emphasized two points particularly: one is the unique capacity of the sector to use scattered labour, equipment, scrap and raw materials that, because of their small size or seasonal availability, could not be made available to the centrally-planned Sector A; the other is that local control releases initiative, with the effect that resources available to Sector B are used more intensively, and produce goods more adapted to local needs than is the case with resources given to Sector A. A more recent argument for Sector B is that, since rural industries such as food processing and machinery repair are operated from the Commune and Brigade level to provide services to Teams, they may be used as a lever to *control* the Teams. Thus rural industrialization is seen as a means of achieving more centralization *within* the Communes.[21]

China's small-scale sector has had many foreign admirers who have found sophisticated economic arguments for Sector B. They point out, for example, that even if small-scale enterprises are 'inefficient', in the sense that the costs of production in a Sector A enterprise are higher than in a Sector B enterprise, *provided that* Sector B products need less transportation, and *provided that* Sector B enterprises can be established in small towns and rural areas where there is no need to build housing and facilities of the kind that have to be provided in large industrial cities, then 'total' costs may be lower in Sector B than in Sector A. It can also be argued that if expansion of Sector A requires certain minimum supplies of skills, knowledge, or foreign capital equipment, it may be that the maximum possible growth of Sector A is at a rate at which the economy fails to use all the domestic resources available for industrial expansion. In this case, there may be no choice between Sectors A and B, and resources have to be used in Sector B, or lie idle.

The contribution of Sector B to industrial output and employment

Table 47 collects together data that indicate the contribution of Sector B to China's industrial sector. It can be seen that the main contribution is made in fertilizers, in cement, and in agricultural machinery. All are commodities of particular importance to agriculture, and this output will mainly be produced by units in the rural areas or County Townships. Sector B's contribution to employment is hard to estimate. About 20 million workers (22 per cent) are employed in rural industry.

Table 47: *The contribution of small-scale industry*

Industry	Share of total output (per cent)		Description of plants
Fertilizer			
(nitrogenous)	·60	(1974)	'locally run'
(phosphorous)	80	(1974)	'small'
Cement	57	(1975)	'small'
Iron ore	28	(1971)	'small mines'
Pig iron	28	(1974)	'medium and small'
Crude steel	13	(1974)	'medium and small'
Agricultural machinery	67	(1966)	'local, small and medium'
Hydroelectricity generating capacity	34	(1975)	'small'
Coal	28	(1974)	'small'

Note: These figures tend to exaggerate the share of the *value* of output since the *quality* of small-scale plant output is usually lower than that of large-scale plant.

Sources: JEC (1975), pp. 166-67, 269, 276; Sigurdson, the same passim; *Peking Review,* 1972, No. 49, p. 22; *Peking Review,* 1975, No. 45, p. 23; Foreign Broadcast Information Service, June 30, 1976, CHI-76-127; New China News Agency, November 11, 1975; The same, October 29, 1974.

Much of this employment will be seasonal, and rules have been published limiting the proportion of the rural labour force employed in rural industry to 5 per cent of the total.[22]

Problems and recent developments

Because the development of Sector B is based on current limitations on Sector A ways of achieving growth, it is vulnerable to future competition from Sector A. The reason for this is that the core technical processes in small-scale production are frequently inefficient. In both metallurgy and fertilizers, for example, the technical evidence shows that small-scale production needs more men, more capital equipment, and more raw materials, to produce the *same* level of output as a large-scale plant. For example, capital costs per unit of nitrogen fertilizer are two to three times as high in small-scale Chinese plants as in imported large-scale plants; and coal required per unit of output in small-scale steel and pig iron plants is 45 per cent and 36 per cent higher than in large plants. Thus when a choice is available for new expansion, these cost considerations will have to be weighed carefully against other advantages that small-scale enterprises may have. For this reason, observers predict that when the new large-scale fertilizer plants come on stream, many small-scale plants will be closed down. On the other hand, the transportation factor is likely to protect the small-scale cement sector for a long period of time.

Another problem with Sector B is that when small-scale enterprises expand to the point where they are no longer local (in the sense of using local materials and of serving local customers), the question of coordination between sectors A and B has to be faced. This problem emerged in the 1970s. Whereas in the 1960s Mao emphasized the importance of 'relatively independent industrial systems', since 1972 there has been a campaign to ensure that local and small-scale industry develops *within centrally planned limits*.[23] This new policy has met some opposition from local planners, and handling the gradual merger of Sector A with viable parts of Sector B is likely to be a difficult problem of indefinite duration.

THE REGIONAL DISTRIBUTION OF INDUSTRY

The development of small-scale local industry has had the effect of distributing industry more widely. The regional distribution of industry has also been changed as a result of a deliberate policy in the allocation of investment for large-scale industry. Before 1949 nearly all of China's industry was located in Shanghai, Tientsin, and Manchuria.

The left-hand side of Table 48 illustrates the share of total industry and population held by the different regions in 1952. Within these totals, five Provinces — Liaoning, Kirin, Heilungkiang (Manchuria), Hopei (including Tientsin), and Kiangsu (including Shanghai) — accounted for 55 per cent of all output. East and North-East China appear as the two regions with the most disproportionate shares of output.

The change that occurred between 1952 and 1972 is estimated on the right-hand side of Table 48. This shows that change has been significant. The two 'over-industrialized' regions have lost, relative to the others, and the Northern Region has gained decisively. Particularly large gains have been made by Inner Mongolia and the city of Peking. Nonetheless, particularly since 1957, the traditional industrial regions have held their positions remarkably well in relation to the early promises to change the distribution of industry radically, and the heavy industrial areas are now Manchuria, Shanghai and East China, and the North China plain. South and South-West China remain relatively deprived as a result of their lack of fuel, their distance from existing centres of population and industry and their lack of tradition in industrial skills.

CONCLUSIONS: INDUSTRIAL PERFORMANCE AND PROSPECTS

China's industrial performance has been rather erratic; but for most of the past twenty-five years progress has been rapid. Three industries have performed particularly well in terms both of the speed of their growth and of their capacity to absorb modern techniques; these are electricity, machine tools, and petroleum. In contrast, coal, iron and steel, and textiles have, for various reasons, become serious problems. In the case of textiles, a partial solution may lie in man-made fibres; for coal, and for iron and steel, the future will continue to be difficult.

Two factors will be particularly important in determining China's industrial prospects for the next few years. One is the willingness and ability of China to absorb new techniques from abroad — whether through trade or by other means. In the past few years, foreign specialists with access to China have observed that *average* technology in electronics, machine tool, iron and steel, aircraft, and textile industries, is seven to twenty years behind Western standards. These judgements imply that the *potential* for further industrial growth is very great, provided that the relatively open policies of the first half of the 1970s are maintained. The other factor is industry's internal morale

Table 48: *The regional distribution of industry and population, 1952-72*
(per cent)

	Share of industrial output 1952	Share of population 1952	Change in share of industrial output, 1952-72
North-East	19	8	19→ 18
Liaoning			
Kirin			
Heilungkiang			
North	21	30	21→ 32
Hopei			
Shantung			
Honan			
Shansi			
Inner Mongolia			
Peking			
Tientsin			
East	32	17	32→ 28
Kiangsu			
Anhwei			
Chekiang			
Shanghai			
Central	7	13	7→ 7
Hupei			
Hunan			
Kiangsi			
South	7	12	7→ 7
Kwangtung			
Kwangsi			
Fukien			
South-West	7	17	7→ 6
Szechuan			
Kweichow			
Yunnan			
North-West	2	6	2→ 3
Shensi			
Kansu			
Tsinghai			
Sinkiang			
Ningsia			

Note: Figures do not add up to 100 per cent owing to rounding.

Sources: Based on data in R. M. Field, J. P. Emerson and N. R. Lardy, 'Industrial output by Province in China, 1949-1973', *The China Quarterly,* No. 63 (1975), pp. 422-23; population data from, J.S. Aird, JEC (1967), p. 370.

and efficiency. It is no accident that some of China's weakest industrial performers are precisely those industries in which the relatively high wages of their workers have been eroded by a twenty year pay freeze and by campaigns for greater income equality. The prospects for steady growth could also be damaged by violent controversies about the way in which industry is organized, or by failure to handle training and educational matters properly. It is clear that in the early 1970s Chou En-lai and Teng Hsiao-p'ing constructed a plan for China's industrial growth that took account of these considerations, and it seems likely that economic pressures are now such as to ensure that this plan will be adhered to, at least for several years.

5
Foreign Trade

'As to its foreign Trade, it is scarcely worth mentioning; for
the Chinese finding among themselves all Things necessary
for the Support and Pleasure of Life, seldom go far from
home.'

Thomas Astley, *A New General Collection*
of Voyages and Travels

China's foreign trade abounds in paradoxes. Many of these arise from
the conflict between an instinctive dislike of trade and the discovery
that if modern industry and a credible military machine are to be
established, and if the population is to be adequately fed, then the
expansion of trade and the elaboration of China's economic
interdependence with the rest of the world are inescapable. One reason
why the Chinese traditionally dislike trade is that for thousands of
years they managed quite well without it. China is a vast country,
endowed with almost every resource necessary for life. Thus, until
relatively recently, the only trade that was necessary was internal;
foreign countries might have their value as suppliers of exotica to the
ruling classes, but that was all. 'Self-sufficiency' became a habit of
mind; part and parcel of China's belief in the flawless superiority of its
civilization. After 1840 this abruptly changed. The tentacles of
European and Japanese economic expansion reached out to China,
where they led to the establishment of foreign economic bases in the
Treaty Ports, and later to foreign industrial expansion in Manchuria.
In this way the economic progress of China was in many ways distorted
and impeded. At the same time, however, the expansion of Western
industrial technology created a storehouse from which, ultimately,
China was to draw resources for an economic revolution of her own.
This chapter describes ways in which the Chinese have attempted to tap
this storehouse, and to forge beneficial links between China and the
world economy. In the first section, the main phases of foreign trade
policy are discussed; in the second, the development of foreign trade
organization and business practices; while the third and fourth sections
analyse the importance of trade to agriculture and industry, and the
changing pattern of China's trade partnerships.

THE EVOLUTION OF TRADE AND TRADE POLICY, 1950s–1970s

During the First Five Year Plan the Chinese expanded foreign trade rapidly. They did this to obtain a block of industrial plant that they could not manufacture for themselves. The centrepiece of this strategy was a series of agreements by which the Soviet Union extended loans to China valued at $1.4 billion (of which £430 million were for economic purposes), and undertook to supply China with industrial plant and technical assistance. The loan programme was phased so that between 1950 and 1955 China was a net recipient of Soviet credit; thereafter, repayments exceeded new credits. The loans were finally paid off in 1965.[1]

Plant exports and technical assistance were planned to support the construction of 291 major projects, to be completed by 1967. These projects were valued at $3.3 billion. By 1959, when the break with the Soviets occurred, only 1.35 billion dollars' worth had been delivered and only 130 projects completed; and of the 68 plants promised from Eastern Europe, only 27 had been completed. Such was the impact of this support that it has been estimated to have been responsible for half of the growth of China's National Product during the First Plan. The implications for individual industries will be discussed later.

This remarkable transfer of industry required the Chinese to commit themselves to long-term foreign trade plans, and to squeeze exports to pay for this out of their economy — primarily from agriculture. As the Minister of Foreign Trade put it in 1955, 'Exports are for imports, and imports are for the country's industrialization.'[2]

By 1957 the weak and erratic growth of agriculture could support this strategy no longer; for at this time agricultural products and industrial products using agricultural raw materials still accounted for almost all of China's exports. In 1956 the State's plan for procuring exports was underfulfilled by 5 per cent. In 1957 underfulfilment was over 10 per cent, and critics complained openly that the export of food and other agricultural products was excessive, and was damaging the standard of living.[3]

In 1959 and 1960 the break with the Soviet Union led to the withdrawal of Soviet technical assistance and the abandonment of 161 planned projects. This coincided with a drastic setback in grain production. As a result, the Chinese were forced to reduce trade, to import food instead of machinery, and thus to abandon the whole strategy of achieving rapid economic growth by exchanging agricultural exports for imports of industrial equipment. The collapse of the special relationship with the Soviet Union was complete, for not only did the Soviet Union stop supplying industrial goods, it *could not* supply the grain China now needed. In 1961 the break was symbolized by the withdrawal of Chinese observers from meetings of the Council for Mutual Economic Assistance: a body controlled by the Russians in which the Chinese had never played the satellitic role of full members.

These basic policy changes were justified by a new ideology — the ideology of 'self-reliance'. Self-reliance had origins in the guerilla wars when the Party followed a policy of making its bases in North-West China economically self-sufficient. In the 1960s the military advantages of self-reliance were re-emphasized and, whereas in the 1940s the Party had felt itself a prisoner in a hostile China, in the 1960s China felt itself a prisoner in a hostile world. In both situations a high degree of economic independence was deemed invaluable. The new policy was summed up thus:

A country should manufacture by itself all the products it needs whenever and wherever possible . . . [self-reliance] also means that a country should carry on its general economic construction on the basis of its own human, material, and financial resources.[4]

In the mid-1960s the Chinese began to plan a new expansion of foreign trade. A number of complete plants were ordered; handbooks were provided to guide the bureaucrats in their negotiations with new capitalist trading partners; enquiries for imports of many kinds began to filter round the world; and, despite the absence of diplomatic relations, trade with Japan began to grow rapidly.[5] During the Cultural Revolution these developments were suspended. Disruption in 1967 led to failure to fulfil export contracts properly, and attacks on embassies and outbreaks of anti-foreign hysteria caused a definite setback in foreign trade relations.

China's economic position in the 1970s made a resumption of trade essential. The abandoned Soviet projects were at last coming on stream (some of them nearly ten years behind schedule) so that China had the capacity to absorb new major industrial projects. Such projects were particularly needed in the transport, oil, chemical, metallurgical, and mining industries, all of which had either developed bottlenecks, or had potential for exceptional growth provided that an injection of advanced technology could be made to them. The economic imperative for trade expansion coincided with — and may well have propelled — the round of diplomatic initiatives that accompanied China's entry into the United Nations. These initiatives led to the opening of trade with the United States, a new era of diplomatic and commercial relations with Japan, and improved relations with a large number of other countries. For while it is true that the Chinese have never allowed the absence of diplomatic relations to impede *indispensable* trading relationships, the opening of diplomatic relations between China and other countries provided a natural moment for the fostering of trade — often on terms favourable to the Chinese.

The result of these developments was a sharp upturn in total trade and an enormous expansion of imports of machinery and plant. Thus in spring 1973 it appeared that China was set for a new phase of industrial and foreign trade expansion; a phase parallel to that of 1953 to 1959, except that this time China's trading partners would be capitalist rather than socialist economies. Events, however, did not unroll so smoothly. The economic shocks of the Arab-Israeli War, and the quadrupling of oil prices in the autumn of 1973, had important repercussions for China. Inflation in the industrial countries led to sharply increased prices of China's imports, while China's export prices went through a confusing period in which some fell, some remained constant, and even those that rose achieved rises less than the increases in import prices. The nature of this crisis is illustrated by price movements of the main commodities exchanged in Sino-Japanese trade. If we take 1973 as 100, by 1975 Chinese imports of Japanese steel pipe and urea rose to 194 and 329 respectively; in contrast, the export price of Chinese silk fell to 76, and the prices of soya beans and textiles rose to 132 and 107.[6] These adverse price movements, combined with weak demand in China's export markets, produced an unprecedented balance of payments deficit in 1974; a deficit that had to be covered by borrowings from foreign banks, by sales of gold, and by legitimate but novel manipulation of trade payments and credits ('leads and lags').[7]

These external developments were accompanied by internal disagreement. The policy of trade expansion was associated with Chou En-lai and Teng Hsiao-p'ing, and the appearance of the trade deficit in 1973, and its inordinate expansion in 1974, provided powerful ammunition for those who opposed them and distrusted reliance on trade as a means of achieving industrial growth. The Chou-Teng group were accused of 'selling out China's natural resources', and the critics argued that if the present policy was developed further, 'then eventually, shall we not turn our country into a market for imperialists to dump their goods in; a raw material base; a repair and assembly shop; and a centre for foreign investment?'[8]

Supporters of the Chou-Teng policy were, however, never in serious trouble. There were no setbacks in trade that cannot be explained as part of a policy to reduce the trade deficit, and time and again the case for trade was given in the press. In these arguments self-reliance was described as a state of mind and a capacity for innovative and creative behaviour, rather than as a policy of restricting imports and exports. As an article in the Peking *Enlightenment Daily* put it:

If socialist construction needs it, foreign equipment and technology must be imported on conditions of equality and mutual benefit . . . we must emphasize self-reliance; but this does not mean that we have no need for learning and borrowing foreign things.[9]

Immediately after the death of Mao current trade negotiations were suspended. But most observers agree that future trade policy is likely to reflect China's need for modern industrial technology, and for a rational exchange of agricultural commodities. The limits to trade will be set by China's exports and willingness to accept credit; on the latter, China has shown increasing flexibility, and abstract dogma currently appears less important in trade policy than careful calculation of self-interest.[10]

Table 49: *Total trade, exports and imports, selected years, 1950-76, and a forecast for 1980*
($ billion)

	Total	Exports	Imports	Balance
1950	1.210	0.620	0.590	0.030
1952	1.890	0.875	1.015	−0.140
1957	3.055	1.615	1.440	0.175
1959	4.290	2.230	2.060	0.170
1960	3.990	1.960	2.030	−0.070
1961	3.015	1.525	1.490	0.035
1962	2.670	1.520	1.150	0.370
1965	3.880	2.035	1.845	0.190
1966	4.245	2.210	2.035	0.175
1968	3.765	1.945	1.820	0.125
1970	4.290	2.050	2.240	−0.190
1971	4.720	2.415	2.305	0.110
1972	5.920	3.085	2.835	0.250
1973	10.090	4.960	5.130	−0.170
1974	13.950	6.570	7.380	−0.810
1975	14.320	6.930	7.385	−0.455
1976	13.529	7.214	6.314	0.899
1980 (est.)	21.700	11.300	10.400	0.900

Notes:
1. Exports are measured FOB; imports are CIF.
2. 1976 data are provisional estimates.

Sources: CIA, *International Trade Handbook* (1976), p. 13; JETRO, *China Newsletter,* 1976, No. 12, p. 18; the same, 1977, No. 13, pp. 2-3.

Trends in total trade, exports, imports, and the balance of payments

The variable performance of exports, imports, and total trade since 1950 is shown in Table 49. The data suggest that this history may be divided into four periods. In the first, between 1952 and 1960, there was expansion at 12.42 per cent per annum, which reflected the Soviet link. Trade then fell, and did not approach the 1959 level again (even in money terms) until 1966. During the Cultural Revolution trade stood still; but after 1970, trade again grew very rapidly. Between 1970 and 1975 the growth was 27.26 per cent per annum in money terms — about 9 per cent in real terms. It is interesting to observe that in both expansionary periods (the 1950s and 1970s) trade grew more rapidly than the domestic economy (see also Figure 1).

The history of the *balance* of trade (exports minus imports) statistic falls into three rather than four phases. In the first (1951-55) Soviet credits allowed China to accumulate a deficit of $1.21 billion. Thereafter, from 1956 to 1972, China earned a cumulative surplus of $2.455 billion. During this phase there were deficits in only three years — 1960, 1967, and 1970. Then, between 1973 and 1975, China ran a cumulative deficit of $1.434 billion. Thus in three years China incurred a deficit equivalent to 58 per cent of the surplus earned over the previous sixteen years. This is the most telling indicator of the gravity of the recent crisis in foreign trade. It appears to have taken the Chinese completely by surprise. For in October 1974 the Chairman of the China Council for the Promotion of International Trade wrote an article in the *Peking Review* in which he described the trade balance as 'even'. Actually, the deficit in 1974 approached $1 billion.[11] According to some estimates, this crisis reduced China's foreign exchange reserves from around $400 million in 1972 to virtually zero by 1975. By 1976 China was reported to be in surplus again. Indeed, had it not been for the timing of payments on machinery and plant deliveries to which the Chinese had committed themselves in 1973 and 1974, the balance might have been restored in 1975.

One aspect of China's trade balance requires further comment. This is the irregular, inter-country distribution of surpluses and deficits. Table 50 shows that China's deficit with developed capitalist countries was $2.87 billion in 1975; with Japan alone, the deficit was $0.91 billion. This deficit was offset by surpluses with each of the three other major groupings of trading partners; particularly striking is the surplus with Hong Kong of $1.05 billion. Table 50 also illustrates how important it is to China to maintain friendly relations with the developing countries, since, apart from Hong Kong, they are now the major source of the currency earnings necessary to buy grain and technology from the advanced economies.

To conclude, let us put China's trade data into broader perspective. At the international level trade is quantitatively small and has been declining for fifty years. In the early 1920s China accounted for over 2 per cent of world trade; in the later 1950s the share was 1.5 per cent; in the 1970s the share has been between 0.7 per cent and 0.8 per cent. This recent decline reflects China's lack of trade growth during the 1960s, a

Table 50: *China's trade balances with major partners, 1975-76*
($ billion)

Class/Country	1 1975	2 1975 part year comparable to 1976	3 1976
Developed capitalist countries: Total	—2.870		
Japan	(–0.910)	(–0.910)	(–0.451)
West Germany	(–0.406)	(–0.294)	(–0.436)
France	(–0.283)	(–0.149)	(–0.245)
Australia	(–0.277)	(–0.160)	(–0.105)
Developing capitalist countries	+0.980		
Hong Kong (and Macao)	·+1.050	874	1.034
Communist countries	+0.380		
Soviet Union	(+0.021)	+0.874	+1.034

Note: 1976 data are based on partial returns, except for Japan, for which 1976 data are full-year January-December. The second column of 1975 data shows returns *for that part of the year for which 1976 data are available.* Comparison of columns 2-3 therefore indicates the trend of change between the two years.

Sources: CIA, *International Trade Handbook* (1976), p. 15; JETRO, *China Newsletter*, 1977, No. 13, pp. 2-3.

period in which world trade was expanding rapidly. At the national level, in 1975 the value of trade was only 4.8 per cent of the estimated Gross National Product. By comparative standards too, China's trade is a small-scale affair. Total trade in 1976 was considerably smaller than that of Norway or Denmark and even of Taiwan — although in population, mainland China is about 65 times larger than Taiwan.

THE ORGANIZATION OF FOREIGN TRADE

The Chinese foreign trade system has served the economy well. Central control has enabled the planners to use foreign trade to effect rapid structural change in the economy, and also to achieve a high degree of success in keeping trade in balance. The localization, specialization and flexibility that have been allowed to develop in recent years enable the system to solve at least partially the most serious problems associated with socialist trade systems.

In a socialist economy the tasks of foreign trade organization are the following:
(1) Within the framework of the national plan and budget, to devise and implement an import plan, ensuring that the *level* of imports is appropriate and that their utilization maximizes their impact on the economy.
(2) Similarly, to devise a realistic export plan and ensure that the

production and procurement of exports are in accordance with it. In the longer run, new export possibilities must be developed in accordance with domestic capabilities and world demand.

(3) To supervise the commercial, financial, and legal machinery needed for communication, the making of contracts, adjudicating disputes, and handling foreign exchange and credit.

In most socialist economies, foreign trade decisions are monopolized by a small group of central institutions: (1) the Ministry of Foreign Trade; (2) Foreign Trade Corporations that specialize in particular commodities, i.e. raw materials, machinery, etc.; (3) a banking institution specializing in trade matters, and responsible for the exchange rate and other financial aspects of the foreign trade sector. This type of system is effective where choices are technically simple, where trade accounts for a small share of the economy, and where producers of exports and consumers of imports are relatively few. In both the Soviet Union and the East European economies, however, centralized trade has become progressively less satisfactory as the choices involved in trade multiply, and as the intermediary role of foreign trade agencies becomes a serious obstacle to the flow of information essential to efficient trading relationships.

In China, the basic institutions of foreign trade were modelled on Soviet example.[12] These are shown in Figure 8. The most important institution is the Ministry of Foreign Trade. The Ministry is subordinate to the highest administrative and political authorities, i.e. to the Office of Finance and Trade of the State Council, and to the Department of Finance and Trade of the Central Committee of the Chinese Communist Party. Since 1973 the Minister of Foreign Trade has been Mr Li Ch'iang. Subordinate to the Ministry is the China Council for the Promotion of International Trade (CCPIT). Established in 1952, the CCPIT is the socialist equivalent of a Chamber of International Commerce. The current Chairman of the CCPIT is Mr Wang Yao-t'ing.

The Ministry of Foreign Trade is divided according to functional and regional principles. Five regional bureaux cover the Soviet Union and Eastern Europe, Western Europe, Asia and Africa, and Latin America. Functional bureaux deal with exports, imports, planning, personnel, and accounting. The Ministry also controls a training college, a market research institute, the administration of customs, and a publications organization. At one time, inspection certificates of origin, testing, and related duties were also the Ministry's responsibility; recently, these were given to a separate organization directly under the State Council.

The Ministry's tasks are defined by the national economic plans

Figure 8: *China's foreign trade organization*

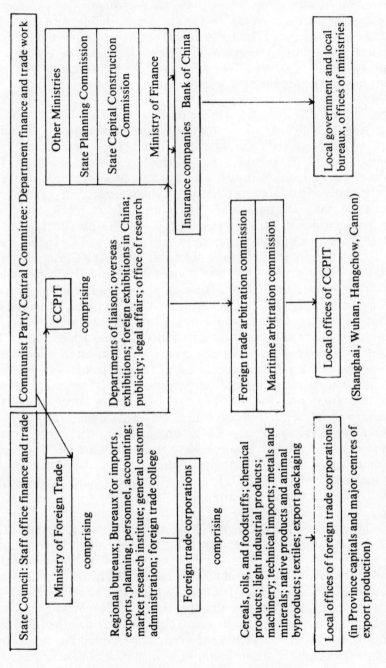

Note: Arrows represent lines of authority.

made by the State Planning Commission and the State Capital Construction Commission. These plans vary in length (see Chapter 2) but the crucial plan is annual. These plans set guidelines and limits for the trade plan, and even after these are set the Ministry has the difficult problem of evaluating the demand by Chinese industrial enterprises for foreign goods — particularly machinery. The correctness of their evaluation is critical to the efficiency of the whole system.

Foreign Trade Corporations   Detailed work on trade plans (including the drafting and signing of contracts) is undertaken by the Foreign Trade Corporations (FTCs). Nine in number, these specialize in the following groups of commodities: Cereals, Oils and Foodstuffs; Chemical Products; Light Industrial Products; Machinery; Metals and Minerals; Native Products and Animal By-products; Textiles; and the Export Packaging Corporation. The ninth is the Technical Import Corporation, which is the key organization responsible for imports of complete plants. Other corporations with responsibility for trade matters are those responsible for books and films; the China National Chartering Corporation and the China National Foreign Trade Transport Corporation. Central foreign trade organizations usually have local offices. In 1976 an incomplete listing reported 97 local FTC branches (excluding branches in Hong Kong and Macao). Many of these branches have sub-branches and offices. The work of local FTC branches is to liaise closely with customers for imported goods, and with producers of exports. A great deal of foreign trade work involves the dissemination to industrial enterprises of information about foreign machinery and, in the final stages of planning, decisions on the relative merits of rival 'bids' for imports. This could not be done without a complex, local network of organization. Similarly, on the selling side, purchasers at local Chinese trade fairs are likely to meet representatives of the local Bureaux of the Ministry of Foreign Trade, of the local office of the CCPIT, and of the local industrial Bureaux responsible for the exporting enterprises.

The China Council for the Promotion of International Trade   The CCPIT is composed of six departments concerned with international trade liaison, technical exchanges, promotions and exhibitions, publicity and publications, legal affairs and research. Its functions are less distinct than those of the Ministry. When it was established in 1952 the Council consisted of 17 prominent officials and experts experienced in trade matters. This group was replaced during the Cultural Revolution, but the organization survived. The Council has no powers to engage directly in trade, although it has made a variety of agreements and non-contractual arrangements. The Council's main work is to handle the diplomacy of trade (often in countries with whom China has no formal relations); to organize trade exhibitions abroad and in China; to issue publications; and to deal with legal matters including trademark registration. Local CCPIT organizations operate in Shanghai, Wuhan, Hangchow, and Canton.

The Council has two subordinate commissions which arbitrate disputes: the Foreign Trade Arbitration Commission and the Maritime Arbitration Commission. Only in exceptional circumstances do China's foreign trade contracts allow for arbitration outside China, and, in practice, the Chinese greatly prefer disputes to be settled by informal discussion rather than by formal arbitration.

The Bank of China   The financial side of China's trade is conducted by the Bank of China.[13] The Bank predates the 1949 revolution and its current articles of association state that it is a corporation of joint public-private ownership, with limited liability. Although a third of its shareholders are apparently private, the Bank is the Chinese Government's instrument for conducting its external financial relations and is the foreign exchange branch of the People's Bank of China. Its main work is to handle the international value of China's currency, to issue letters of credit and guarantee, and to borrow foreign currencies which, in effect, give China a line of international short-term credit other than that available from suppliers of imports.

Trade expansion in the 1970s has been accompanied by rapid expansion of the Bank's work. Liabilities under letters of credit and guarantee have increased severalfold and bankers' estimates are that during 1974 and 1975 the Bank borrowed at least half a billion dollars from Western and Japanese banks; these sums are in addition to mutual deposits exchanged by the Bank with other major foreign banks. At present the Bank's only overseas branches are in London, Singapore, and Hong Kong; eventually the Bank will probably open branches in other financial centres. To complete the picture, China has three insurance firms: the China Insurance Co. Ltd, the People's Insurance Company of China Ltd, and the Taiping Insurance Company Ltd. These companies write normal transport and shipping policies and although little is known of their operations, it has been reported that they are seeking to expand and increase their international links, particularly in the reinsurance market.

The institutions sketched above are all highly professional in their procedures, staff training, and organization. They work closely with each other and with other planning agencies, and are subject to common controlling authorities. An interesting indication of their complementarity and closeness is their practice of exchanging officials. Interchange of this kind is particularly common between the Ministry of Foreign Trade and the CCPIT.

Change in the organization of foreign trade

By comparison with other parts of China's planning system, foreign trade organization has not altered greatly since the 1950s. The basic framework of institutions has remained the same, although methods of work and organizational detail have undergone modification as the inadequacies of the Soviet practices came to light. The most important change took place in 1957-58, when the Chinese abandoned fixed, long-term commitments to import or export. By this system, since exports were fixed in advance, year-to-year fluctuations in agriculture (from which most exports were produced) were reflected in unplanned fluctuations in the population's standard of living. The strain of this became insupportable. The new system aimed to stabilize domestic consumption first, and then allow year-to-year fluctuations in agricultural output to be reflected in fluctuations of exports and, thereby, of imports. Since imports were at this time largely goods required by industrial expansion, this change could be described as an attempt *to substitute variations in the rate of growth of industry for variations in the standard of living.*[14] During the Great Depression the situation was so desperate that the planners were reduced to stabilizing the domestic food supply (by limiting exports and by importing grain), and to otherwise maximizing exports to repay Soviet credits. The latter involved exporting textiles to an extent that led to a drastic contraction of supply to the population.

In the 1970s the Chinese modified their preference for planning foreign trade on an annual basis, for in practice the import, construction, and payment for large-scale industrial plants cannot be planned in this way. Nonetheless, whereas in the 1950s the Chinese made five- and six-year plans (and outline plans for up to thirteen years), today the time horizon is far shorter and as flexible as possible.

It was mentioned earlier that the efficiency of socialist foreign trade systems is commonly affected by lack of communication and incentives; to some degree, these problems are unavoidable in a system where output is primarily determined by central administrative order rather than by response to profitability. Since 1971, rapid expansion of trade—particularly of imports—has encouraged the Chinese to modify and expand their foreign trade organization in a flexible and imaginative way. These changes have been made to improve the circulation of information, to allow closer contact between foreign buyers and sellers and their Chinese counterparts, and also, I believe, to provide more powerful incentives for producers and planning intermediaries to maximize their export effort. One of the most important developments has been the multiplication of local branches of the FTCs and the appearance of a small number of new agencies which appear to violate the monopoly of the old FTCs. Between 1975 and 1976 alone, the number of local FTC branches appears to have increased by at least half. These branches deal directly with foreign customers and have a monopoly of trade in their own commodities in their areas. There is evidence that these branches work very hard—particularly on the stimulation of exports. For example, they call local conferences at which representatives of enterprises and Communes discuss export plans; they encourage exporting enterprises to build up networks of subcontracting units, including many small-scale, rural enterprises; and they provide exporters with a wide range of technical advice, material supplies, and transport facilities. There is evidence that this development was a direct result of the unexpected trade deficits in 1973 and 1974, which made the central authorities desperate to maximize exports.

In the case of agricultural products, local foreign trade organizations often agree with Communes the area of land to be allocated to the production of exports. The Communes thus provide the labour and the land, and the trade organizations provide everything else necessary for production, transport, and marketing. Foreign trade corporations can also make advances of up to 25 per cent of contract value.

Our evidence indicates that China's trade system now provides large incentives to exporters. This has always been so to some extent, but has been increasingly true in the past decade. Visitors to China can observe for themselves the exceptional standard of living enjoyed in Communes that specialize in export products such as tea, silk, fruit, fish, vegetables, etc., and articles in the Chinese press rarely fail to point out the material advantages given to exporting Communes. An illustration of the profitability of these Communes is the account of the fishing Brigade in a Shanghai Commune, which at one time had average incomes below that for the Commune as a whole. After being persuaded to develop fresh water crabs for export, average incomes in the Brigade were reported to have risen to 50 per cent above those of the Commune average.[15] In industry, too, exporting is rewarded. Wage levels reported in factories providing light industrial exports are substantially higher than average wages in that sector; moreover, enterprises with a good export record are likely to earn high profits and to rate high in planners' investment priorities. They are therefore likely to attain the many benefits of expansion, modernization, and enterprise level investment in welfare facilities.

Not all recent changes have been at the local level. The increase in the number of central purchasing agencies—in particular the re-emergence of the Technical Import Corporation as the key agency responsible for imports of industrial plant—has already been mentioned (the Corporation disappeared as a separate entity during the Cultural

Revolution). Another change, less understood, but detected by experienced businessmen, has been a rise in the importance of the CCPIT. At one time it was believed that the CCPIT's role would diminish as China's formal diplomatic ties expanded. In the event, it seems that the CCPIT still finds important functions to perform.

Other aspects of China's foreign trade practices

Trade fairs and technical exhibitions   For many years the Canton Fair has played an important rôle in China's foreign trade, and the enlargement of its facilities in the early 1970s was one of the firmest indications of China's plans to increase foreign trade.[16] The Fair is held twice a year and both import and export transactions are made there. Recently, as many as 28,000 visitors attended the Fair; of these, about a quarter are traders and the rest are Chinese visitors. The Japanese now form the largest individual group of participants. The Chinese do not report the percentage of their foreign trade finalized at the Fair. In 1973 contracts equal to two-thirds of the year's exports were reported as being signed at the Fairs, and Japanese sources say that one-sixth of Sino-Japanese trade is concluded in Canton. In 1975 the Fair's share of trade probably declined.

The recent decline of the Fair is a result of the expansion, localization, and growing flexibility of China's trade organization. It may also reflect the wish of the Chinese to avoid an excessive concentration of contract making activity which, in the event of recession or disturbance, can be very embarrassing. This was a serious problem in the autumn of 1973, when declining world demand, combined with the disenchantment of Japanese and other new trading partners, were the main causes of an unsuccessful Fair.

The multiplication of local branches of FTCs has encouraged the Chinese to stage a number of smaller-scale, more specialized fairs. At these, problems and business can be more carefully controlled and the particular needs of foreign buyers more easily met.

Another major development is the expansion of special exhibitions and seminars by foreign countries. The rate at which exhibitions have been held has tripled in the 1970s. In the seminars (which are sometimes in conjunction with exhibitions and sometimes separate), the theory, design and application of foreign equipment is discussed by visiting specialists and potential Chinese users. The Japanese have been particularly active in these, and in 1975 put on no less than 140. The Chinese refer to these seminars as 'technical exchange'; the element of exchange is actually minimal and, for the Chinese, the presentations are an effective and inexpensive way of acquiring technical information.

Prices and pricing policy   Foreign trade pricing policies have evolved as China moved through various phases in her relationship to the world economy. Isolated in the 1960s, courted in the 1970s, China is now settling into a larger, more realistic role in world trade. In the 1960s her trade was small; and in search of new friends the Chinese frequently set selling prices for raw materials and specialized products below world prices. Thus for those engaged the business was exceptionally profitable although turnover was low. The diplomatic offensive of 1971-73 brought potential trading partners to China in great numbers, and a combination of official goodwill and private expectation of future profitability led foreign sellers and buyers to trade at prices exceptionally favourable to the Chinese. Thus while China's export prices for chemicals, metals, vegetable oils, clothing, and textiles were above world prices, imports were frequently purchased at prices more favourable than those available to the rest of the world. At this time, discriminatory prices for China's exports were also common. 'Old friends' (the Chinese term for favoured customers) could purchase at prices well below regular prices. This phase reached its climax at the spring Canton Fair in 1974. By autumn of that year the tide had turned. Lack of world demand, some disenchantment with Chinese delivery performance (particularly of textiles), and the gross over-pricing of the spring Fair, all led to a retreat. Chinese negotiators were forced to abandon 'non-negotiable fixed prices' and their take it or leave it attitude. Official prices became 'negotiable reference prices', and the prices of minerals, metals, and other products moved down to world levels. This was even true of commodities in which China has a powerful world position, such as antimony, cassia, and anise oil. A similar cycle has been reported for oil prices in Sino-Japanese trade.

China's export pricing since 1974 has been realistic and the fruit of carefully researched enquiry into world and trading partner markets. On the import side too the honeymoon is over, and China's trading partners generally apply the same considerations to the Chinese market as they do to any other.

A by-product of China's incorporation into the world price system has been the growth of Chinese interest in the way in which the prices of traded raw materials and industrial goods are fixed. China has been an unwavering supporter of higher oil and raw material prices. This is not surprising since China relies heavily on raw material and agricultural exports, and may in future do so even more. China's interest in this problem has been particularly acute since 1973 when the prices of her imports began to rise more rapidly than those of her exports.

Bilateralism and barter   The Chinese maintain that one of their cardinal principles is that trade between China and each of her partners be balanced. As we have seen, this is far from being the case at present. China earns surpluses with developing countries and the socialist bloc; these finance large deficits with the industrial economies and suppliers of agricultural products such as Australia, Canada, and the United States. China clearly dislikes this, and in recent years has attempted to correct bilateral deficits by putting pressure on trading partners to increase imports from China, and by encouraging barter deals.

On the import side, the United States, Japan, Britain, France, and Hong Kong have all made efforts to encourage importers to take an interest in China, and to suggest ways to the Chinese in which they can make their products more acceptable in foreign markets. This has not been easy since, until recently, China has adopted a rather lofty attitude towards safety and other regulations governing their export commodities such as toys, pharmaceuticals, and food.

Most of China's trade is conducted on a cash basis; recently, however, there are reports that the growth of bilateral imbalances has led the Chinese to limit import and export activities and even to negotiate barter deals of various kinds. Thus at the simplest level one finds that major exporters to China are encouraged to purchase Chinese goods wherever possible. For example, Komatsu (the Japanese construction equipment manufacturer) has made large purchases of Chinese cotton overalls. But the most serious developments in barter appear to have been connected with oil. There have already been reported exchanges of Chinese oil for Romanian urea and Thai rice, and during the past two years Japanese exporters of steel have been trying to get an arrangement whereby Chinese oil and Japanese steel are subject to long-term barter agreements. So far, no major progress has been made on this.

Credit The Chinese consistently favour a conservative approach to credit—indeed they themselves do not use the term at all. In the 1950s China had a deficit in trade for five years; since then there have been only six overall deficits, each due to exceptional or unexpected factors. Recently this approach has been reflected in Chinese criticism of developing countries that find themselves with intractable foreign debts. The conservative approach has, however, come under pressure. In the 1960s strict balancing of the trade account made sense; it was consistent with both annual planning and a low level of industrial imports. In the 1970s two factors have changed the situation: the resumption of imports of whole plant, which require several years of negotiation and installation and involve progress payments, and the trade deficit of 1973-75. For plant imports, the Chinese have taken full advantage of normal suppliers' credit—indeed the terms they have obtained have often been exceptionally favourable. For example, Japanese exporters have asked for 20-30 per cent down payments with balances spread over five years, interest being charged at 7.5 per cent. Since they themselves have had to raise money from private banking consortia (as well as from the Japanese Export-Import Bank) these terms probably represent a subsidy to the Chinese. This is certainly the case if the normal prices of plant make no allowance for these terms.[17] The Chinese have also been able to arrange 12-18 month terms for grain purchases.

Two other aspects of China's new flexibility to credit are worth mentioning. One is the success with which the Bank of China has attracted net foreign deposits and has raised loans in international money markets. In Hong Kong, estimates of the value of private deposits made by the Communist banks range from half to 2 billion dollars—mainly from overseas Chinese, including those resident in Hong Kong. Total Chinese borrowings from international money markets are a closely guarded secret, but at their peak in 1974 they are unlikely to have been less than half a billion dollars. The other change has been that China has been manipulating payment leads and lags by requiring up to 180 days usage on credit instruments. In conjunction with gold sales, these techniques have enabled the Chinese to handle their overall trade deficit.

In future it is probable that China's attitude to credit will become even more flexible. We cannot predict the forms that this flexibility will take, but it is significant that China's attitude to the major international financial institutions, the IMF and the World Bank, is surprisingly open. China has joined neither, but the obstacles to this are narrow diplomatic ones that could disappear overnight.

The renminbi *and its international value*   The Chinese frequently refer to the fact that trading partners from sixty countries use the *renminbi* as the unit of settlement. In general, this reflects the wishes of the Chinese rather than of their trading partners; indeed, insistence that contracts are denominated in the *renminbi* has at times been a serious obstacle to trade. The international value of the *renminbi* used to be linked to sterling, but in recent years rates against other currencies have been decided unilaterally by the Chinese authorities. Foreign analysts have been unable to identify any definite pattern in the rate, except to note that the *renminbi* has a tendency to follow movements of the strongest European currencies and the US dollar.[18] Foreign customers have to find the daily rate from broadcasts and announcements by the New China News Agency. Some forward facilities are available, but they are still fairly restricted. These facilities are mainly available to importers of Chinese products who get forward quotations from select banks in London and Hong Kong. Recently, forward *yen-renminbi* contracts also became available.

In practice many trading partners take out hedges in dollars or other strong currencies in lieu of contracts in the *renminbi*. All this has created considerable uncertainties, particularly for foreign exporters, and has resulted in the Chinese having to agree to the denomination of some contracts in dollars. This practice is still restricted, but unless the Bank of China solves the problem by abandoning unilateral determination of the *renminbi*, or by offering full forward facilities, it may well grow.

TRADE AND THE ECONOMY

The relationship between exports, imports, and the strengths and weaknesses of China's economy is illustrated in Table 51. This shows how the shares of the four main groups of traded commodities varied between 1959 and 1975. The 1959 pattern is typical of the period of Soviet-assisted industrialization; 1962 was the worst point of the Great Depression, and 1970 was the year in which the value of trade regained its 1959 level. The data for 1975 illustrate the situation that has resulted from a period of exceptionally rapid growth of trade.

The salient features of Table 51 may be summarized as follows:

(1) On the import side the share of *manufactures* fell dramatically during the Great Depression, but by 1975 had regained the peak of 1959; within the 1975 total, however, the share of *machinery and equipment* was still below that of 1959.

(2) The share of *foodstuffs* in imports rose between 1959 and 1962 from zero to 39 per cent; in 1975 foodstuffs accounted for only 13 per cent of imports, and the trend has been downwards.

(3) The pattern of exports has been relatively stable; however, within the *crude materials* group, oil has become an important commodity.

(4) China has a large deficit in trade in manufactures and a moderate one in chemicals. These are offset by surpluses earned in foodstuffs and crude materials. The whole of this surplus in foodstuffs is accounted for by sales to Hong Kong and the less developed economies, while the bulk of raw material exports go to developed economies. Put another way, in 1975 exports based on agriculture (i.e. agricultural products and manufacture using agricultural raw materials) accounted for 64 per cent of all exports; the exports paid for imports of which 78 per cent were industrial products. From this we may conclude that the process of strengthening China's industry by trade still depends on both the performance of agriculture, and on the ability of the planners to mobilize agricultural exports.[19]

Table 51: *Structure of trade by major commodity groups, selected years, 1959-75 (per cent of total)*

Imports	1959	1962	1970	1975	Exports	1959	1962	1970	1975	Net balance (exports–imports) 1975 $ billion
Foodstuffs	0	39	16	13	Foodstuffs	28	13	31	30	+1.17
Crude materials	20	33	17	14	Crude materials	28	21	21	27	+0.865
textile fibres	(6)	(10)	(5)	(4)	oil	(0)	(0)	(0)	(11)	(+0.105 ex oil)
Chemicals	8	17	15	11	Chemicals	2	2	5	4	–0.515
fertilizers	(3)	(3)	(10)	(5)						
Manufactures	60	10	52	62	Manufactures	30	41	43	37	–1.995
machinery & equipment	(41)	(5)	(18)	(30)	textiles, clothing, footwear	(19)	(40)	(25)	(20)	
iron and steel	(n.a.)	(n.a.)	(18)	(21)	Other	12	23	0	2	+0.015
Other	12	11	0	0	Total	100	100	100	100	overall deficit –0.46
Total	100	100	100	100	Index of growth of value	100	68	92	311	
Index of growth of value	100	56	109	359						

Sources: N.R. Chen, JEC (1975), pp. 646-47; Alexander Eckstein, *Communist China's Economic Growth and Foreign Trade*, pp. 106-07, 114-15; CIA, *International Trade Handbook* (1976), pp. 16-17.

Trade and industry

Imports There have been two phases during which foreign trade played a crucial role in the development of Chinese industry; 1952 to 1960, and 1972 to 1976. The best indicator of the timing of these phases—the share of manufactures, machinery and equipment in total imports—can be seen in Table 51. In 1959 manufactures, machinery and equipment accounted for 60 per cent and 41 per cent of imports respectively; in 1962 these shares fell to 10 per cent and 5 per cent; and in 1975 their share had risen again to 62 per cent and 30 per cent. In the 1950s imported industrial goods, in particular the Soviet whole plant purchases, were crucial in consolidating and equipping basic industries such as iron and steel, transport, and mining. Imports were also responsible for the creation of virtually new industries including machine building, electrical power generation, chemicals, and crude oil production. So important was the Soviet role that, during the Five Year Plan, the Chinese reported that the share of *additional production capacity* supplied by the Soviet projects was 100 per cent in the case of trucks, 83 per cent for steel, and about 50 per cent for crude oil, metallurgical, and electrical generating equipment. These figures tell us why the Soviet withdrawal, halfway through the agreed programme, virtually halted China's industrial progress for a decade in some sectors.

The expansion in industrial imports in the 1970s is important, but not in exactly the same way as that of the 1950s. The scale of imports, for example, is relatively modest. As Table 52 shows, if inflation is allowed for, the average value of machinery and transport imports between 1970 and 1973 was below the average for 1952 to 1960; and the value of imports in the single year 1973 was little more than half the value of the goods imported in 1959. Moreover, since domestic output of these commodities has increased severalfold between the two phases, the imported share of the total value of deliveries of machinery and transport equipment has fallen dramatically; from about 39 per cent in 1957 to 6 per cent in 1973.[20] In spite of these contrasts, the significance of industrial imports must not be underplayed. Table 53 lists the

Table 52: *Imports of machinery and transport equipment, annual averages,*
1950s-70s at constant prices
($ million)

1952-60	540
1964-66	289
1970-73	445
peak years: 1959	931
1973	574

Source: CIA, *Foreign Trade in Machinery and Equipment since 1952* (Washington, 1975), p. 6.

Table 53: *Summary of China's whole plant purchase agreements/contracts: values in current and constant prices*
(*values in $ million*)

	number of projects/ contracts	value of projects/ contracts	individual value at current prices	individual value at constant prices	annual rate: value at current prices	annual rate: value at constant prices	annual rate: number projects/ contracts
1950-59	198	2,060	10	10	343	343	33
1963-65	30	167	6	6	56	56	10
1973	24	1,259	52	37	1,259	906	24
1974	15	831	55	30	831	449	15
1975	11	371	34	18	371	200	11
1976	10	170	17	9	170	92	10
1973-76	60	2,631	44	24	658	412	15

Notes:

1. Data for 1950-59 refer to the 130 Soviet plants that were delivered and largely completed, and to 68 East European plants that fall into the same category. Value of Soviet plants was $1.35 billion. I have assumed that East European average plant prices were the same as the Soviet plants. Since all the plants related to agreements made between February 1950 and April 1956, to obtain 'annual' rates for these commitments I have divided by six.

2. Many recent contracts are for more than one plant or project. As far as can be ascertained the 60 plant contracts cited here cover about 80 projects/plants.

3. Contracts for 1973 were deflated by the imported machinery price index. Adjustments for 1974-76 were made on the basis of prices of machinery exports from Japan to China.

Sources: CIA, *International Trade Handbook* (1976), pp. 21-23; *US-China Business Review*, July-August 1976, pp. 40-43; Robert L. Price, JEC (1967), pp. 591-92; 603; CIA, *Foreign Trade in Machinery and Equipment since 1952*, pp. 1-6; Hans Heymann Jr, JEC (1975), pp. 714-21; JETRO, *China Newsletter*, September, 1975, p. 20.

Chinese imports of complete plant. For this category the value of deliveries in the 1970s is high compared to the 1950s. Moreover, although small in relation to China's *total* industry, these imports are crucial in relation to *particular* industries (Table 54). Indeed, almost all of the $2.631 billion spent between 1973 and 1976 has been to support two industries: chemicals and steel. In chemicals, imports are adding over a third to the capacity of the chemical fertilizer industry (as it existed in the early 1970s) and in the case of man-made fibres and petrochemicals, imports are virtually creating new industries. Output of ethylene, for example, (the most versatile basis for producing a range of artificial materials) is to be trebled as a result of imported plant.[21]

Table 54: *Breakdown of whole plant contracts by industry, 1973-76*

	Number of contracts	Value $ million	Per cent of total contract value
Chemical (inc. petrochemical)	26	943	36
Man-made fibres	5	130	5
Chemical fertilizer	8	512	19
Chemicals sub-total	(39)	(1,585)	(60)
Power equipment	9	247	9
Engineering	4	197	7
Steel	8	602	23
Totals	60	2,631	100

Sources: As Table 53.

The steel situation is quite different. As discussed in Chapter 4, steel is a well-established industry which, due to serious planning errors, is technically inefficient and unable to satisfy domestic demand. The significance of this is shown in Table 51 which shows that steel imports now account for a fifth of China's imports. These imports are at the expense of imports of machinery. Further, a broader viewpoint, including the whole metals sector, reveals that imports of metal ores, scrap, and products in 1975 exceeded exports by $1.850 billion—an enormous sum in the perspective of China's balance of payments. The effect of imports of steel plant should be to increase steel finishing capacity by about a third as compared to the early 1970s; imports will also improve mining and processing facilities to enable China to make better use of indigenous raw materials.

The reason why industrial imports are more important than their quantitative level suggests is that they have the capacity to provide cumulative, *qualitative* improvement in China's industry. The Chinese absorb foreign technology in many ways. They read literature; they send specialists to study abroad; they encourage foreign firms to give expositions in China. They even purchase prototypes which they try to copy in substantial quantities. All of this is useful, although prototype copying has proved more difficult than anticipated. For example, in 1963 the Chinese purchased a Dutch urea plant which they planned to replicate in a twin plant, but were unable to do so. In some products, however, the Chinese have succeeded in prototype copying. Two examples are a very advanced British fuel injection unit for tractor engines, and the Swedish Hasselblad camera.[22]

As a *general* solution to technology acquisition, prototype copying is not feasible. The Chinese, therefore, have also had to purchase substantial quantities of equipment and to obtain the technical assistance necessary to adapt and integrate specialized equipment into their industrial systems. Interest in this type of import has been markedly apparent in recent years. One side of this was the re-establishment of the Technical Import Corporation in 1972; less well known, but equally important, are the growing number of import choices made, not by the staff of industrial enterprises, but by the staff of technical research organizations. German and Japanese specialists report that these organizations scan the market for advanced technology, make complex technical and economic comparisons, and then persuade Chinese enterprises to buy particular products.[23] The most outstanding deal that reflects China's need to upgrade her technical expertise is the $200 million Rolls Royce contract concluded in 1975. This will enable China to produce aero engines ten years more up-to-date than those produced at present. To accomplish the transfer of technology necessary for this, the deal has included a training programme for Chinese engineers as well as the import of machinery and equipment. Another aspect of this deal is that it shows that the prohibition of exports to China for defence reasons (the COCOM regulations) are a dead letter.

Exports   China's exports of industrial commodities remain modest. In 1975 they accounted for 37 per cent of total exports. This was *lower* than their share in the early 1960s; moreover over half of these exports were textiles. In making the textile industry the major industrial exporter China is following a pattern common among developing countries. China undoubtedly has a comparative advantage in this industry, although several factors make it hard for her to compete in the upper end of the market with sophisticated competitors such as those in Hong Kong. Dyeing and weaving are weak, and deliveries are slow. The latter is a serious problem in a market where fashions change rapidly. Importers report that the Chinese take two to five months for rush orders, but that Hong Kong manufacturers can deliver in three weeks.

Textiles apart, China produces a wide range of manufactured exports. These include all types of machinery, transport equipment, and consumer goods. China sells textiles, clothing, and footwear to both developed and underdeveloped countries, and to communist customers. Handicrafts are popular in developed countries; manufactured consumer goods and machinery are nearly all sold to the less developed countries.

Table 55: *Foreign trade in agricultural products and products using agricultural materials, 1975 ($ million)*

Exports		Imports		Balance	
Foodstuffs	2,100	Foodstuffs	930	Foodstuffs	+1,165
grains	(745)	grains	(680)		
meat, fish,					
live animals	(615)	fruit, vegetables	(35)		
fruit, vegetables	(340)	sugar	(185)		
other	(400)				
Total to Hong Kong	(605)				
Crude materials	640	Crude materials	525	Crude materials	+115
(hides, oilseeds,		textile fibres	(275)		
textile fibres,		crude rubber	(140)		
animal materials,					
vegetable oils)					
Manufactures	1,670	Manufactures	170	Manufactures	+1,500
leather, dressed					
skins	(50)				
paper	(45)				
textile yarn, etc.	(985)				
clothing	(330)				
footwear	(55)				
handicrafts	(205)				
Total	4,410	Total	1,625	Agriculture's	
Total exports	6,930	Total imports	7,385	balance	+2,785
Agriculture's share		Agriculture's share		Total balance	−455
(per cent)	64	(per cent)	22		

Source: CIA, *International Trade Handbook* (1976), pp. 16-17.

Trade and agriculture

Agriculture's role in China's foreign trade is summarized in Table 55. This shows details of the principal imports and exports that are either agricultural products, or are products for which agriculture provides raw materials. In 1975 such products accounted for 64 per cent of exports and 22 per cent of imports. Thus in a year in which China's trade deficit was $455 million, the surplus from agriculture was $2,785 million. In 1975, for the first time since the 1950s, there was even a net profit on trade in grains in the sense that the *value* of exports exceeded that of imports—although in *weight*, the reverse was true. As long as this dependence on agricultural foreign exchange earnings remains, trade planning will be difficult since such plans can be upset by fluctuations in harvests and, in the long term, by population growth that limits the availability of agricultural products for export.

To understand the role of grain in trade we need some additional information. On the import side grain imports since 1961 have averaged 5 million metric tons per year. The peak was 1973 when China imported 7.68 million metric tons. In terms of cost, the peak year was 1974 when imports cost $1.18 billion. In 1975 and 1976, imports fell to their lowest level — 3.5 and 2 million metric tons. These low figures reflect good harvests, exceptional pressure on China's ability to pay, and a tripling of prices between 1971 and 1975. The effect of price rises has been that, whereas in 1971 China bought 3 million metric tons for $205 million, in 1975, 3.3 million metric tons cost $680 million. Fortunately, rising prices have increased receipts from rice exports as well. Low purchases in the past two years have been achieved by China taking minimum quantities (and even less) stipulated under long-term agreements with Australia, Canada and Argentina. The Chinese have also demonstrated their willingness to be active in the futures market by paying appropriate penalties when cancelling forward grain contracts made with American exporters.

Apart from grains, agricultural imports include rubber from South-East Asia and Sri Lanka, sugar mainly from Cuba, and cotton mainly from the United States. An interesting commodity is the soya bean, whose trade role varies from year to year. In 1974, for example, net *imports* cost China $87 million, whereas in 1975 net *exports* earned $58 million. These figures probably reflect variations in the need for foreign currency. By any objective standard China needs all the soya beans produced for domestic consumption (except for some special varieties exported to Japan). However, if foreign exchange is short, the domestic consumer is squeezed, imports are stopped, and an export surplus earned.

In the longer term China will try to reduce the role of agriculture in exports. This is already being done by exporting oil and manufactures other than textiles. This transformation of trade will, however, take time, and until the mid-1980s at the very least, agriculture's performance will remain central to China's foreign trade situation.

Table 56: *China's trading partners: rank, value, and shares of total trade,*
average 1973-75
(values, $ million)

	Rank	Value	Per cent share
Japan	1	3,047	24
Hong Kong	2	909	7
USA	3	802	6
W. Germany	4	629	5
Malaysia Singapore	5	513	4
Canada	6	471	4
France	7	375	3
Australia	8	374	3
Romania	9	335	3
UK	10	327	3
Soviet Union	11	277	2
Italy	12	230	2
Others		4,498	34
Total		12,787	100

Sources: *Current Scene,* September 1976, p. 5; Table 49.

CHINA'S TRADING PARTNERS

Japan

In the past decade Japan has emerged as China's most important trading partner (Table 56). Between 1960 and 1972, trade (value and volume) grew at approximately 10 per cent per annum — double the rate of China's overall trade growth. Since 1972 the value of trade has increased three-and-a-half-fold, and volume increases have also been substantial. As Table 57 shows, recent growth has been one-sided; China's imports have outstripped exports with the result that the cumulative trade deficit for 1972 to 1975 was $1.4 billion. The deficits in 1974 and 1975 reflect the fact that upward movements of China's export prices have not kept up with import prices — particularly those for fertilizers and some categories of steel.

The result of this rapid expansion has been that Japan now supplies more than a third of China's imports, and has won a similar share of the value of the contracts for whole plant imports to China (Table 58). China is less important to Japan; although by 1975 China had become Japan's third largest export market, accounting for 4 per cent of total exports. China's importance to Japan's steel, chemical, and plant manufacturing industries is considerably greater than the 4 per cent figure suggests.

The commodities traded between China and Japan are shown in Table 59. On the import side the figures are typical of recent years with

Table 57: *China's trade with Japan: values and volumes, selected years 1961-76 (values in $ million)*

	Exports value	Exports volume	Imports value	Imports volume	Total trade value	Balance value	Per cent growth value of total trade	Per cent growth volume of exports	Per cent growth volume of imports
1961	29		17		46	+12			
1966	300	100	331	100	631	−31			
1972	468	140	640	249	1,108	−172	10 (1966-72)	6 (1966-72)	16 (1966-72)
1973	928	155	1,093	305	2,021	−165	71	11	22
1974	1,305	161	1,985	360	3,290	−680	82	4	18
1975	1,531	n.a.	2,259	n.a.	3,790	−728	15	n.a.	n.a.
1976	1,371	n.a.	1,663	n.a.	3,033	−292	−20	n.a.	n.a.

Note: Exports FOB, Imports CIF.

Sources: N.R. Chen, JEC (1975), p. 650; *Current Scene*, September 1976, p. 9; JETRO, *China Newsletter*, September 1975, p. 11.

Table 58: *Breakdown of whole plant contracts by exporting country, 1973-76*

	Number of contracts	Total value $ million	Per cent total value
Japan	30	986	37
France	6	571	22
West Germany	11	420	16
UK	2	208	8
USA	2	205	8
Other	11	241	9
Total	60	2,361	100

Source: Table 53.

over 90 per cent of China's imports being metals, chemicals, and machinery and equipment. On the export side, this table reflects the recent appearance of oil (included in mineral fuels). In 1973 petroleum exports to Japan earned China $33 million; in 1974 $411 million; and in 1975 $740 million. Without these exports, China's trade deficit with Japan would have reached $1 billion. Apart from oil, China's exports are food, raw materials, and manufactured products based on agricultural raw materials. Indeed, if one excludes mineral fuels, 84 per cent of China's exports to Japan are related to agriculture.

There are powerful economic reasons that explain the growth of Sino-Japanese trade. The two economies are close and in many ways complementary. On the Japanese side, the China market provided an excellent outlet for capacity built up during the economic expansion stimulated by the Vietnam war. Since 1973 China has had the added attraction of being a trading partner that may have the potential to diversify Japan's sources of crude oil, payment for which would solve the problem of China's inability to pay for imports from Japan. On the Chinese side, Japan has been cast in a role similar to that occupied by the Soviet Union during the 1950s. For, through Japan, China can

Table 59: *Commodity structure of Sino-Japanese trade, 1975*

Imports from Japan		Exports to Japan	
Commodity	Per cent share	Commodity	Per cent share
Fibres and fibre manufactures	5	Fibres and fibre manufactures	19
Metals and metal manufactures	40	Foodstuffs	13
Chemicals	20	Raw materials	10
Machinery and equipment	31	Mineral fuels	50
Other	4	Other	8
Total	100	Total	100

Source: JETRO, *China Newsletter,* April, 1976, pp. 10-12.

obtain access to almost the whole range of modern industrial technology. It was the economic rationale that pushed Sino-Japanese trade ahead between the mid-1960s and 1972; a period in which the two countries had no proper diplomatic relations and were involved in a series of disputes over Taiwan, over Japan's relations with America, and over the treatment of Japanese nationals caught up in the Cultural Revolution.

After Nixon had reopened American links with China, Japan followed suit. The chief executives of Japan's most powerful corporations paid visits to China, amended their Taiwanese links, and undertook to observe principles of trade stipulated by China. These ceremonial reconciliations were climaxed by a visit to China (in September 1973) of a group of leading businessmen led by Kogo Uemura, President of the Keidanren. There is no doubt that the Japanese business community had a sense of guilt about Japan's pre-war involvement in China, a sense that the Chinese exploited by declining to accept even token material reparations for the damage done during the Sino-Japanese war. The Chinese made it clear that Japanese goodwill was to be manifested in trading relations; they agreed almost immediately to trade, fishing, and shipping agreements, while still declining to sign a treaty of peace and friendship.

The future growth of Sino-Japanese trade will be determined by oil. On the Chinese side there are no serious limits to imports from Japan. Availability of skilled manpower controls the pace at which new whole plant facilities are imported; but these apart, China's absorptive capacity for other types of machinery is practically limitless. The question is, therefore, what can China pay for? Apart from oil, the prospects for Chinese exports are not good. Agricultural imports are restricted by Japan's protection of farming. Protection of Japan's silk industry, for example, has recently become a serious obstacle to China's exports. Some Chinese commodities, moreover, have to compete in Japan with exports from America and elsewhere. Since China has in recent years accounted for up to two-thirds of Japan's imports of agricultural produce, the Japanese will find it difficult to agree to any expansion that increases this share further. Among manufactured products, Chinese textile exports have proved harder to sell than was expected. Thus in 1974 Japanese importers failed to complete contracts (mainly for textiles) valued at up to $300 million.

In 1973 and 1974 oil was widely regarded as the commodity that would facilitate further rapid growth of Sino-Japanese trade. In 1975 imports were over 9 million tons and Japanese traders forecast that imports of crude oil could reach 100 million tons by the early 1980s. (At this level they would account for about a third of Japan's consumption.) By 1976 the situation had changed considerably. The

Japanese were less anxious as purchasers since Chinese prices were still marginally higher than prices from elsewhere. Transport costs from China were still as high as those from the Arabian Gulf (because China cannot handle supertankers) and Japanese refining facilities remained unsuited for Chinese oil. On the Chinese side, officials informed Japanese enquirers in the spring of 1976 that future supplies of oil to Japan were to be *reduced*. The reason given for this was that domestic demand was growing, but this statement also reflected the declining rate of growth of China's oil output. These complications notwithstanding, there remains a real possibility that by the 1980s Chinese exports of oil could exceed 50 million tons, and that Japan's share of these will be large.

Finally, trade strategy in both China and Japan will depend on a variety of other factors. Relations with the Soviet Union, for example, are crucial to both countries. China may well continue to decline Japanese offers of close involvement in the development of her oil and other extractive industries. The Soviet Union, by contrast, may extend offers of this kind which the Japanese will find it difficult to refuse. For in effect China and the Soviet Union are competitors; both being relatively underdeveloped economies seeking a complementary relationship with an advanced economy — Japan. Japan also has close trade and investment ties with Taiwan, the United States, the OPEC group, and Western Europe. All of these provide a network of limitations that affect China's relations with Japan. On the Chinese side, too, there are problems. For example, the Chinese wish to avoid relationships which impose on them the role of suppliers of raw material and consumers of finished goods. Also, feelings about Japan are ambiguous; indeed, while entertaining Japanese businessmen with every courtesy, the Chinese take other foreigners to see films and plays in which the Japanese are portrayed as cruel and ridiculous and, in their media, they describe the Japanese economy as being in the last delirious throes of capitalist collapse.[24] Thus, although relations have been good and trade has expanded to the benefit of both parties, future Sino-Japanese trade will have to be worked out in a minefield of possible complications arising out of history, politics, and the evolution of the world trading system.

The United States

Between 1950 and April 1971 an American embargo forbade all exports to China; for most of this period imports were also forbidden. The embargo was relaxed as a preliminary to the revolution in Sino-American relations that followed from Nixon's visit and the communiqué that concluded this: the Shanghai Communiqué of

February 1972. By 1973 America was China's second largest trading partner, a position maintained in 1974 when two-way trade reached a peak of just over $1 billion. In the same year China's trade deficit with the United States was $610 million. In 1975 two-way trade fell to $460 million.[25]

The composition of Sino-American trade is surprising. The United States has the world's most advanced industry; China is one of the world's most agricultural economies—in both absolute and relative terms—yet American exports to China are mainly agricultural products, and China's principal exports to America are manufactured cotton goods. Table 60 lists the five main exports and imports in 1974.

Table 60A: *China's five main imports from the United States, 1974 (value $ million)*

	Value	Per cent share
Wheat and corn	330	40
Cotton	186	23
Soya beans	140	17
Aircraft	50	6
Steel scrap	9	1
Other	105	13

Table 60B: *China's five main exports to the United States, 1974 (value $ million)*

	Value	Per cent share
Cotton goods	18	16
Tin	9	8
Rosin	8	7
Antiques	7	6
Bristles	6	5
Other	60	52

Source: US-China Business Review, March-April, 1975, p. 19.

The Americans have made some important sales of industrial products; notably ten Boeing 707 aircraft ($150 million) and eight ammonium fertilizer plants ($2.5 billion). But the Americans have not succeeded in getting a major foothold in the market for machinery and whole plant which is still dominated by the Japanese and West Europeans.

The decline in 1975 is an interesting example of how unpredictable trade with China can be. The decline was a result of China's cancellation of contracts to import grain, and the reduction by two-thirds of cotton imports. To some extent, these reflected a better harvest in China, a squeeze on China's ability to pay, and China's dissatisfaction with the size of the trade imbalance. However, Chinese officials also made it clear that until political relations improve, the United States will be regarded as a residual supplier rather than an 'old friend'. Improvement of political relations will have to include full exchange at ambassadorial level. There will also have to be settlement to resolve American claims of 197 million dollars' worth of assets in China and 77 million dollars' worth of frozen Chinese assets in the United States, and the extension to China by America of Most Favoured Nation treatment. Withholding of the latter has caused the Chinese particular anger, since they assumed that extension of Most Favoured Nation treatment would follow directly from the Shanghai Communiqué, which referred to trade conducted 'under conditions of equality and mutual benefit'. When diplomatic relations are improved, America's role in China's trade will become important again. The extension of Most Favoured Nation treatment will lower tariffs sharply on a number of Chinese exports, and should result in an improvement in total sales—particularly if domestic American demands for control of textile imports are contained. As an exporter to China, America is in the unique position of being able to supply both agricultural and non-agricultural goods. Thus if China needs further agricultural imports, American trade will be good; conversely, if China can keep a high proportion of foreign exchange for industrial products, the Americans still have strong points to press.

Prospects for American industrial exports will be particularly good if more satisfactory arrangements can be made for licensing. At present the handling of patented rights is regarded as reasonably satisfactory; the Chinese either add 20 to 30 per cent to the purchase price to account for patents, or they agree to mutually acceptable limitations on re-exporting to third countries. Satisfactory licensing agreements are not yet common, but, if they were, this would open new prospects for American exporters in such sophisticated fields as aerospace, electronics, and offshore oil drilling and prospecting.

Western Europe

Politically, China is inclined to have close relations with Western Europe, which is regarded as an ally (often in need of prompting) against the super powers, the Soviet Union and the United States. Western Europe's capacity to supply machinery and plant of high technical sophistication adds to the region's attractiveness. In 1975 China opened diplomatic relations with the European Economic Community, and although EEC regulations do not allow for bilateral trade agreements of the type favoured by China, there is a reasonable prospect that some form of close, formal economic relations between China and the Community will be constructed. Western Europe is a traditional supplier to China and, even in the 1950s when trade was dominated by the Eastern bloc, total trade reached $630 million in 1959, accounting for 15 per cent of China's total trade.

The Europeans were among the first to begin exporting industrial goods to China during the 1960s. Twenty-three out of the thirty whole plant purchases recorded for 1963 to 1965 were European sales. In the 1970s Europeans have continued to play an important role as exporters. In 1975 total trade was $2.755 billion, with a surplus of $1.075 billion in Europe's favour. This accounted for 19 per cent of China's total trade. As can be seen from Table 56, the best performers have been West Germany and France, who ranked fourth and seventh in total trade over the three years 1973-75. Both countries also figure prominently in whole plant sales (see Table 58). The Germans in particular have cultivated China assiduously. They have sent a steady flow of top politicians on visits, and backed this with imaginative planning and sales work that looks to the 1980s as carefully as to the 1970s. Apart from steel plant, valued at $250 million, German exports have been spread across a wide range of industrial product groups, including chemicals, helicopters, oil and mining equipment.

In spite of the long history of a China trade, the most conspicuously weak European performer has been Britain. Between 1970 and 1975 Britain's share of China's trade fell from 5 per cent to 2 per cent, and, even in monetary values, total trade actually declined in 1974 and 1975. The one area of outstanding British success has been aeronautics. The Hawker Siddeley contract for Tridents, and the 1976 Rolls Royce engine contract, are together valued at $300 million. The Rolls Royce contract is not yet included in published trade figures, but payments to Hawker Siddeley are. Without the Hawker contract Britain's role as an exporter to China would have diminished to vanishing point.

The Soviet Bloc and other socialist countries

Table 61 records the deep fall, and slight rise since 1970, of China's trade with other socialist countries. The share of this group reached its peak in 1959 when it accounted for 70 per cent of China's total trade. This figure reflected China's close relationship with the Soviet Union and the CMEA (Council for Mutual Economic Assistance) bloc. In general, this trade was an exchange of raw materials, agricultural produce, and textiles from China, for machinery and industrial imports from the bloc. Trade collapsed when political links collapsed, and when China's primary need was for foodstuffs, which other socialist countries could not supply.

Some recovery of trade has taken place in the 1970s. Romania is now China's largest socialist trading partner, accounting in 1975 for 32 per

Table 61: *Distribution of total trade, by socialist and non-socialist countries, selected years, 1957-75 (per cent)*

	USSR	E. Europe	N. Korea N. Vietnam Mongolia	Total socialist	Rest of world
1952	51	17	0	68	32
1959	48	16	6	70	30
1970	1	8	4	20	78
1975	2	7	5	16	84

Note: Total socialist trade for 1970 and 1975 includes Albania, Cuba, Yugoslavia. In the 1950s, trade with these countries was negligible.

Sources: N.R. Chen, JEC (1975), p. 648; CIA, *International Trade Handbook* (1976), p. 14.

cent of total socialist trade. Other important partners are the Soviet Union, East Germany, and Czechoslovakia. Romanian trade reflects a combination of China's desire to help Romania weaken links with the Soviet Union, and China's need to acquire Romanian oil technology. China gave $300 million aid to Romania between 1970 and 1971 and, very unusually, made a three year trade agreement for 1972 to 1975. With European socialist economies, China continues to buy industrial products with textiles, agricultural goods, and raw materials. These exchanges are normally conducted by annual agreements.

Trade between the Soviet bloc and China remains a hostile and unpredictable activity. China continues to use trade to press political points, although the Soviet Union apparently prefers to keep trade and politics in separate compartments. It is unlikely that, as a group, the socialist countries will succeed in expanding their share of China's trade very much in future.

The Third World

China has good political reasons for seeking economic links within Third World countries. Third World countries—along with socialist ones—are the only markets in which China's manufactured goods are readily acceptable, and, as a result, China's annual trade surplus with certain Third World countries has risen steadily. In 1975 it amounted to $980 million. This surplus sustains imbalances with suppliers of grain and advanced industrial commodities.

In relations with the Third World, aid and trade go closely together. Between 1970 and 1974 China dispensed economic assistance amounting to $2.4 billion; two-thirds of this went to Africa, and approximately one-fifth of it was allocated to one project—the Tanzam railway. Repayment of China's aid usually involves purchases of Chinese exports. In the Tanzam case, 52 per cent of the total cost was to be repaid in this way.

In 1975 Third World countries accounted for 19 per cent of China's trade and 27 per cent of exports. Within the total the most important regions were South-East Asia and Africa, accounting for 39 per cent (26 per cent of total trade). China's trade with this group of countries is likely to grow. Latin America has minerals (including high quality iron ore) in which China is deficient. And there are many other economic complementarities between Third World countries and China that have not yet been exploited.

Conclusion: trade and politics

Throughout this chapter I have emphasized the sense and rationality of Chinese trading. It must be remembered that this rationality is always subject to international political considerations. The infrequency of 'political' trading must not blind us to its existence. The Chinese have described trade as 'a weapon for international political struggle'.[26] Examples of political trading include cotton purchases from Egypt (in 1956), sugar purchases from Cuba (the 1960s), the switch from Australia to Canada as a major supplier of grain (1971) as protest at Australian involvement in Vietnam, and the cutback on imports from America (1975) due to lack of progress in political reconciliation. Above all, there was the Sino-Soviet break. The Chinese made this decision in full awareness of the grim economic consequences, and it illustrates decisively that, if need be, they are prepared to sacrifice the economic for the political good.

6
Incomes, Prices, and the Standard of Living

'They have Recourse to all Manner of Contrivances, for
Means of Subsistence; and as there is not a Spot in all the
Empire that lies untilled, neither is there one Person, Man
or Woman, though ever so old, deaf, or blind, but what
may easily gain a Livelihood.'

Thomas Astley, *A New General Collection
of Voyages and Travels*

THE PROBLEM OF MEASURING LIVING STANDARDS

The measurement of living standards in China is difficult. Little
research has been done on the subject in the West and the Chinese have
not published much useful material on the subject since 1958. Lack of
data is not the only problem, for it is not always clear how we should
go about using more statistics even if we had them. Populations
consume different bundles of goods at different times. Their needs
change and may differ from those in other cultures. How then can we
measure improvement through time; make comparisons between the
Chinese and others; or between what the Chinese consume and what
they 'need'? Also, if we are concerned with welfare in the widest sense,
how do we value greater equality of distribution or greater security of
supply?

There are no simple answers to these questions. But in this chapter
the problem will be approached in three ways. First, the size and
composition of income per head will be considered; secondly, estimates
of the consumption of a small but important group of commodities
and services; thirdly, Chinese materials on the incomes of different
groups within the population. These throw light not only on the
standard of living but also on questions of equality and inequality. This
leads naturally to the final section of the chapter which will discuss
changing Chinese policies towards incomes.

Income per head

The starting point for measuring income per head is customarily taken to be Gross Domestic Product. This is a measure of the total value of an economy's output, i.e. the value of all its agricultural and industrial output; of its transportation, communications, commercial and financial activities; and of all Government, education and other social services. (It is 'gross' in the sense that no allowance is made for the fact that the provision of output and services incurs a cost in terms of equipment and natural resources. If this figure is in turn adjusted to take account of income earned from investment abroad and from aid, the final result is the Gross National Product (GNP). In China's case, net income from aid and investment has been so small in recent years (slightly negative in fact) that the difference between Gross Domestic Product and GNP is unimportant.[1]

Table 62: *Gross National Product, 1949-75*
($ 1975)

	1949	1952	1957	1965	1970	1975
GNP (billion)	49	82	115	163	219	299
Population (million)	538	570	640	750	813	901
GNP per head	91	144	180	217	269	332

Sources: A.G. Ashbrook, JEC (1975), pp. 42-43; CIA, *Handbook of Economic Indicators* (1976), p. 1; Table 2.

Table 62 shows the best Western estimate of GNP per head for various years between 1949 and 1975. It will be seen that in 1975 the estimated income was $332 (£195). Alone, this figure does not mean much—an income of this amount would not suffice for human existence in Europe or the United States. What is wrong is that the income measured in Chinese *yuan* has been converted to US dollars at an official exchange rate that *understates* the purchasing power of the *yuan*. To translate the Chinese income into a figure with meaning to ourselves, we need some idea of the extent of this undervaluation. One American scholar has tried to find this by estimating what it would cost for a Chinese family to consume the goods and services it enjoys in China *if it were living in America*. His conclusion was that a family earning 166 *yuan* a month in China (quite a high income) would need $4,800 (or £2,824) per annum to enjoy the same goods and services in the United States. This suggests tenfold undervaluation. This is far too high, but the calculation illustrates an important point.[2]

In spite of this difficulty, estimates of GNP are useful because although it is difficult to interpret the *level* of income they indicate, they do tell us whether income is *growing*, and if it is, how rapid the progress is. Table 63 shows the rate of growth of GNP, and GNP per

Table 63: *Rate of Growth of Gross National Product, selected periods, 1949-75*
(per cent per annum)

	1949-52	1952-57	1952-75	1957-65	1957-75	1965-75
GNP	18.72	7.00	5.79	4.46	5.45	6.25
GNP per head	16.53	4.56	3.70	2.36	3.46	4.36

Source: Table 62.

head, for several periods between 1949 and 1975. If the period 1952 to 1975 is taken as representative of the long-run trend, the rate of progress indicated — if maintained — would be a rate exceeded in modern times only by the economies of Japan and the Soviet Union[3] (excluding the special cases of small economies such as Taiwan that had exceptional potential for growth through foreign trade). A look at the different items that make up the GNP reveals that nearly *all* the growth that occurred has taken the form of industrial production and services. Thus between 1952 and 1975 population and grain production increased by 58 per cent and 71 per cent respectively, but industrial production increased tenfold. Gains in income per head in the form of food were therefore small, while gains in the form of industrial production were large. This means that if we wish to understand what the growth of GNP has meant in terms of personal *living standards* we need to scrutinize its composition and use very carefully. For if, for example, we found that it took the form of machine tools, armaments, or exports, living standards might not have increased at all, or might even have declined. In the world's first socialist industrialization in the Soviet Union, declining living standards and a growing GNP were combined for twenty years. The Chinese have done better than this, as will now be shown with reference to the consumption of specific products.

THE CONSUMPTION OF GRAIN, COTTON CLOTH, AND HOUSING

The commodities and services listed in Table 64 include the most important components of personal consumption in China. This section will discuss grain, cotton cloth, and housing individually, and then present an estimate of the total improvement in consumption which has taken place since 1952.

Grain Grain accounts for four-fifths of China's total supply of food. In 1974 the output of unhusked grain per head in China was 308 kg. After making allowance for a) grain used for seed and the feeding of animals, and b) net imports of grain, the average number of calories

Table 64: *Consumption of grain, cotton cloth, and bicycles, 1949-74*

	1949	1952	1957	1965	1974
Population (million)	538	570	640	726	894
Output of grain (million metric tons)	111	161	191	204	275
Kilograms of grain per head available from domestic sources (per annum)	206	282	298	281	308
Supply of calories from domestic and imported grain (per day)	n.a.	2,024	2,116	2,095	2,287
Consumption of machine-made cotton cloth per head (metres per annum)	n.a.	5.24	6.21	n.a.	6-8
Output of bicycles per annum (000's)	14	80	806	1,792	4,859
Number of persons per bicycle	n.a.	3,584	266	57	21

Sources: Population Table 2; grain Table 19; calories from estimates supplied by Professor K.R. Walker based on his estimates of the structure of grain output; cotton cloth, 1952 and 1957 from N.R. Chen, *Chinese Economic Statistics,* p. 436 and Table 46. The 1974 cotton consumption estimate is based on reports of ration standards and an estimate of the level of ration free cloth distributed to workers and members of the forces based on informants' reports. Bicycles from CIA, *Handbook of Economic Indicators* (1976), p. 25. The number of persons per bicycle is estimated by calculating the stock of bicycles produced since 1949, assuming that there is no depreciation — the latter is not unreasonable in a society where most bicycles are fairly recent and are treasured by their owners as a major personal asset.

available per day from grain was approximately 2,287.[4] Actual *consumption* would be somewhat less since grain is also added to store in normal years.

An interesting benchmark for evaluating this standard is the level of grain consumption in Bangladesh. Bangladesh is generally recognized to be one of the world's poorest countries, and foreign donors attempt to make imports of grain available to ensure that consumption per head averages 0.44 kg of husked grain per day. In China the minimum quantity of husked grain guaranteed to those unable to work or to earn sufficient to pay for what is regarded as an absolute minimum, is approximately 0.30 kg per day. The average consumption of about 0.55 kg achieved in the 1970s is, therefore, 25 per cent above the Bangladesh average.[5]

However, although the *average* level of grain consumption appears adequate, two considerations must be borne in mind. One is that there is no evidence of a rising standard. For if we compare average consumption for the six year periods 1953 to 1958 and 1970 to 1975 we find that the level has remained virtually unchanged, and that in recent years even this level has only been achieved with the help of imports. Thus, although such imports account for only 3 per cent to 4 per cent of supplies, the fact that they have been just sufficient to keep consumption constant in the face of rising population suggests that they have been carefully calculated and are rather important.

The other qualification to this estimate concerns distribution. The grain supply is adequate *provided that* it is distributed so that those doing heavy physical work, and those living in cold places, get an above average share. For those living in the cities, the rationing system tends to ensure this is so. But in the countryside, natural variations in the availability of food make this sort of redistribution difficult. Grain production per head in the richest Provinces is thought to be about double that of the poorest, and even after redistribution, differences are substantial.[6] Thus it is possible that in the poorer regions those engaged in heavy agricultural work do not always get adequate extra grain.

If these remarks are taken in conjunction with the view that the supply of vegetables and other foods has increased more rapidly than grain itself, the conclusion must be that the Chinese diet is fairly adequate. This has been confirmed in the case of city dwellers, by visiting nutritional experts familiar with other countries in Asia and Africa. Their reports note the absence in China of the symptoms associated with malnutrition. Unfortunately there are no relevant Chinese data on this. Neither are there likely to be, since an official of the Chinese Academy of Sciences recently told a visiting nutritionist that nationally directed nutritional surveillance had been stopped in 1972.

Cotton cloth The data in Table 64 suggest some improvement in the consumption of cotton cloth during the 1950s, but very little improvement since then. This is explained by the fact that the growth in the textile industry since 1959 has largely been used to increase exports. The data in the table reflect only quantitative changes, they do not reflect the qualitative improvements in textiles that have been made in recent years.

Housing Visitors to China are usually taken to see impressive new housing estates, and from time to time the authorities publish the number of square metres of housing constructed in individual cities. There is, however, no official account of the overall housing situation. We know from many articles published in China that using space as the criterion, during the 1950s urban housing standards fell by 40 to 50 per cent (i.e. that was the fall in space available per person). By the end of the Plan (1957) millions of Chinese had less than 3 sq. metres per person, and in the fastest growing cities figures as low as 1.8 sq. metres were quoted—the latter being about room for a bed and a chair. These standards may be compared with current standards of 20 sq. metres per person in Western Europe, 11 sq. metres in the Soviet Union, and 8 sq. metres in Japan.

In the countryside, the upheavals of collectivization must have discouraged investment in housing, and the events of the Great Leap and the Great Depression cannot have left many resources for this kind of construction. However, the slower growth of population in the countryside will have meant that the decline in urban standards had no rural parallel.

Lack of official information since the 1950s does not exclude the possibility of estimates for the later period. In 1965 and 1974 Chinese officials gave me detailed information on housing in Shanghai (a 'large' city) and in Foshan (a 'medium' city in South China). Combined with published information, these figures have enabled me to calculate the change in the housing situation in these two cities since 1949. In Shanghai, by reducing population and pressing ahead with building, the housing stock has increased to the point where, by the 1970s, standards were slightly above those of 1952. In Foshan the sharp deterioration of the 1950s has still not been compensated for, and in 1974 housing availability per head was 24 per cent lower than it had been in 1949. Since few cities have actually reduced their populations in the way that Shanghai has done, and since cities of Foshan's size account for 60 per cent of China's urban population, the conclusion must be that for the urban population, housing standards are probably still slightly worse than in the early 1950s[7] in terms of space available. In some other respects—availability of piped water and sewage—the situation will have improved.

Rural housing, in contrast, may now be somewhat better. Population growth has been much slower, and since the late 1960s informants have been reporting a minor boom in housing construction. This has been mainly for the benefit of cadres, of households with relatively large amounts of labour power, and of the 'sent down' youth. Taking the rural and urban sectors together, therefore, the long-run change in the housing situation has probably been minimal.[8] This is a result of investment policies that emphasize construction for productive purposes, and of the increase in demand due to the growth of population.

An index of personal consumption

In Table 65 data from various sources are shown that can be used to provide an estimate of changes in total personal consumption. Consumption is divided into seven categories. The first six are categories commonly used by the Chinese. The extra category is the value of benefits received from all types of social funds: health, education, poverty relief benefits, etc. For each category I have an estimate of (a) its importance (or 'weight') in the total household budget, and (b) the

Table 65: *An index of consumption per head, 1952-74*

Item	Share of household expenditure (per cent)	'weight'	Rate of growth per head per annum
1. Main foodstuffs	33	0.33	0.56
2. Secondary foodstuffs	25	0.25	1.93
3. Clothing	16	0.16	1.33
4. Fuel	9	0.09	0
5. Other consumer goods	9	0.09	5.99
6. Housing	4	0.04	0
7. Health, education and welfare benefits and services	4	0.04	6.03
Total	100		1.66

Notes and sources:
1. *Main foodstuffs:* Table 64.
2. *Secondary foodstuffs:* Based on official statistics and author's estimates of probable changes in availability of edible oil, salt, pork, vegetables and fish — weighted by relative expenditure share in budget.
3. *Clothing:* Table 64.
4. *Fuel:* I assume no increase in fuel per head available for domestic use. There may actually have been a decline.
5. *Other consumer goods:* the index of output for all consumer goods, Table 32.
6. *Housing:* Estimate based on details for numerous cities up to 1957. These indicate a decline in housing area available per head. For the period since 1957, details for cities representative of the 'large' and 'medium' types of city (see text).
7. *Health, education and welfare:* For 1952 to 1959 the estimate is based on published data for central and local budget expenditure, *plus* an estimate of expenditure on these items by enterprises and organizations. For the period since 1959, we know that welfare expenditures have approximately kept their share of budgetary expenditures and that *total* expenditures increased even more rapidly than this owing to (a) successful mobilization of health and education funds through the Commune system (I assume 2 per cent of income from agriculture allocated for these expenditures), and (b) a reported rise in the percentage of enterprise incomes allocated to welfare to offset the wages freeze. Budgetary and wages data from N.R. Chen, *Chinese Economic Statistics,* pp. 441, 446-47, 491; New China News Agency, September 25, 1972; and recent budget sources cited in Chapter 1, Table 1.
Household expenditure shares: Estimated from several surveys of rural and urban household expenditure made in the mid-1950s. The survey data were adjusted for the share of the rural and urban populations and for the value of welfare expenditure. Because of the predominance of the rural population, the budget pattern shown is more typical of rural than urban families.
Population: Table 2.

rate of growth of its consumption per head. From these a figure may be calculated that expresses the growth of the whole bundle of goods and services.

My estimate is that personal consumption grew at 1.66 per cent per annum between 1952 and 1974. This figure involves some guesswork, but about 60 per cent of the consumption data are 'firm'. It is unlikely that more accurate information would move the rate above 2 per cent or much below 1½ per cent. It will be seen that, if the figures are correct, China owes its improving standard of living mainly to increases in secondary foodstuffs, manufactured consumer goods, and to growing expenditures on health, education and welfare. Insofar as health, education and welfare improvements are allocated according to need, human welfare may have increased by more than the expenditure figures by themselves suggest.

THE STANDARD OF LIVING OF CITY WORKERS

Workers in the city population may be divided into two groups. The most important is the group described by the Chinese as 'workers and staff'. Originally a Russian classification, this term describes people working for a wage or salary in Government organizations and in the more modern, large-scale economic organizations. Such people account for about two-thirds of the urban workforce, i.e. about fifty-five million people. Workers engaged in smaller-scale, more traditional trades—transport, services, handicraft production, and so forth—are usually organized in some form of cooperative. Payment in cooperatives varies according to results. In general, the pay, conditions of work, and fringe benefits of workers and staff are better than those applying to other urban workers. The fixing of wages of workers and staff involves several operations. First, workers are divided into broad occupational *groups* such as production workers, engineering-technical personnel, managerial, administrative and professional staff, etc. Official tables for these groups show how much everyone from janitors to the Chairman of the Republic should earn. Secondly, the pay specified for an *occupation* within a broad group varies according to the size and importance of the organization in which it occurs. And thirdly, pay for an *individual* in such an occupation will additionally depend on his training, experience, educational qualifications, and political history. There are also allowances for working in harsh conditions, for local variations in living costs, and for special skills. Piecework seems largely to have disappeared, but in 1975 'bonuses' for good performance were still being paid in many organizations and enterprises.[9]

The national wage tables have not been published since 1956, but amended versions of these are still used and Chinese officials and diplomats are often willing to describe their own position in them. We also have many wage charts for factories and organizations visited by foreigners since 1972.[10]

Once workers and staff are placed in a wage chart, pay improvements depend on being upgraded, or on benefits from a general rise in wages. In practice, regrading and general rises in wages only occur when the Party orders them. Since the wage system was established in

1955 there have been three important wage adjustments: in 1956 there was both a general rise and a general regrading; in 1963 lower paid workers were raised a grade; and in 1971/72 there was regrading for the bottom three of the eight grades of industrial worker, and for the bottom six of the thirty-grade system for workers and staff in State administration. In October 1977 over 40 per cent of workers received rises in a fourth adjustment.

The system of fixing wages and incomes for those outside the categories described above is more flexible and informal. Responsibility for this sector belongs to the Labour Bureau, and policies follow the pattern of those applied to workers and staff.

The Chinese have published some information about the average level of money wages for workers and staff, and a summary of this, together with an index of retail prices and an index of real wages based on the first two items, is shown in Table 66.

It will be seen that the Chinese have not published an official index number for retail prices since 1963. Fortunately, one of the by-products of the opening of China to visitors has been the collection of price data. The estimates in Table 66 and the detailed prices in Tables

Table 66: *The average wages of workers and staff, 1952-74*
(1952=100)

	1952	1957	1963	1971	1972	1974
Wages (money)	100	143	n.a.	128	141	142
Index of retail prices	100	109.1	118.5	n.a.	n.a.	124 (estimate)
Wages (real)	100	131	n.a.	n.a.	n.a.	115

Notes and sources: Money wages for 1952-59 are from *Ten Great Years,* p. 216; for 1971, *Peking Review,* 1971, No. 40, p. 14 reported a figure of 650 *yuan* as the average wage, 'except for those who started working in recent years'. We know that there has been a freeze on the relatively higher paid salaries and on promotion to those. This has meant that, as the higher paid retired or died, they were not replaced. It follows that, without actually reducing any *individual* wage, *the average wage of all workers and staff must have fallen.* To disguise this fact, *Peking Review* has to omit the low paid, recent entrants to the workforce from the average. On the basis of detailed information about wage rates and the number of workers earning them in the iron and steel industry, I have calculated that between 1957 and 1971 the average wage fell by a minimum of 12 per cent. I have used this piece of information to estimate the average fall for workers and staff in all industries and organizations. In 1971/72, there was a 10 per cent increase in average money earnings and the effect of this on wages was confirmed in a report published by New China News Agency on December 1, 1975.

Retail prices: The index for the years 1952-63 comes from official figures in *Ten Great Years,* p. 174 and New China News Agency, December 3, 1964, *Peking Review,* 1964, No. 47, p. 7. There are no official figures for recent years. It is probable that the high prices reported for 1963 moderated somewhat as supplies became available after the collapse of 1960-61. However, since 1972, visitors and informants have reported rises in the prices of some consumer goods, meat, edible oil, secondary foodstuffs and canteen meals. Also reported are reductions in the quantities of some goods available at low, rationed prices. This implies that consumption can only have been maintained by extra-purchase at the higher, unrationed prices. My estimate of a net 5 per cent rise in prices between 1963 and 1974 is conservative, and implies that the rate of inflation has dropped by two-thirds compared to the rate reported by official statistics for 1952-63.

67, 68, and 69 are based on over 800 prices reported by British, American, and German visitors between 1973 and 1975. We also have reports on the price situation as it appeared to residents who subsequently left China. These give an idea of the price situation as it actually appeared to the consumer.

The growth of real wages between 1952 and 1957 was 5.5 per cent per annum. After 1957 the 'rational low wage policy' was adopted. This has meant a freeze in wages, alleviated only by the two adjustments mentioned above. The effect of this freeze, combined with some upward movement in prices, has been a slight fall in the real average wage of workers and staff. (This is explained in the notes to Table 66.) Thus for the whole period since 1952, I estimate that real wages have increased by 15 per cent.

Judgement of these figures depends on the criterion used. It is certainly a slower rate of advance than that achieved by some comparable groups in other developing economies in the same period. On the other hand, the Chinese workers and staff have done much better than their counterparts in the Soviet Union whose real wages did not begin to rise at all until thirty years after the beginning of the First Five Year Plan in 1928. And in terms of social justice, the recent decline in the wages of the better-paid can be regarded as a desirable development, reflecting a policy of reducing inequalities between rural and urban workers. Finally, it is important to observe that by raising the proportion of the urban population in employment, the planners will have ensured that *household* incomes have increased by more than the increase in income of *individual* workers. Indeed, increased household income due to employment expansion has probably more than compensated for the fall in real individual incomes since 1957.

Wage differences between different types of urban workers

The information in Table 67 illustrates the range of incomes earned among the 20 per cent of China's population who live in cities. Teachers, administrative staff and technicians working in the countryside would also be on the scales indicated in the table. Except for the salaries in State administration, all the details are recent. The situation in State administration is believed to have remained substantially as quoted, except for a possible reduction of the highest salaries of about 100 *yuan* per month.

It is clear that, senior ministerial and judicial salaries aside, the top bracket is 200 *yuan* to 400 *yuan* a month. Only a minute proportion of the workforce earns this much; it includes managers and engineers in large, important enterprises, top local bureaucrats, and a few people engaged in cultural work. Down the scale, quite a large number of

Table 67: *Incomes recently earned among city-dwellers*

Yuan per month	1 State Administration (1956)	2 Heavy Industry	3 University	4 The People's Daily Newspaper	5 People's Liberation Army	6 Workers in traditional occupations in the cities and others
	Prime Minister 560					
500	Senior Judiciary 505 ← 280					
400	Ministers and Vice-Ministers 400 ← 250					
300	City Mayors and Vice-Mayors 360 ← 220		Professors 350			
200		Engineering and technical staff 230 ← 34		Editor 250		
100	Section chiefs and deputies in State Council 190 ← 108	Managerial and administrative staff 180 ← 37	Associate Professors 170 / Instructors 120 ← 100	Section chiefs 100	Divisional Commanding Officers 180	Cart pullers 157 ← 61
50	Office staff in State Council 48.5 ← 32.5	Skilled manual workers 104 ← 33	Assistants (newly graduated) 70		Lower ranking men 60 ← 50	Vegetable traders 80 ← 20

Category	Wage (yuan/month)
Apprentices	28 ↑ 24
Cub reporters	40
Dependants of PLA soldiers working in PLA factories	33
Female workers in 'street factories'	25 ↑ 18
Temporary construction workers	40 ↑ 20
Labour camp workers	30 ↑ 16
Shanghai shoe cleaners	15
	0

Notes and Sources: *State Administration:* These data come from Tables published in *The 1956 compendium of Central Government financial laws and regulations* (Peking, Financial Publishing House, 1957). Since that time it has been reported, but not confirmed, that the 30 grade system of bureaucratic salaries has been reduced to 24 grades, with a maximum of 400-500 *yuan* per month in place of 560 *yuan* per month quoted here.

Heavy Industry: A typical, but exceptionally detailed, example of a factory wage system reported to visitors in 1972. Mitch Meisner, 'The Shenyang transformer factory', *The China Quarterly*, No. 52 (1972), p. 731. Meisner was not given the rates for apprentices and the lowest rate for technical staff. I have inserted probable figures for these, based on regulations and reports of wages in other heavy industry factories.

University: Visitors' reports from Futan University, Shanghai. Reports from other universities confirm that this structure is typical. Top university salaries were those paid to professors whose salaries were left unchanged. Younger professors who succeed to these positions are unlikely ever to earn more than 200 *yuan* per month.

The People's Daily: This information was given to visiting British journalists.

The People's Liberation Army: As above.

Workers in traditional occupations and others: Cart pullers and vegetable traders from *Labour* (Ch.), 1958, No. 3, p. 30. The Labour camp workers are probably persons who have not committed crimes; they are persons sent to camps by administrative order for political 're-education'. Data quoted in Martin King Whyte, *Small Groups and Political Rituals in China* (University of California Press, 1974), p. 184; *Planned economy* (Ch.), 1958, No. 4, p. 27. All other data are visitors' reports.

The average wage: The 'official' average wage was 60 *yuan* in 1976; actually it is about 53 *yuan* (see note to Table 66).

administrators and technical specialists are in the 100 *yuan* to 200 *yuan* per month bracket, but the majority of wage earners get between 40 and 100 *yuan* a month. The last 'official' statement about the average wage for workers and staff was in 1976 when it was reported as being 60 *yuan* per month. (See notes to Table 67.) Below the average wage are the extremely low incomes reported in street factories and in traditional urban trades and services; the wages of persons undergoing corrective training in labour camps; and the wages paid to gangs of 'People's Workers' who are engaged for temporary construction jobs.

Table 67 shows that it is actually possible to earn more as a Labour Camp inmate than as an ordinary worker. This remarkable point is confirmed in a letter to the journal *Planned Economy*, in which the writer complained that 'People's Workers' on a construction job were getting 0.8 *yuan* a day, compared to the 1 *yuan* being paid the workers from the Labour Reform Brigade.[11]

No one could live in a Chinese city on the wages quoted towards the bottom of Table 67. These workers must be part of family groupings that include other, better paid members, or have other sources of income, such as remittances from relatives. One interesting aspect of the earnings of some of the workers in the unorganized trades is that they *can* be very high. Clever operators in hawking and the manufacture of simple goods earn considerable sums. The size and significance of this group has been confirmed by recent articles in the Chinese press. These articles confirm that official policy is to tolerate such people (because they render some useful services), but to ensure that they do not recruit less well paid workers and peasants who are needed for other work.

Rationing and prices in the cities

The total number of rationed items in China is large. A detailed article on rationing in Canton puts the number at about 200, and an informant from Szechuan reports that there are 300 items presently rationed and that there is a Provincial target to reduce the number to three by 1980. The major, permanently rationed items are grain, vegetable oil, meat, sugar, and cotton cloth. The precise rations vary depending on supply conditions, and minor food items are sometimes rationed and sometimes not.

Grain rations vary according to sex, age and work. Typically, children get 12.5 kg per month, while a man engaged in heavy work could get up to 25 kg. At one time it was possible to escape the ration by eating out. Now, however, meals in canteens and restaurants are only obtainable if ration coupons are surrendered. Another aspect of the ration is that, although the ration specifies minimum *quantities*, it avoids the question of *which* grains shall be consumed. This is very important. The 'fine grains' (rice and wheat) are much preferred by consumers as compared to the 'coarse grains' (which include maize and potatoes). In the cities, about 80 per cent of the ration is taken in 'fine' form, although if times are bad, the share of the 'coarse' rises. The price of grains has remained stable since the early 1950s, and since the procurement price paid to peasants has risen by about 50 per cent, this means that grain is subsidized by the State to an extent equal to the costs of distribution and transport.

The current ration for edible oil is 0.25 kg per month and *households* are allowed a meat ration of between 0.5 and 1 kg per month. The meat ration will be purchased at a price one half to one third of the price at which 'free' meat (sometimes fish) may be purchased. The cloth ration varies from year to year according to conditions. In 1976 the ration in Central China was 6 *chih* (5.28 metres), but in recent years other reports indicate a ration within the range of 4.5 to 6 metres length of cloth per year. (The standard cloth width is 0.8 of a metre.) Some urban workers also benefit from the provision of clothing at work, and it is possible to obtain extra cotton by purchasing ration coupons from peasants who have not got the cash to buy their full ration.[12]

One way to assess the meaning of these rations is to consider what foods a typical consuming family could buy *after* it has bought its rationed supplies. If, for example, we take the case of a four person family with one worker earning the official average wage (60 *yuan* per month), the cost of buying the ration would be 16 *yuan* to 18 *yuan* a month. Since surveys show that average expenditures on food for such a family would total 26 *yuan*, there is a balance of 6 *yuan* to 8 *yuan* for other food purchases. What would this buy? Tables 68-70 show a selection of food and vegetable prices from which some possibilities can be calculated. In using the Shanghai or Peking vegetable prices, it should be remembered that incomes and prices in these cities are higher than average, so that it would be more appropriate to see what could be bought for 8 *yuan* to 11 *yuan*, rather than for 6 *yuan* to 8 *yuan*.

Inspection of Tables 68-70 leads to the inevitable conclusion that a family such as that cited above could at best supplement its rations with items such as eggs and inexpensive vegetables. In contrast, a two-income family, earning, say, 100 *yuan* to 160 *yuan*, would have considerable possibilities for food consumption beyond the ration as well as for buying consumer goods.

To provide a more exact idea of the typical expenditures of Chinese families, Table 71 gives two estimated budgets for families in Shanghai. The budget for the 'well off' family has been constructed from data reported to him by Professor Bruce Reynolds. The 'average' family budget is a construction by myself; this estimates expenditure on

Table 68: *Consumer goods prices in Peking and other cities, 1974/75*
(yuan)

	Peking	Range of prices quoted in twelve other cities, 1973/75
Cotton cloth (per metre)	1.8	0.3 – 2.5
Plastic raincoat	4.0	1.2 – 6.0
Trousers	13.0	4.0 – 15.0
Shirt	10.0	3.0 – 8.0
Padded jacket	—	10.0 – 25.0
Men's leather shoes	12.0	12.0 – 23.0
Bicycle	160.0	140.0 – 250.0
Radio	100.0	30.0 – 150.0
Ballpoint pen	0.2	0.16 – 0.7
Watch (Chinese)	120.0	38.0 – 150.0
Watch (Swiss)	900.0	200.0 – 650.0
Umbrella	3.0	2.0 – 9.0
Frying pan	2.0	0.9 – 2.0
Television set	—	450.0

Note: Most of the variations in the right-hand column reflect size and quality differences.

Sources: Reports from British, American and German travellers in China.

Table 69: *Food prices in Peking and other cities, 1974/75*
yuan per chin (0.5 kg)

	Peking	Range of prices quoted in twelve other cities, 1973/75
Pork	0.90 (R)	0.68 – 1.0
Beef	0.75 (UR)	0.56 – 2.0
Fresh fish	0.50 (UR)	0.22 – 1.80
Salted fish	—	0.15 – 8.0
Chicken	—	0.96 – 1.80
Rice	0.21 (R)	0.09 – 0.187
Wheat flour	—	0.09 – 0.18
Vegetable oil	0.85 (R)	0.54 – 1.0
Salt	0.14 (UR)	0.13 – 0.19
Sugar	0.80 (UR)	0.56 – 1.0
Eggs	0.90 (UR)	0.68 – 0.95
Vegetables (green)	—	0.02 – 1.20
Potatoes	—	0.065 – 1

Notes:
1. The range of prices in the right-hand column includes rationed and unrationed prices.
2. The letters (R) and (UR) in the Peking column indicate that the reported prices referred to rationed or unrationed respectively.
3. A wide range of vegetables is not quoted in this table, since regional and seasonal variations make the prices difficult to interpret.

Sources: Reports from British, American and German travellers in China.

Table 70: *Food prices in Shanghai, 1973*
yuan per chin (0.5 kg)

Item	Price
Ham	1.38-1.42
Shellfish	0.60
Lettuce	1.20
Duck	0.98
Chicken	1.25
Runner beans	0.16
Cauliflower	0.13
Apples	2.50 – 4.60
Beets	0.045
Potatoes	0.065
Dried fish	0.15 – 0.31
Fresh fish	0.22 – 0.31

Source: Bruce Reynolds, *Observations on the Chinese Economy* (New Haven, 1973) (mimeo).

the same items by a family of average size, with the average family income. Given that the average family would not be able to reduce expenditures on items 1 to 4 of the budget (rent, transport, medical insurance, and school fees) and that items 5 and 6 (food and clothing) could only be subject to marginal economies, the conclusion is that the balance of income for other items — such as helping relatives, entertainment, spending on consumer goods and saving — is extremely small. Indeed, if the 10 *yuan* remittance to relatives was an 'essential', no balance is left at all.

This exercise reinforces the conclusion that high income families are comfortably off and can enjoy a wide variety of unrationed food and consumer goods. For the average family, however, the margin above basic living is very small. For them, saving and the acquisition of consumer goods is hard, and even finding the cash for items such as school fees may be difficult.

Families whose incomes are below average must find life very hard indeed. For them, there is no margin above subsistence and no ability to make private provision for emergencies. This does not mean that such families are always in trouble. Informants report that trade union welfare payments to poor families can be as high as 100 *yuan* to 200 *yuan* per year. Some poor families may also be the recipients of remittances from relatives living abroad. Because they are in hard currency, these remittances are encouraged by the Government, and families sending them confirm that they often amount to many hundreds of *yuan* a year.

Finally, looking at the tables of prices, the reader might well ask how *anyone* in China can afford a Swiss watch that would cost a skilled worker a year's earnings, a television set that costs nearly as much, or any of the Japanese electronic goods that circulate on the black market at very high prices. One answer to this puzzle is that many official and army personnel who spend time 'down on the farm', away on duty, or even in disgrace, accumulate large sums which are available to them when they return to normal work. Considerable savings were built up during the Cultural Revolution in this way, and the highly priced consumer goods that appeared in the 1970s probably represent an effort to mop them up. It must be remembered also that families with two or more earning members have considerable surpluses for buying consumer goods; and, according to some reports, the younger generation are much less interested in saving than their frugal parents.

Table 71: *Average monthly expenditures of Chinese urban families*

Item	Monthly expenditure cost		Per cent of monthly income	
	'well off'	*'average'*	*'well off'*	*'average'*
1. Housing and fuel	28	28	17	21
2. Transport	10	10	6	7
3. Medical insurance	2	2	1	2
4. School fees	7	7	4	5
5. Food	64	61	39	45
6. Clothing	25	18	15	13
7. Remittance to relatives	10		6	
8. Entertainment	5		3	
	} 30	} 10	} 18	} 7
9. Miscellaneous	5		3	
10. Saving	10		6	
	166	136	100	100

Notes and Sources: The 'well off' family data are Bruce Reynolds' (Table 70). My estimate of the 'average' family is based on data for the average income of Shanghai's employed population given in *Liberation Daily* (Ch.), August 11, 1956, updated with Table 66. The estimate of average family income is based on data for population and employment cited in Chapter 1. I have assumed an average family size of 4.8 persons — a figure agreed in most sources.

Working conditions, welfare and housing allocation

Workers in organizations and industrial enterprises employing more than a hundred people have their working conditions and welfare benefits prescribed in detail. There are regulations that govern hours of work, physical conditions, and expenditures on medical benefits, canteens, clubs, crèches, and poverty assistance for those in need of it.[13] Smaller organizations, too, have some rules on working conditions. However, welfare in these cases is paid out of self-financing schemes and the benefits approach the standards of the large organizations only as far as financial circumstances permit. The cost of welfare schemes varies, but figures in the Chinese press suggest that a sum equal to 12 to 36 per cent of an organization's total wage expenditure is commonly put into welfare.

The model rules for working conditions are: (1) an eight hour day (two and three shifts are common); (2) a six day week with four additional public holidays; (3) special leave for workers whose families still live in the countryside; (4) 56 days maternity leave; (5) retirement at 55 for women and 60 for men on 60 to 70 per cent of their final pay; (6) free medical attention for workers, and workers' families either getting treatment at half price, or being able to join a supplementary insurance scheme.

These benefits, together with the recreational facilities, constitute a sizeable addition to the security and economic welfare of those who get them. We do not know quite how many people this is. In 1956, 7.4 million workers were covered by the full labour insurance legislation.[14] If their families are included, this number rises to about 20 million. This was less than one in five of the urban population of that time, and less than one in thirty of the total population. Today the figure would be higher, probably by about 30 per cent, and the number who benefit from some form of scheme may now be a high proportion of the urban population. Nonetheless, workers and staff in the larger organizations remain a privileged group, even within the cities. And in general, welfare privileges *increase* differences created by wages.

The other factor that reinforces differences between workers is housing allocation. In the older cities, housing built since 1949 still only accommodates 20 to 25 per cent of the urban population. Conditions in this newer housing are much superior to those in the older buildings. Since most new housing is allocated directly to enterprises and organizations, the chance of being well housed is much enhanced for those in important organizations.

The system described above might well be described as a socialist version of the Japanese system of labour organization, in which the key to a comfortable life is attachment to a large, influential corporation. It is certainly true that in China big organizations have remarkable powers to look after their staff. Two examples will illustrate this. During the Cultural Revolution, the Peking broadcasting system had to send members of its staff down to the inhospitable countryside of south Honan. During the first winter the party nearly perished. To help them, the system then organized a supply of tractors and other modern farming aids — largely by going to factories and using threats of unfavourable media comment to extract help. The railway system is another organization with surprising capacities. For example, not only do the railways run an independent health system, but they have three medical schools to train the staff. Needless to say, other big industrial organizations (and the armed forces) create similar islands of security and privilege whenever they can. In many ways this large-scale paternalism is a good system. Once in, workers can rely on management to train and care for them for the rest of their lives. This encourages hard work, loyalty, and a flexibility towards learning new techniques which other forms of organization do not seem to inspire so efficiently.

The role of the trade unions in wages and welfare

The Chinese trade unions have had a chequered history. The All China Federation of Trade Unions (ACFTU) is a national organization. When last reported in 1965, the ACFTU had eighteen constituent industrial unions and a membership of 22 million — about 75 per cent of all eligible workers.

In China, as in Russia, trade unions are described as a propaganda 'transmission belt' between the Party and the workers. To some extent the belt works both ways. The unions transmit Party orders, but also feed back the reactions of the workers. In practice, the job of the unions is to mobilize workers to fulfil their tasks, and an article published in 1975 explained how this was to be done. Unions were to seek involvement in planning and organization, run spare time education in politics and technical subjects, and administer the provision of welfare arrangements.

The unions are emphatically not supposed to press for better wages (a deviation known as 'economism'). Nor are they to supplant the Party as the organization directly responsible for the leadership of the working class. In practice, the unions seem inevitably to become the means by which industrial workers covertly press their claims for improved wages and welfare. This is not surprising. The article referred to above describes how union organizations are expected to operate in a 'model' plant: the Peking, February 7th Rolling Stock Plant. This has 9,000 union members. Union committees operate at the level of the factory and the workshop; and even at the lowest level, 'the Team', there is a Trade Union 'Group'.[15]

These close links with the workforce are bound to make the unions sensitive to popular pressure and in 1951 and 1957 they were purged for pressing the economic interests of their members and seeking an independent role as representatives of the workers. There is some evidence that Liu Shao-ch'i wanted a more substantial role for the unions, and in 1966/67 the leadership of the Cultural Revolution dissolved the ACFTU completely. It did this on the ground that the unions put too much emphasis on material rewards and were a pressure group for already privileged sections of the urban labour force. A new organization of 'Revolutionary Rebels' was set up to replace the official ACFTU leadership.

In 1973 the old union organization was revived at the local level — partly to allow it to resume its diplomatic role of making contacts with the working class in other countries. Actually, the 1967 dissolution may not have meant all that much. In 1974 I was passing the impressive offices of ACFTU in the city of Sian. I enquired of the official who was accompanying me what had gone on in this building between 1967 and 1973. His reply was, 'They just changed the name on the gates.'

RURAL INCOMES

The gap between rural and urban incomes

It is difficult to make direct comparisons between rural and urban incomes. Physical conditions and consumption habits are so different. Also, peasant production varies, is consumed directly, or exchanged in rural markets where no records are kept. Thus whereas change in urban incomes can be measured by looking at figures for wages and prices, no such yardstick exists for rural incomes.

In the 1950s the flow of peasants to the cities was widely thought in China to be a reflection of the increasing difference between peasant and worker incomes. In 1956 and 1957, therefore, investigations were undertaken into this problem, and the reports published at that time are the most revealing accounts of peasant income that we have. The investigations attempted, first, to summarize the rural-urban gap in money terms. The most authoritative report concluded that in 1956 the average wage of workers and staff in the cities was 95 per cent higher than the average peasant income.[16] This compared to an 85 per cent difference in 1952. Even more revealing were differences between the two groups in the consumption of specific products. In the case of grain and vegetables, consumption was reported to be about the same; although more detailed analysis confirmed that urban consumption of the preferred 'fine' grains was two to three times that of the rural population. In the case of other foodstuffs and of cotton cloth, the gap was dramatic. Urban dwellers consumed twice as much pork, eggs, and cotton cloth as peasants; three times the quantity of sugar; and four times the quantity of vegetable oil. A few crude calculations were also made of the difference in benefits from expenditures on health, education and welfare but, in reality; these differences were so large that no comparison was possible.

In the 1960s this crisis of inequality led directly to countervailing policies. In the rural areas more consumer goods were made available (often at lower prices), and at the same time rural incomes were increased by paying higher prices for rural products and by reducing the costs of some production goods such as fertilizers. There was also a reallocation of heath, education and welfare expenditures towards the countryside.[17]

Overall, one estimate has it that rural incomes increased by 10-15 per cent between 1957 and the early 1970s. In the cities, on the other hand, average incomes have been frozen and the evidence of current rationing standards suggests that some of the gross inequalities in consumption have been removed.

In spite of these changes, urban-rural difference in living standards is still large. Urban workers get ration-free clothes for work, but it is reported that the rationing of consumer goods in the countryside is still so severe that the peasants in some areas draw lots for the chance to buy their Commune's allocation of popular items such as bicycles and sewing machines. The fact is that urban incomes cannot be reduced too much, and that the growth of rural incomes is limited by both the improvement of agriculture and the speed with which the planners can make more consumer goods available to the population. Thus while it was relatively easy to raise the living standards of the 15 per cent of the population in the cities in the 1950s, raising the living standards of the 80 per cent who live in the countryside in the 1960s and 1970s has been a much slower and more difficult process.

Income differences within the countryside

The problem of rural incomes is not just that the average level is low. Variations between Provinces, within Provinces, and within villages and Teams, are also serious. In a country such as China, peasant living standards are bound to reflect differences in natural conditions. Where soil and climate are favourable, living standards will tend to be high. Where they are poor and harsh, they will be low.

The scale of differences *between* Provinces is indicated by the fact, mentioned above, that grain availability is twice as high in the richest Provinces as it is in the poorest. Some idea of the differences *within* Provinces was given by a survey of Kiangsu Province in East China. This found that the eight Administrative Districts had average incomes ranging on a scale from 36 to 100.[18] A survey of Shensi, a poorer Province, reported an even wider range on a scale in which the highest income was 100, the income in the poorest areas was 15.4; this rose to 34 in the mountainous districts; to 60 in the main grain producing areas; and the maximum of 100 was found in favoured districts that specialized in market gardening for the cities.[19]

When we move down to the smaller unit of the village or Team,

Table 72: *Inequality in the village of Lung Chung, Kwangtung Province, 1956*

Type of household	Total population in each group (no. and percentage)	Number of households in each group	Average no. in household	Average net income	Grain consumption	Pork consumption	Oil	Clothing	General comment
'Well off'	195 (8.3)	44	4.43	100	100+	100	100	100	Very comfortable
'Middle'	1,840 (78.36)	464	3.97	77	100	77	77	43	No savings for illness or exceptional expenditure
'In difficulties'	282 (12.01)	77	3.66	57	50	n.a. (none?)	49	29 (less than)	Lacked grain for three months a year. Could not afford to buy cloth ration
'In receipt of aid'	31 (1.32)	28	1.11	38	61-71 (aid)	n.a. (none?)	n.a. (none?)	n.a. (none?)	Very hard life, needing assistance to survive
Total	2,348 (100)	613							

Note: Average income and consumption of grain, pork, oil, and clothing have been expressed as a percentage of the income and consumption of the 'well off'. The relative advantage of the 'well off' and 'middle' peasants with respect to grain consumption is understated. This is because the survey reported that the 'middle' group consumed grain almost entirely in 'fine' (i.e. rice) forms, rather than in the form of sweet potatoes and taros — the main items of consumption of the poorer groups.

Source: 'A report on an investigation into the standard of living in the village of Lung Chung', *New China Semi-Monthly* (Ch.), 1957, No. 10, pp. 71-74.

inequalities remain. Table 72 shows the situation in a village in Kwangtung Province in 1956. Unfortunately the survey is not as useful as it might be, because the investigators grouped too many peasants in the 'middle' category, although they admit in the report that differences within the group were substantial.

Apart from throwing light on village inequality, a most interesting feature of this survey is that when one puts the Households in order by standard of living, *this turns out to be the same as putting them in order by Household size.* In other words, the bigger the Household the higher the living standards. The prevalence of this relationship may well be one of the reasons why it is so difficult to get rural families to accept the practice of birth control.

Since most of these surveys and statistics relate to the 1950s, it might be asked whether things have not changed markedly for the better since then. The answer is that they have not. There are two reasons for thinking this. One is that since the 1960s there has been a policy of concentrating new supplies of fertilizer and mechanized equipment in areas which could most easily achieve 'high and stable yields' of crops. Since these areas were *initially* relatively prosperous, further support must have widened the gap between them and the rest.

The reality of rural inequality at the present time is also confirmed by informants and by articles in the press. Among the latter, a good example was recently published in the journal *Study and Criticism*. This piece contained a series of reflections on the progress made since the publication of Mao's call for agricultural collectivization in 1955. The article illustrated its points with reference to a County near Shanghai — a locality in which one would have anticipated that many of the inequalities found in backward parts of China would have been ironed out. However, the article reported that in this County the difference in average income between the poorest and wealthiest *Commune* was 64 per cent; between the poorest and wealthiest *Brigade* the gap was 130 per cent; and between the poorest and wealthiest *Team* the gap was 270 per cent. It continued:

The explanation of this situation is that, at our present, generally low level of development of agriculture within the development of the collective economy, there remains an imbalance, and a gap between rich and poor, which may be said to be unavoidable.[20]

POLICIES TOWARDS WAGES AND INCOMES

Chinese incomes policy has been concerned with three questions: To what extent should incomes be increased to improve living standards? How far should the planners use differences in incomes to control people's economic behaviour? Irrespective of what may seem *desirable*, to what extent is the control of incomes *possible*?[21]

Between 1949 and 1957 the policy was to raise urban and rural incomes quite rapidly. For wage earners, it was also intended that wage differences should be used as incentives. Since wage and salary earners in the 1950s were such a small group in the labour force (increasing from eight to twenty-five million in a total labour force of about four hundred million), decisions about their incomes could be implemented by administrative order. The food and consumer goods necessary to supply demand created by these rising incomes were initially modest in relation to supply. But raising incomes of hundreds of millions of peasants depended on the growth of agricultural output. This in turn depended on many factors: human, technical and climatic. This problem was acknowledged in the First Five Year Plan. The Plan set a specific target for the incomes of wage earners (a 33 per cent increase over five years), but summed up peasant prospects with the sentence: 'the development of agriculture during these five years will enable the peasants to enjoy a still higher standard of living.'

In the event, urban incomes moved rapidly ahead, but there was little or no increase in peasant incomes. As a result, a very serious situation arose. For not only was inequality increasing, but by 1957 the growing incomes of the now much enlarged number of wage earners were making demands on food and other supplies that could not be met.

This economic crisis was compounded, in Mao's eyes, by political dangers. In 1956 Mao had stated that it would be 'improper to ignore' the demands for higher wages, but he soon became a supporter of what was officially called the 'rational low wage policy'. This policy was designed to stop further rises in urban wages; to lessen differentials between peasants and workers; and to reduce differences between wage earners. This became so important to Mao that, in his private notes on a book by Stalin, he described as 'most incorrect' the theory that continuously rising wages 'is where socialism is fundamentally superior'.

The labour situation in 1974-76 has appeared far from settled. Reports suggest that skilled manual workers and white collar staff are demoralized by the lack of wage improvements for so many years, and that this is a factor in the labour unrest reported in 1974 and 1975. While these frustrations are understandable, it is difficult to see what the remedies can be. There are few resources available for improving incomes, and if urban incomes were increased, the urban-rural gap would increase again, with social and political consequences.

Early in 1975 a series of rather sensational articles appeared, which revealed that part of the leadership favours trying to escape from the impasse by even more egalitarianism. These articles were part of a campaign against 'bourgeois rights' and they reflected much of the hostility that Mao developed in the 1960s towards the use of material incentives. This attitude was put in its starkest form by a Party spokesman who addressed a visiting group of British sinologists in November 1974 as follows:

There is a contradiction between the standard of living of the people and the growth of production. We have resolved this by putting production first in accordance with Chairman Mao's principles of taking grain as the key, digging tunnels, storing grain and serving the people. We [in Kweilin] are not planning any more multi-storey workers' flats. We shall build factories.

The new leadership is more cautious and has made definite statements undertaking to raise living standards, and it seems unlikely that the critical state of the coal, iron and steel, and transport industries would allow further experiments in egalitarianism.* The price of a serious dislocation would be too high. In the countryside, however, while the leadership may wish to raise incomes, there may well be an effort to shift agricultural organization in such a way as to make the equalization of incomes rather easier. But here, as in the towns, there can be no major changes until the economy reaches a level of development where it is possible to improve the standard of living of one group without reducing that of another.

*See p. 176, first paragraph.

Appendixes

Chronology of Important Economic, Technological and Political Events, 1949-77

1949	October	Government of Chinese People's Republic established.
	December	Mao visits Moscow to seek aid.
1950	January–December	A series of laws and regulations on finance, trade, taxation, grain, control of the private sector.
	February	First long-term agreement on Soviet credits for China.
	June	*Land Reform Law* adopted.
		Measures taken to alleviate unemployment.
	October	China enters the Korean War.
1951	May	Public security conference adopts proposal to set up Labour Reform camps.
	October	The economy reaches full capacity in many sectors.
	November–Summer 1952	Political campaigns against the private economic sector and corruption in public administration ('The Five Antis' and 'Three Antis').
1952	February	First campaign for agricultural collectivization begins.
	October	Work on control of Yellow River begins.
	November	State Planning Commission established.
	December	Chou En-lai announces that the *First Five Year Plan* will begin in January 1953.
1953	Spring	Land Reform completed in South China.
	March	Death of Stalin.
	June	National Population Census taken.
	July	Korean Armistice.
	November	Regulations for the compulsory purchase of key agricultural commodities introduced.
	December	Second campaign for agricultural collectivization begins.
1954	September	First National People's Congress; Constitution approved; State Council established; People's Bank of China established.
	October	Second (long-term) agreement on Soviet credits for China.

1955	February	Campaign for agricultural collectivization halted.
	March	Announcement of purge of Kao Kang (Pro-Soviet, Party Chief of Manchuria).
	March-Autumn	Series of purges against political, cultural, and religious dissidents.
	Summer	First major campaign to send population to the countryside (*Hsia Fang*).
	July 5	Chairman of the State Planning Commission speaks on the publication of the *First Five Year Plan* to the National People's Congress.
	July 31	Mao calls for agricultural collectivization in his speech *On the Problem of Agricultural Cooperativization.*
	September	Adoption of the first *Twelve Year Plan for Science.*
	October	Decision taken to accelerate collectivization of industry and commerce.
	November-Spring 1956	The 'High Tide' of cooperativization in agriculture and in the private commercial and industrial sectors.
1956	January	Mao introduces his *Twelve Year Programme for the Development of Agriculture 1956-1967* (known as the *Forty Articles*).
		Chou En-lai speaks *On the Problem of Intellectuals* to mobilize support for economic upsurge.
	February	The State Planning Commission announces a 60 per cent increase in 1956 in construction investment (compared to 1955).
	April	Mao speaks *On the Ten Major Relationships.*
	June	Wage Reform to increase wages and improve the system.
	September	Chou En-lai reports on the draft *Second Five Year Plan.* Management of enterprises transferred from individual Directors to Party Committees.
1957	February	Mao speaks *On the Correct Handling of Contradictions Among the People* (an analysis of how to govern China *after* the socialization of the economy).
	May	The 'Hundred Flowers' campaign—three weeks during which intellectuals were encouraged to speak out.
	June	A 'Rectification' campaign begins to suppress dissent.
	August	Large-scale campaign to send unemployed workers, graduates, and officials to the countryside.
	October	Revised *Twelve Year Plan for the Development of Agriculture* adopted.
	November-December	Mass campaign for rural water conservation works started.

		Measures announced to decentralize industry and finance, and to control employment and population migration.
	December	Revised targets for the *Second Five Year Plan* announced.
		Purge of local Party leadership begins.
1958	February	The *People's Daily* calls for a 'Leap Forward'.
	April-July	A few large-scale collectives and public messhalls appear.
	May	Mao announces steel targets to catch up with the United States in eight years.
	August	Party supports the nationwide extension of the People's Communes (at Peitaiho).
	September	98 per cent of the rural population reported in Communes.
	December	Mao resigns as Chairman of the Republic; a retreat on Communes and the Great Leap Forward begins. Party claims grain output of 375 million metric tons and publishes ambitious 'leap' plans for 1959. China trial produces electronic computers and television equipment.
1959	February	Mao warns of dangers of Leap policies and calls for abolition of much small-scale industry.
	March	The *Sixty Articles of Commune Management* (first version) make the Brigade the basic unit of ownership and accounting.
	Spring	Revival of central coordination of the economy under the slogan 'The whole country is one chessboard'.
	April	Hsüeh Mu-ch'iao and Sun Yeh-fang convene economists' conference to discuss economic problems.
	June	Decision to encourage the development of vegetable growing near cities for urban 'self-sufficiency'.
	August	The Party dismisses Peng Te-huai for criticism of Mao and the Leap, but lowers 1959 economic targets (at Lushan).
	November	Soviet built Loyang No. 1 Tractor Plant begins production.
		Production of diesel locomotives begins.
		Production of 50,000 kW generating sets and large scale steel rolling and smelting equipment begins.
		Successful oil strike at Taching.
1960-1962		Reports of mass transfers of population to the countryside.
		The *Revised* (September 1962) *Sixty Articles of Commune Management* make the Team the basic

rural unit and with the *Seventy Articles of Industrial Policy* provide a framework for an expansion of incentives in agriculture, and a reimposition of technical, financial and organizational discipline in industry.

1960

Statistical blackout begins.

Agreement to rephase repayments of Soviet credits.

June–September
Campaign 'Agriculture is the foundation of the economy' begins.

August
Soviet technicians leave China.

Chou En-lai discusses the expansion of trade with representatives of the Association for the Promotion of Sino-Japanese trade.

November
Twelve articles of the *Urgent Directive on Rural Work* make the Brigade the key unit.

December
First trade deficit since 1955.

1961 January
Party announces full retreat from the Great Leap; the Brigade confirmed as the basic unit of ownership and accounting in agriculture and free markets for agricultural products reopened.

July
Teng Hsiao-p'ing orders the Party to support scientific work.

September–December
Campaign to restore proper accounting in industry.
Import of food grains begins.

October
Liu Shao-ch'i orders that free markets be expanded (by legalizing black markets).

December
Conference of industrial leaders to discuss implementation of the *Seventy Articles.*

1962 June
National Conference on Accounting Work.

Summer
Teng Hsiao-p'ing and others continue to advocate individual farming.

September
Mao speaks on need to attack corruption and 'restoration of reactionary classes': beginning of the Socialist Education Movement.

The *Revised Sixty Articles of Commune Management* make the Team the basic unit of ownership, accounting and labour organization.

December
Liu Shao-ch'i reports on the poor situation in the countryside.

1963

Work starts on control of the Haiho river.

Imports of whole plant resume.

The Liao-Takasaki agreement with Japan for five years trade comes into operation.

The second *Twelve Year Plan for Science* adopted.

February
National conference calls for new efforts to raise the technical level of agriculture and solve problems of fertilizer, water, etc.

	May	Party promulgates a directive on *Some Problems in Current Rural Work* (known as the *First Ten Points*) to launch the 'Four Cleansings' campaign against rural corruption and private economic activities.
	Summer	Police check of population registers. Wage rises for lower paid and some other workers and staff.
	September	Circulation of *Second Ten Points* and intensification of the 'Four Cleansings'.
	October	Agricultural Bank established. State Planning Commission strengthened by the addition of three Politburo members (T'an Chen-lin, Po I-po, Ch'en Po-ta) and Teng Tzu-hui.
1964	January	New Year editorial in the *People's Daily* calls for concentration on agricultural 'High and Stable Yield' areas. France and China establish diplomatic relations.
	Spring	New Political Departments established in transport, finance, and trade as part of a campaign to increase political and military control of the economy.
	May	Shengli oilfield comes on stream.
	June	Travel and Tourist Administration Bureau established. Mao calls for an end to grain imports.
	September	Purge of about two million rural cadres begins.
	October	China tests first nuclear bomb.
	December	Chou En-lai reports to the Third National People's Congress that the economy has recovered from the setback of 1960-1961; calls for the 'Four Modernizations' with appropriate use of foreign technology.
1965	January	Mao advises economic planners to move cautiously but ensure international technological standards are reached. Debts to the Soviet Union paid off. Self-sufficiency in oil achieved.
1966	January	*Third Five Year Plan* announced (no details).
	May-June	The Cultural Revolution begins.
	August	Liu Shao-ch'i and Teng Hsiao-p'ing purged.
	October	Campaign to take the Cultural Revolution to the economy begins. China tests a nuclear missile.
	December	All China Federation of Trade Unions abolished. Chinese scientists are the first to manufacture benzene by synthetic means.
1967	January	First Provincial Revolutionary Committees established.

	February	'Revolutionary Rebels' take over industrial enterprises from Party Committees. Press articles attack the *Seventy Articles of Industrial Policy*.
		PLA take over Public Security Bureaux in several areas.
	June	Attack on universities begins.
		China explodes first hydrogen bomb.
	July	Five Japanese businessmen arrested.
	August	British Embassy in Peking burned out.
	September	Teams take the Cultural Revolution into schools and universities. China involved in diplomatic disputes with 32 countries.
	October	Transistorized digital computer trial produced.
	December	Press reports of demands for higher wages and of loss of economic control.
		Output of industry falls (the only fall between 1961-75).
1968	January	Serious measures taken to reimpose political and economic order.
		Conference of railway workers held to plan restoration of communications.
	April	Rural Red Guards returned to the countryside.
	April-September	Political stability returns to the Provinces.
	July	Vickers-Zimmer fined £650,000 and contract with China National Technical Import Corporation annulled after Mr George Watt beaten and tried for alleged 'espionage'.
	October	China makes large export contracts at Canton Fair.
	December	Several millions returned to countryside.
1969	February	Breakdown of Sino-Japanese trade negotiations for 1969 following Chinese attack on Premier Sato.
	April	The end of the 'First Phase' of the Cultural Revolution. Provincial conference called to restore industrial production.
	October	German engineers sentenced to 10 years imprisonment for 'espionage'.
1970	April	China launches first earth satellite.
	May	The *People's Daily* quotes Mao in a call for recentralization of economic planning.
	July	Population limitation campaign begins.
	August	Attacks on Po I-po (former Chairman of State Planning Commission).
	September	Student enrolments at universities begin again.
	October	Lin Piao calls for preparation of the *Fourth Five Year Plan*.
	November	Attacks on 'anarchy' in industry and calls for reimposition of rules and proper accounting.

December	Pai Hsiang-kuo identified as new Minister of Foreign Trade.
	Completion of major projects for Huai River and to bring the South-Western parts of the Haiho under control.
	Trade deficit (first since 1960).
1971	Fourth Five Year Plan announced in New Year editorials (no details).
February	Publication in Italy of economic statistics given to Edgar Snow by Chou En-lai (first detailed data since 1960).
April	Campaign in agriculture to 'learn from Tachai' attacks 'left' deviations including suppression of peasants' side activities.
July	Kissinger visits China in secret.
September	Chinese Minister of Foreign Trade visits France.
November	China joins United Nations.
December	Major campaign to reassert leadership by Party Committees in the economy and industrial enterprises.
1972	Campaign to restore skilled workers and staff to their pre-Cultural Revolution jobs.
	Wage rise for low paid workers and staff.
	Chou En-lai launches a movement to improve education and science work.
January	Publication of grain output data resumed.
February	Nixon visits China; the *Shanghai Communiqué* agreed.
March	Britain and China establish full diplomatic relations.
April-May	China outlines economic policies at UNCTAD.
September	Lin Piao dies fleeing to the Soviet Union.
	Sino-Japanese Communiqué announces establishment of diplomatic relations.
	Media report that the 1956 *Programme for the Development of Agriculture* is still in force.
October	Yu Ch'iu-li identified as Minister in charge of State Planning Commission.
	The *People's Daily* instructs that the 'autonomy' of agricultural production Teams be respected.
	German Federal Republic and China establish full diplomatic relations.
Autumn	Decision to strengthen fertilizer industry by importing thirteen of the world's largest scale ammonia-urea complexes.
1973 January	Articles in media indicate serious economic anxieties (grain production *declined* in 1972).
April	Teng Hsiao-p'ing reappears in public.

		Local Trade Union Congresses held in Peking and other cities.
	June	Ku Mu reported as Minister in Charge of the State Capital Construction Commission.
	August	Chou En-lai calls for increased centralization. Attacks on 'Lin Piao and Confucius' begin.
		New Constitution adopted confirming the existing structure of agricultural organization and the use of economic incentives.
	October	Delegation of the China Council for the Promotion of International Trade tours Europe.
		Li Chiang reported as new Minister of Foreign Trade.
		Exports of oil begin.
		Trade deficit.
1974	January	Teng Hsiao-p'ing rehabilitated.
	May	Development of Takang oilfield announced.
	Summer	Disruption in rail and iron and steel industries. Widespread factional disputes reported in industrial enterprises.
	September	New China News Agency predicts the collapse of the existing international economic order following the oil crisis.
	November	Chinese representatives at UN World Food Conference claim that China is self-sufficient in grain.
	December	Steel output falls for the first year since 1967.
1975	January	Fourth National People's Congress; Chou En-lai introduces new plans for economic modernization.
	February	Completion announced of China's largest hydro-electricity station at Luchiahsia on the upper Yellow River.
	May	Establishment of relations between China and the European Economic Community.
	June	Completion of the Tanzam Railway.
		Reports that the military have been called in to handle disorder on the railways.
	August	At an UNCTAD conference China supports the formation of an organization to raise raw material prices.
	September	China supports OPEC price rise for oil.
	October	Hua Kuo-feng sums up at the National Conference on Learning from Tachai in Agriculture.
		Ministry of Coal calls a large conference to discuss the industry's problems.
		West German Chancellor Schmidt visits China.
	November	Chinese media publicize claims to sovereignty over oil in the South China Sea.

1976	January	Chou En-lai dies. Memorial speech made by Teng Hsiao-p'ing.
	February	Campaign against Teng Hsiao-p'ing gathers pace.
	March	American visitor reports China's progress in laser technology.
	April	Dismissal of Teng Hsiao-p'ing following demonstrations in favour of 'moderates' (the 'Tien An Men incident').
		Appointment of Hua Kuo-feng as Premier.
	Spring	Completion of the oil pipeline linking Taching oilfield and the port of Darien.
	May	Major article in *Red Flag* attacking current foreign trade policies.
	July	Earthquake in Tangshan region.
	September 9	Mao Tse-tung dies.
	October	Hua Kuo-feng appointed Chairman of the Central Committee of the Chinese Communist Party.
		The 'Gang of Four' denounced.
	November	Beginning of campaign describing the role of the 'Gang of Four' in dislocating economic development.
	December	Second National Conference on Learning from Tachai in Agriculture.
		Release for the first time cf official text of Mao's *On the Ten Major Relationships* (April 1956).
1977	January	New Year editorials promise 'prosperity', 'political liveliness', renewed blooming of 'a hundred red flowers', and 'comprehensive modernization'.
		State Council gives New Year's Eve reception for foreign experts to thank them for their 'valuable contribution' to China's construction.
		Chen Yung-kuei reports that the 'Gang of Four' caused serious agricultural production losses in six Provinces, and for 'years' 'sabotaged' the iron and steel industry.
		New 300,000 ton capacity ethylene plant reported on stream in Peking.
	February	Conference held by PLA Science and Technology Commission and Third Ministry of Machine Building to discuss defence production.
		JETRO estimates that China achieved a trade surplus in 1976.
	May	Yu Ch'iu-li announces plans for a new industrialization drive including a huge expansion of oil production.
	August	Eleventh Party Congress sets guidelines for China's future development. Addressed by Chairman Hua and the rehabilitated Teng Hsiao-p'ing.

Sources: This chronology is based on many sources. Particularly valuable English publications were *Current Scene*, 1961- ; *Chronicle and Documentation* sections of *The China Quarterly*, 1960- ; Kenneth Lieberthal, *A Research Guide to Central Party and Government Meetings in China 1949-1975* (New York, 1976). Chinese sources included compendiums of laws and regulations, and indexes to the *People's Daily*, and to editorials in the *People's Daily*.

Biographical Notes on Persons Frequently Referred to in Literature on the Chinese Economy*

CHANG CH'UN CH'IAO   See 'Gang of Four'.

CHANG NAI-CH'I   A non-communist financier and industrialist who was Minister of Food responsible for introducing food control and rationing in 1955; disgraced in 1957. Mao later claimed that Chang deliberately caused an 'uproar' in China by mishandling the rationing policy.

CHAO TZU-YANG   Leading Party official in South and South-West China from 1950s onwards. A specialist in agriculture who became First Secretary of Kwangtung Party Committee in 1965. In the Cultural Revolution was described as 'Krushchev's agent in Kwangtung'. Reappeared in 1973 and transferred to Szechuan Province in 1975 where he was still reported to be active in 1977. Promoted to Politburo, August 1977.

CH'EN PO-TA   For many years the leading interpreter of the Thought of Mao. A controlling force in academic and cultural life and Editor of *Red Flag*. Promoted to Politburo in 1956 and played a key role in the Great Leap. In late 1966 was China's fourth ranking politician and Head of the 'Group in Charge of the Cultural Revolution'. Later disgraced, and last heard of in 1970.

CH'EN YÜN   Played a major role in economic policy, 1949-1957. In 1954 negotiated Soviet loans with Chou En-lai and made Vice-Premier. Favoured stable growth and use of financial incentives in controlled markets. Made Chairman of the State Capital Construction Commission in 1958 but eclipsed in the Great Leap. In 1960s Mao said that 'old Ch'en was right' (after the Leap). Still being reported in mid-1976.

CHEN YUNG-KUEI   Vice-Premier and Politburo member. Former First Secretary of the Tachai Production Brigade Party Committee. China's foremost spokesman on agricultural affairs.

CHIANG CH'ING   See 'Gang of Four'.

CHOU EN-LAI   Prime Minister from 1949 to his death in 1975. Crucial in economic affairs. Appears to have preferred cautious, technically sound policies, but bent with the wind in the High Tide (1955), the Great Leap (1958),

---

* Chinese sources frequently spell names without apostrophes, i.e. 'Ping' for 'P'ing'.

and the Cultural Revolution (1966-69). Author of the current strategy of achieving the 'Four Modernizations'.

FANG YI Minister for Economic Relations with Foreign Countries and a leading figure in China's foreign aid programme until January 1977. Was in charge of China's trade office in Hanoi, 1956-60. Joined the Central Committee in 1960 and has played the major role in the Tanzam Railway project. Fluent in several languages. Promoted to Politburo, August 1977.

FEI HSIAO-T'UNG China's most celebrated anthropologist. Author of studies of rural society in pre-communist China. Worked for many years in the Peking Nationalities Institute where he has met several foreign visitors who subsequently wrote up their conversations with him.

'GANG OF FOUR' Wang Hung-wen, Chang Ch'un-ch'iao, Yao Wen-yuan and Mao's widow—Chiang Ch'ing. A group of 'radicals' based in Shanghai who rose to prominence in the Cultural Revolution. The group exercised great control over the media in the mid-1970s. After Mao's death the four were arrested and accused of plotting to gain power.

HSÜ TI-HSIN An influential economist who played an intermediary role between communist and non-communist leaders before and after 1949. Worked as a supervisor of the Bank of China and as a member of the CCPIT. Hsü's most famous book, *An Analysis of the National Economy during the Transition Period*, was published in three editions reflecting the pre-Leap, the Leap, and the post-Leap points of view. Last reported active in 1976.

HSÜEH MU-CH'IAO Became Head of the State Statistical Bureau and member of the State Planning Commission in 1952. Established China's statistical administration and wrote prolifically on the subject in the 1950s. Became Vice-Chairman of the State Economic Commission in 1958. Disgraced and dismissed in the Great Leap. Reappointed to State Planning Commission in 1960 and made Director of National Commodities Price Commission in 1963.

HUA KUO-FENG Believed born about 1920. Early career as a Party leader in Hunan Province where he implemented agricultural collectivization. A survivor of the Cultural Revolution, Hua joined the Politburo in 1973. Appointed Minister of Public Security in 1975. Appointed Acting Premier after the death of Chou En-lai in 1976, and Party Chairman after the death of Mao.

KAO KANG Established himself as the major authority in Manchuria in 1948-49 where he set up a Soviet style government. Brought to Peking in 1952 to be the first Chairman of the State Planning Commission. Purged in 1954-55 for pro-Soviet treason.

K'O CH'ING-SHIH Long career of Party leadership in Shanghai and East China. Joined the Central Committee in 1956. Became Mayor of Shanghai and Politburo member in 1958. Close to Mao, K'o played the central role in the reversal of Shanghai's economic fortunes that began in 1956. Died in 1965.

KU MU Minister in charge of the State Capital Construction Commission since 1973. Became Vice-Chairman (under Po I-po) of State Construction

Commission in 1954. From 1956 to 1965 was Vice-Chairman of State Economic Commission specializing in heavy industry and is also known to have worked on the Scientific Planning Commission under the State Council. Worked on the State Capital Construction Commission from its inception in 1965. Described as a 'big renegade' during the Cultural Revolution. Reappeared in public at the funeral of Teng Tzu-hui in 1972.

LI CHIANG Minister of Foreign Trade. Vice-Minister since 1952, and adviser on the Soviet aid agreements while Commercial Counsellor in the Chinese Embassy in Moscow. A specialist in scientific planning work with particular expertise in communications and electronics. Has worked closely with Fang Yi on aid matters. China's principal spokesman on a variety of international trade and economic issues.

LI FU-CH'UN One of China's chief economic administrators since the mid-1940s. Negotiated with the Soviets in 1950, 1952, and 1953. Signatory of the 1954 agreement by which the Soviet Union supplied 141 projects to China. Placed at first in charge of Ministry of Heavy Industry, and in 1954 appointed Chairman of State Planning Commission. Principal author of China's *First Five Year Plan* and, by 1959, China's top economic official. Acting Vice-Premier in 1970s. Died in 1975.

LIAO CH'ENG-CHIH President, China-Japan Friendship Association. Born in Tokyo in 1908. Studied at Waseda University and is fluent in Japanese. Co-author of the Liao-Takasaki Agreement of 1962 under which Sino-Japanese trade was developed after the Sino-Soviet collapse.

LIAO LU-YEN Former Minister of Agriculture and key spokesman on agricultural affairs in the 1950s. Eclipsed in the Great Leap. Made a small recovery in the 1960s, but finally disgraced in the Cultural Revolution.

LI CHING-CH'ÜAN Long career in Szechuan Province and South-West China (originally under Teng Hsiao-p'ing). Joined the Central Committee in 1956. Attacked in the Cultural Revolution when he was accused of attempting to isolate Szechuan in an economic 'kingdom'. He was accused of 'travelling in fleets of cars surrounded by escorts', and of saying that 'some people eat Szechuan rice and insult us too.' Rehabilitated in 1973, but believed subsequently removed from office.

LI HSIEN-NIEN Vice-Premier with long, influential career in finance and economics. Post-1949 career began in Hunan. Minister of Finance from 1954. Appointed Politburo member in 1956, and Vice-Chairman of State Planning Commission in 1962. An acting Vice-Premier in 1970s. Member of Politburo.

LIN PIAO Military leader who played an important political role until his death in 1971. Controlled the Central-South Region of China, 1950-54. Appointed to State Planning Commission in 1952. Took charge of People's Liberation Army after the disgrace of Peng Te-huai in 1959 and began to cooperate with Mao to build up the political and economic role of the Army. Became heir apparent to Mao after fall of Liu Shao-ch'i. Died fleeing to the Soviet Union in 1971.

LIU CHIEN-HSÜN Early career under Teng Tzu-hui and Li Hsien-nien. First Party Secretary of Kwangsi in 1957. Joined the Central Committee in

1958 and moved to Honan in 1961. Attacked in the Cultural Revolution for deriding Mao and his policies. Rehabilitated in Honan in 1970s.

LIU SHAO-CH'I Obtained enormous political and administrative experience before 1949, and from 1956 was China's leading political figure after Mao. Succeeded Mao as Chairman of the Republic in 1959 and played a central role in leading China out of the Great Leap. The most sensational victim of the Cultural Revolution. Never heard of again after his disgrace. Presumed dead.

MA YIN-CH'U China's most celebrated economist. Educated in America, Ma wrote prolifically on economic matters before 1949. In the 1950s he held many political and academic offices and summarized his views in a book, *My Economic Theory, Philosophical Thoughts and Political Standpoint*. Ma emphasized population problems and advocated 'balanced growth'. Violently attacked in 1957 and 1958. Made his last public protest in 1960 and was dismissed as President of Peking University in the same year.

MAO TSE-TUNG Master-minded the novel strategy by which the Chinese Communist Party captured power in the countryside and then moved into the cities. Dominated China's political life from the 1930s to his death in 1976. Adopted Soviet economic strategies in the 1950s, then tried to accelerate growth between 1955 and 1959. Lost influence and power after the Great Leap, but in 1966 initiated the Cultural Revolution to regain power. Mao's role in the 1970s remains unclear.

PAI HSIANG-KUO Minister of Foreign Trade, 1970-73. Subsequently Deputy Director, PLA Logistics Department.

P'ENG TE-HUAI One of China's greatest military leaders. Minister of Defence, 1954-59. In 1959 attacked Mao's policies of the Great Leap. Mao counter-attacked and P'eng was replaced by Lin Piao.

PO I-PO For many years one of China's top four economic administrators (with Li Hsien-nien, Li Fu-Ch'un, and Teng Tzu-hui). Member of State Economic Commission from 1956. Vice-Chairman of the State Planning Commission from 1962. Denounced in Cultural Revolution and the object of sporadic attacks in early 1970s. Author of numerous speeches and articles on economic affairs.

SHA FENG Minister of Agriculture and Forestry.

SUN YEH-FANG An economist who wrote several important articles in the early 1960s advocating the use of profit as an indicator of enterprise performance. Often described as 'China's Libermann' and at one time Director of the Economic Research Institute of the Chinese Academy of Sciences. Attacked in Cultural Revolution for travelling on a train in 1925 with Wang Ming (a pro-Soviet 'traitor') and for describing the thought of Mao as 'chauvinistic'.

T'AN CHEN-LIN Agricultural specialist. Early career 1949-52 in Chekiang Province. Became Director of Huai River Harnessing Commission in 1952. Joined Politburo and strongly supported the Great Leap in 1958, and was thereafter the Party's top spokesman on agriculture. Appointed Director of State Council Office for Agriculture and Forestry in 1962 and Vice-Premier.

Attacked in Cultural Revolution, but rejoined Central Committee in 1973.

T'AO CHU   Throughout the 1950s T'ao was the most important leader in South and Central China—particularly in Kwangtung Province. Joined the Central Committee in 1956, and after a record of moderation plunged actively into the Great Leap in 1958. In 1964 wrote an article, *The People's Communes Forge Ahead*, which at the time was the most important official confirmation of the nature of the Communes after their collapse in the Great Leap. In 1966 T'ao moved to Peking as Director of Propaganda in which position he was briefly the fourth ranking official in China. Disgraced in the Cultural Revolution and never heard of again.

TENG HSIAO-P'ING   A leading military and political figure from the 1920s to the present. Served in the State Planning Commission, 1952-54. Became Secretary-General of the Party in 1954 and joined the Central Committee and Politburo. Disgraced as an arch-villain in 1966. Rehabilitated in 1973 and disgraced again at the instigation of the 'Gang of Four' in 1976. Rehabilitated in summer, 1977 as member of Politburo holding key posts.

TENG TZU-HUI ('Old Teng')   Long pre-1949 career and for many years the Party's leading agricultural expert. Appointed Vice-Chairman of the State Planning Commission in 1952 and Head of the Party Rural Work Department in 1953. Opposed rapid collectivization in 1955 and, after opposition to the Great Leap in 1958, was replaced in importance by T'an Chen-lin. As Vice-Chairman of the State Planning Commission, Teng advocated the development of private agriculture from 1962. Disgraced in the Cultural Revolution, but later rehabilitated. Teng's death in 1972 was used to rehabilitate three important economic Ministers all of whom made their first public reappearance at his funeral.

WANG CHIN-HSI   Was China's most famous 'labour hero'. Worked in the oil industry and known as the 'iron man of Taching'. Later became a member of the Central Committee. Died in 1970.

WANG HUNG-WEN   See 'Gang of Four'.

WANG KUANG-WEI   Senior economic planner transferred from Manchuria to Peking to help prepare the First Five Year Plan. Appointed Vice-Chairman of the State Planning Commission in 1956. Author of many important articles on the Chinese economy and one of the first to recognize that China's development must diverge from Soviet and East European patterns. Still active in 1976.

WANG YAO-T'ING   Chairman of the China Council for the Promotion of International Trade since June 1973.

YAO WEN-YUAN   See 'Gang of Four'.

YU CH'IU-LI   Veteran Military administrator, currently Minister in charge of the State Planning Commission, in which post he succeeded Li Fu-ch'un. Director of Finance in the People's Liberation Army, 1956-57. Believed to have favoured an early slowdown of the Great Leap. Appointed Vice-Premier and member of the State Planning Commission in 1965. Disgraced in the Cultural Revolution, but believed to have been recalled to power on the insistence of Chou En-lai. Promoted to Politburo, August, 1977.

Principal Sources: Donald W. Klein and Ann B. Clark, *Biographic Dictionary of Chinese Communism 1921-1965*, two volumes (Cambridge, Mass., 1971); Union Research Institute, *Who's Who in Communist China* (Hong Kong, 1966 and 1969); Malcolm Lamb, *Directory of Central Officials in the People's Republic of China 1968-1975* (Canberra, 1976). Files of cards recording public appearances of important figures are available at the Universities Service Centre, Hong Kong and at some other China centres.

APPENDIX C

Mao Tse-tung:
*On the Ten Major Relationships**
(Parts I-V and X)

In recent months the Political Bureau of the Central Committee has heard reports on the work of thirty-four industrial, agricultural, transport, commercial, financial and other departments under the central authorities and from these reports has identified a number of problems concerning socialist construction and socialist transformation. In all, they boil down to ten problems, or ten major relationships.

It is to focus on one basic policy that these ten problems are being raised, the basic policy of mobilizing all positive factors, internal and external, to serve the cause of socialism. In the past we followed this policy of mobilizing all positive factors in order to put an end to the rule of imperialism, feudalism and bureaucrat-capitalism and to win victory for the people's democratic revolution. We are now following the same policy in order to carry on the socialist revolution and build a socialist country. Nevertheless, there are some problems in our work that need discussion. Particularly worthy of attention is the fact that in the Soviet Union certain defects and errors that occurred in the course of their building socialism have lately come to light. Do you want to follow the detours they have made? It was by drawing lessons from their experience that we were able to avoid certain detours in the past, and there is all the more reason for us to do so now.

What are the internal and external positive factors? Internally, the workers and the peasants are the basic force. The middle forces are forces that can be won over. The reactionary forces are a negative factor, but even so we should do our work well and turn this negative factor as far as possible into a positive one. Internationally, all the forces that can be united with must be united, the forces that are not neutral can be neutralized through our efforts, and even the reactionary forces can be split and made use of. In short, we should mobilize all forces, whether direct or indirect, and strive to build China into a powerful

*Mao's original speech was made in April 1956. This version was published in Peking in December 1976, and the text here printed is the translation published by the Foreign Languages Press, Peking, 1977. The present version has been edited by Chairman Hua Kuo-feng, and differs from earlier versions that have been circulating unofficially for many years. These differences are briefly discussed by Stuart Schram in *The China Quarterly*, No. 69 (1977), pp. 126-35.

socialist country.

I will now discuss the ten problems.

1. THE RELATIONSHIP BETWEEN
HEAVY INDUSTRY ON THE ONE HAND AND
LIGHT INDUSTRY AND AGRICULTURE
ON THE OTHER

The emphasis in our country's construction is on heavy industry. The production of the means of production must be given priority, that's settled. But it definitely does not follow that the production of the means of subsistence, especially grain, can be neglected. Without enough food and other daily necessities, it would be impossible to provide for the workers in the first place, and then what sense would it make to talk about developing heavy industry? Therefore, the relationship between heavy industry on the one hand and light industry and agriculture on the other must be properly handled.

In dealing with this relationship we have not made mistakes of principle. We have done better than the Soviet Union and a number of East European countries. The prolonged failure of the Soviet Union to reach the highest pre-October Revolution level in grain output, the grave problems arising from the glaring disequilibrium between the development of heavy industry and that of light industry in some East European countries—such problems do not exist in our country. Their lop-sided stress on heavy industry to the neglect of agriculture and light industry results in a shortage of goods on the market and an unstable currency. We, on the other hand, attach more importance to agriculture and light industry. We have all along attended to and developed agriculture and have to a considerable degree ensured the supply of grain and raw materials necessary for the development of industry. Our daily necessities are in fairly good supply and our prices and currency are stable.

The problem now facing us is that of continuing to adjust properly the ratio between investment in heavy industry on the one hand and in agriculture and light industry on the other in order to bring about a greater development of the latter. Does this mean that heavy industry is no longer primary? It still is, it still claims the emphasis in our investment. But the proportion for agriculture and light industry must be somewhat increased.

What will be the results of this increase? First, the daily needs of the people will be better satisfied; second, the accumulation of capital will be speeded up so that we can develop heavy industry with greater and better results. Heavy industry can also accumulate capital but, given our present economic conditions, light industry and agriculture can accumulate more and faster.

Here the question arises: Is your desire to depelop heavy industry genuine or feigned, strong or weak? If your desire is feigned or weak, then you will hit agriculture and light industry and invest less in them. If your desire is genuine or strong, then you will attach importance to agriculture and light industry so that there will be more grain and more raw materials for light industry and a greater accumulation of capital. And there will be more funds in the future to invest in heavy industry.

There are now two approaches to our development of heavy industry: one is to develop agriculture and light industry less, and the other is to develop them more. In the long run, the first approach will lead to a smaller and slower development of heavy industry, or at least will put it on a less solid foundation, and when the over-all account is added up a few decades hence, it will not prove to have paid. The second approach will lead to a greater and faster development of heavy industry and, since it ensures the livelihood of the people, it will lay a more solid foundation for the development of heavy industry.

II. THE RELATIONSHIP BETWEEN INDUSTRY IN THE COASTAL REGIONS AND INDUSTRY IN THE INTERIOR

In the past our industry was concentrated in the coastal regions. By coastal regions we mean Liaoning, Hopei, Peking, Tientsin, eastern Honan, Shantung, Anhwei, Kiangsu, Shanghai, Chekiang, Fukien, Kwangtung and Kwangsi. About 70 per cent of all our industry, both light and heavy, is to be found in the coastal regions and only 30 per cent in the interior. This irrational situation is a product of history. The coastal industrial base must be put to full use, but to even out the distribution of industry in the course of its development we must strive to promote industry in the interior. We have not made any major mistakes on the relationship between the two. However, in recent years we have underestimated coastal industry to some extent and have not given great enough attention to its development. This must change.

In the past, fighting was going on in Korea and the international situation was quite tense; this could not but affect our attitude towards coastal industry. Now, it seems unlikely that there will be a new war of aggression against China or another world war in the near future, and there will probably be a period of peace for a decade or more. It would therefore be wrong if we still fail to make full use of the plant capacity and technical forces of coastal industry. If we have only five years, not to say ten, we should still work hard to develop industries in the coastal regions for four years and evacuate them when war breaks out in the fifth. According to available information, in light industry the construction of a plant and its accumulation of capital generally proceed quite rapidly. After the whole plant goes into production, it can earn enough in four years to build three new factories, or two, or one or at least half of one, in addition to recouping its capital outlay. Why shouldn't we do such profitable things? To think that the atom bomb is already overhead and about to fall on us in a matter of seconds is a calculation at variance with reality, and it would be wrong to take a negative attitude towards coastal industry on this account.

It does not follow that all new factories are to be built in the coastal regions. Without doubt, the greater part of the new industry should be located in the interior so that industry may gradually become evenly distributed; moreover, this will help our preparations against war. But a number of new factories and mines, even some large ones, may also be built in the coastal regions. As for the expansion and reconstruction of the light and heavy industries already in the coastal regions, we have done a fair amount of work in the past and will do much more in the future.

Making good use of and developing the capacities of the old industries in the coastal regions will put us in a stronger position to promote and support industry in the interior. To adopt a negative attitude would be to hinder the latter's speedy growth. So it is likewise a question of whether the desire to develop industry in the interior is genuine or not. If it is genuine and not feigned, we must more actively use and promote industry, especially light industry, in the coastal regions.

III. THE RELATIONSHIP BETWEEN ECONOMIC CONSTRUCTION AND DEFENCE CONSTRUCTION

National defence is indispensable. Our defence capabilities have now attained a certain level. As a result of the war to resist US aggression and aid Korea and of several years of training and consolidation, our armed forces have grown more powerful and are now stronger than was the Soviet Red Army before the Second World War; also, there have been improvements in armaments. Our defence industry is being built up. Ever since Pan Ku separated heaven and earth, we have never been able to make planes and cars, and now we are beginning to make them.

We do not have the atom bomb yet. But neither did we have planes and artillery in the past. We defeated the Japanese imperialists and Chiang Kai-shek with millet plus rifles. We are stronger than before and will be still stronger in the future. We will not only have more planes and artillery but we will also have atom bombs. If we are not to be bullied in the present-day world, we cannot do without the bomb. Then what is to be done about it? One reliable way is to cut military and administrative expenditures down to appropriate proportions and increase expenditures on economic construction. Only with the faster growth of economic construction can there be more progress in defence construction.

At the Third Plenary Session of the Seventh Central Committee of our Party in 1950, we already raised the question of streamlining the state apparatus and reducing military and administrative expenditures and considered this measure to be one of the three prerequisites for achieving a fundamental turn for the better in our financial and economic situation. In the period of the First Five Year Plan, military and administrative expenditures accounted for 30 per cent of total expenditures in the state budget. This proportion is much too high. In the period of the Second Five Year Plan, we must reduce it to around 20 per cent so that more funds can be released for building more factories and turning out more machines. After a time, we shall not only have plenty of planes and artillery but probably have our own atom bombs as well.

Here again the question arises: Is your desire for the atom bomb genuine and very keen? Or is it only lukewarm and not so very keen? If your desire is genuine and very keen, then you will reduce the proportion of military and administrative expenditures and spend more on economic construction. If your desire is not genuine or not so very keen, you will stay in the old rut. This is a matter of strategic principle, and I hope the Military Commission will discuss it.

Would it be all right to demobilize all our troops now? No, it would not. For enemies are still around, and we are being bullied and encircled by them. We must strengthen our national defence, and for that purpose we must first of all strengthen our work in economic construction.

IV. THE RELATIONSHIP BETWEEN
THE STATE, THE UNITS OF PRODUCTION
AND THE PRODUCERS

The relationship between the state on the one hand and factories and agricultural co-operatives on the other and the relationship between factories and agricultural co-operatives on the one hand and the producers on the other should both be handled well. To this end we should consider not just one side, but must consider all three, the state, the collective and the individual, or, as we used to say, 'take into consideration both the army and the people' and 'take into consideration both the public and the private interest'. In view of the experience of the Soviet Union as well as our own, we must see to it that from now on this problem is solved much better.

Take the workers for example. As their labour productivity rises, there should be a gradual improvement in their working conditions and collective welfare. We have always advocated plain living and hard work and opposed putting personal material benefits above everything else; at the same time we have always advocated concern for the livelihood of the masses and opposed bureaucracy, which is callous to their well-being. With the growth of our economy as a whole, wages should be appropriately adjusted. We have recently decided to increase wages to some extent, mainly the wages of those at the lower levels, the wages of the workers, in order to narrow the wage gap between them and the upper levels. Generally speaking, our wages are not high, but compared with the past the life of our workers has greatly improved because, among other things, more people are employed and prices remain low and stable. Under the regime of the proletariat, our workers have unfailingly displayed high political consciousness and enthusiasm for labour. When at the end of last year the Central Committee called for a fight against Right conservatism, the masses of the workers warmly responded and, what was exceptional, overfulfilled the plan for the first quarter of the year by working all out for three months. We must strive to encourage this zeal for hard work and at the same time pay still greater attention to solving the pressing problems in their work and everyday life.

Here I would like to touch on the question of the independence of the factories under unified leadership. It's not right, I'm afraid, to place everything in the hands of the central or the provincial and municipal authorities without leaving the factories any power of their own, any room for independent action, any benefits. We don't have much experience on how to share power and returns properly among the central authorities, the provincial and municipal authorities and the factories, and we should study the subject. In principle, centralization and independence forming a unity of opposites, there must be both centralization and independence. For instance, we are now having a meeting, which is centralization; after the meeting, some of us will go for a walk, some will read books, some will go to eat, which is independence. If we don't adjourn the meeting and give everyone some independence but let it go on and on, wouldn't it be the death of us all? This is true of individuals, and no less true of factories and other units of production. Every unit of production must enjoy independence as the correlative of centralization if it is to develop more vigorously.

Now about the peasants. Our relations with the peasants have always been good, but we made a mistake on the question of grain. In 1954 floods caused a decrease in production in some parts of our country, and yet we purchased 7,000 million more catties of grain. A decrease in production and an increase in purchasing—this made grain the topic on almost everyone's lips in many places last spring, and nearly every household talked about the state marketing of grain. The peasants were disgruntled, and there were a lot of complaints both inside and outside the Party. Although quite a few people indulged in deliberate exaggeration and exploited the opportunity to attack us, it cannot be said that we had no shortcoming. Inadequate investigation and failure to size up the situation resulted in the purchase of 7,000 million more catties; that was a shortcoming. After discovering it, we purchased 7,000 million less catties in 1955 and introduced a system of fixed quotas for grain production, purchasing and marketing and, what's more, there was a good harvest. With a decrease in purchasing and an increase in production, the peasants had over 20,000 million more catties of grain on their hands. Thus even those peasants who had complaints before said, 'The Communist Party is really good.' This lesson the whole Party must bear in mind.

The Soviet Union has taken measures which squeeze the peasants very hard.

It takes away too much from the peasants at too low a price through its system of so-called obligatory sales and other measures. This method of capital accumulation has seriously dampened the peasants' enthusiasm for production. You want the hen to lay more eggs and yet you don't feed it, you want the horse to run fast and yet you don't let it graze. What kind of logic is this!

Our policies towards the peasants differ from those of the Soviet Union and take into account the interests of both the state and the peasants. Our agricultural tax has always been relatively low. In the exchange of industrial and agricultural products we follow a policy of narrowing the price scissors, a policy of exchanging equal or roughly equal values. The state buys agricultural products at standard prices while the peasants suffer no loss, and, what is more, our purchase prices are gradually being raised. In supplying the peasants with manufactured goods we follow a policy of larger sales at a small profit and of stabilizing or appropriately reducing their prices; in supplying grain to the peasants in grain-deficient areas we generally subsidize such sales to a certain extent. Even so, mistakes of one kind or another will occur if we are not careful. In view of the grave mistakes made by the Soviet Union on this question, we must take greater care and handle the relationship between the state and the peasants well.

Similarly, the relationship between the co-operative and the peasants should be well handled. What proportion of the earnings of a co-operative should go to the state, to the co-operative and to the peasants respectively and in what form should be determined properly. The amount that goes to the co-operative is used directly to serve the peasants. Production expenses need no explanation, management expenses are also necessary, the accumulation fund is for expanded reproduction and the public welfare fund is for the peasants' well-being. However, together with the peasants, we should work out equitable ratios among these items. We must strictly economize on production and management expenses. The accumulation fund and the public welfare fund must also be kept within limits, and one shouldn't expect all good things to be done in a single year.

Except in case of extraordinary natural disasters, we must see to it that, given increased agricultural production, 90 per cent of the co-operative members get some increase in their income and the other 10 per cent break even each year, and if the latter's income should fall, ways must be found to solve the problem in good time.

In short, consideration must be given to both sides, not to just one, whether they are the state and the factory, the state and the worker, the factory and the worker, the state and the co-operative, the state and the peasant, or the co-operative and the peasant. To give consideration to only one side, whichever it may be, is harmful to socialism and to the dictatorship of the proletariat. This is a big question which concerns 600 million people, and it calls for repeated education in the whole Party and the whole nation.

V. THE RELATIONSHIP BETWEEN
THE CENTRAL AUTHORITIES AND
THE LOCAL AUTHORITIES

The relationship between the central authorities and the local authorities constitutes another contradiction. To resolve this contradiction, our attention should now be focussed on how to enlarge the powers of the local authorities to some extent, give them greater independence and let them do more, all on the premise that the unified leadership of the central authorities is to be strengthened. This will be advantageous to our task of building a powerful socialist country. Our territory is so vast, our population is so large and the conditions are so complex that it is far better to have the initiative come from both the central and the local authorities than from one source alone. We must not follow the example of the Soviet Union in concentrating everything in the hands of the central authorities, shackling the local authorities and denying them the right of independent action.

The central authorities want to develop industry, and so do the local authorities. Even industries directly under the central authorities need assistance from the local authorities. And all the more so for agriculture and commerce. In short, if we are to promote socialist construction, we must bring the initiative of the local authorities into play. If we are to strengthen the central authorities, we must attend to the interests of the localities.

At present scores of hands are reaching out to the localities, making things difficult for them. Once a ministry is set up, it wants to have a revolution and so it issues orders. Since the various ministries don't think it proper to issue them to the Party committees and people's councils at the provincial level, they establish direct contact with the relevant departments and bureaus in the provinces and municipalities and give them orders every day. These orders are all supposed to come from the central authorities, even though neither the Central Committee of the Party nor the State Council knows anything about them, and they put a great strain on the local authorities. There is such a flood of statistical forms that they become a scourge. This state of affairs must be changed.

We should encourage the style of work in which the local authorities are consulted on the matters to be taken up. It is the practice of the Central Committee of the Party to consult the local authorities; it never hastily issues orders without prior consultation. We hope that the various ministries and departments under the central authorities will pay due attention to this and will first confer with the localities on all matters concerning them and not issue any order without full consultation.

The central departments fall into two categories. Those in the first category exercise leadership right down to the enterprises, but their administrative offices and enterprises in the localities are also subject to supervision by the local authorities. Those in the second have the task of laying down guiding principles and mapping out work plans, while the local authorities assume the responsibility and put them into operation.

For a large country like ours and a big Party like ours the proper handling of the relationship between the central and local authorities is a matter of vital importance. Some capitalist countries pay great attention to this too.

Although their social system is fundamentally different from ours, the experience of their growth is nevertheless worth studying. Take our own experience: the system of the greater administrative area instituted in the early days of our Republic was a necessity at that time, and yet it had shortcomings which were later exploited to a certain extent by the Kao Kang-Jao Shu-shih anti-Party alliance. It was subsequently decided to abolish the greater administrative areas and put the various provinces directly under the central authorities; that was a correct decision. But neither was the outcome so satisfactory when matters went to the length of depriving the localities of their necessary independence. According to our Constitution, the legislative powers are all vested in the central authorities. But the local authorities may work out rules, regulations and measures in the light of their specific conditions and the needs of their work, provided that the policies of the central authorities are not violated, and this is in no way prohibited by the Constitution. We want both unity and particularity. To build a powerful socialist country it is imperative to have a strong and unified central leadership and unified planning and discipline throughout the country; disruption of this indispensable unity is impermissible. At the same time, it is essential to bring the initiative of the local authorities into full play and let each locality enjoy the particularity suited to its local conditions. This particularity is not the Kao Kang type of particularity but one that is necessary for the interest of the whole and for the strengthening of national unity.

There is also the relationship between different local authorities, and here I refer chiefly to the relationship between the higher and lower local authorities. Since the provinces and municipalities have their own complaints about the central departments, can it be that the prefectures, counties, districts and townships have no complaints about the provinces and municipalities? The central authorities should take care to give scope to the initiative of the provinces and municipalities, and in their turn the latter should do the same for the prefectures, counties, districts and townships; in neither case should the lower levels be put in a strait-jacket. Of course comrades at the lower levels must be informed of the matters on which centralization is necessary and they must not act as they please. In short, centralization must be enforced where it is possible and necessary, otherwise it should not be imposed at all. The provinces, municipalities, prefectures, counties, districts and townships should all enjoy their own proper independence and rights and should fight for them. To fight for such rights in the interest of the whole nation and not of a local department cannot be called localism or an undue assertion of independence.

The relationship between different provinces and municipalities is also a kind of relationship between different local authorities and it should be properly handled too. It is our consistent principle to advocate consideration for the general interest and mutual help and mutual accommodation.

Our experience is still insufficient and immature on the question of handling the relationship between the central and local authorities and that between different local authorities. We hope that you will consider and discuss it in earnest and sum up your experience from time to time so as to enhance achievements and overcome shortcomings.

X. THE RELATIONSHIP BETWEEN
CHINA AND OTHER COUNTRIES

We have put forward the slogan of learning from other countries. I think we
have been right. At present, the leaders of some countries are chary, and even
afraid, of advancing this slogan. It takes some courage to do that; in other
words, theatrical airs have to be discarded.

It must be admitted that every nation has its strong points. If not, how can it
survive? How can it progress? On the other hand, every nation has its weak
points. Some believe that socialism is just perfect, without a single flaw. How
can that be true? It must be recognized that there are always two aspects, the
strong points and the weak points. The secretaries of our Party branches, the
company commanders and platoon leaders of our army have all learned to jot
down both aspects in their pocket notebooks, the weak points as well as the
strong ones, when summing up their work experience. They all know there are
two aspects to everything. Why do we mention only one? There will always be
two aspects, even ten thousand years from now. Each age, whether the future
or the present, has its own two aspects, and each individual has his own two
aspects. In short, there are two aspects, not just one. To say there is only one is
to be aware of one aspect and to be ignorant of the other.

Our policy is to learn from the strong points of all nations and all countries,
learn all that is genuinely good in the political, economic, scientific and technological fields and in literature and art. But we must learn with an analytical
and critical eye, not blindly, and we mustn't copy everything indiscriminately
and transplant mechanically. Naturally, we mustn't pick up their shortcomings and weak points.

We should adopt the same attitude in learning from the experience of the
Soviet Union and other socialist countries. Some of our people were not clear
about this before and even picked up their weaknesses. While they were
swelling with pride over what they had picked up, it was already being
discarded in those countries; as a result, they had to do a somersault like the
Monkey Sun Wu-kung. For instance, there were people who accused us of
making a mistake of principle in setting up a Ministry of Culture and a Bureau
of Cinematography rather than a Ministry of Cinematography and a Bureau
of Culture, as was the case in the Soviet Union. They did not anticipate that
shortly afterwards the Soviet Union would make a change and set up a
Ministry of Culture as we had done. Some people never take the trouble to
analyse, they simply follow the 'wind'. Today, when the north wind is
blowing, they join the 'north wind' school; tomorrow, when there is a west
wind, they switch to the 'west wind' school; afterwards when the north wind
blows again, they switch back to the 'north wind' school. They hold no
independent opinion of their own and often go from one extreme to the other.

In the Soviet Union, those who once extolled Stalin to the skies have now in
one swoop consigned him to purgatory. Here in China some people are
following their example. It is the opinion of the Central Committee that
Stalin's mistakes amount to only 30 per cent of the whole and his achievements
to 70 per cent, and that all things considered Stalin was nonetheless a great
Marxist. We wrote 'On the Historical Experience of the Dictatorship of the
Proletariat' on the basis of this evaluation. This assessment of 30 per cent for

mistakes and 70 per cent for achievements is just about right. Stalin did a number of wrong things in connection with China. The 'Left' adventurism pursued by Wang Ming in the latter part of the Second Revolutionary Civil War period and his Right opportunism in the early days of the War of Resistance Against Japan can both be traced to Stalin. At the time of the War of Liberation, Stalin first wouldn't let us press on with the revolution, maintaining that if civil war flared up, the Chinese nation ran the risk of destroying itself. Then when fighting did erupt, he took us half seriously, half sceptically. When we won the war, Stalin suspected that ours was a victory of the Tito type, and in 1949 and 1950 the pressure on us was very great indeed. Even so, we maintain the estimate of 30 per cent for his mistakes and 70 per cent for his achievements. This is only fair.

In the social sciences and in Marxism-Leninism, we must continue to study Stalin diligently wherever he is right. What we must study is all that is universally true and we must make sure that this study is linked with Chinese reality. It would lead to a mess if every single sentence, even of Marx's, were followed. Our theory is an integration of the universal truth of Marxism-Leninism with the concrete practice of the Chinese revolution. At one time some people in the Party went in for dogmatism, and this came under our criticism. Nevertheless, dogmatism is still in evidence today. It still exists in academic circles and in economic circles too.

In the natural sciences we are rather backward, and here we should make a special effort to learn from foreign countries. And yet we must learn critically, not blindly. In technology I think at first we have to follow others in most cases, and it is better for us to do so, since at present we are lacking in technology and know little about it. However, in those cases where we already have clear knowledge, we must not follow others in every detail.

We must firmly reject and criticize all the decadent bourgeois systems, ideologies and ways of life of foreign countries. But this should in no way prevent us from learning the advanced sciences and technologies of capitalist countries and whatever is scientific in the management of their enterprises. In the industrially developed countries they run their enterprises with fewer people and greater efficiency and they know how to do business. All this should be learned well in accordance with our own principles so that our work can be improved. Nowadays, those who make English their study no longer work hard at it, and research papers are no longer translated into English, French, German or Japanese for exchange with other countries. This too is a kind of blind prejudice. Neither the indiscriminate rejection of everything foreign, whether scientific, technological or cultural, nor the indiscriminate imitation of everything foreign as mentioned above, has anything in common with the Marxist attitude, and they in no way benefit our cause.

In my opinion, China has two weaknesses, which are at the same time two strong points.

First, in the past China was a colonial and semi-colonial country, not an imperialist power, and was always bullied by others. Its industry and agriculture are not developed and its scientific and technological level is low, and except for its vast territory, rich resources, large population, long history, *The Dream of the Red Chamber* in literature, and so on, China is inferior to other countries in many respects, and so has no reason to feel conceited. However, there are people who, having been slaves too long, feel inferior in everything and don't stand up straight in the presence of foreigners. They are just like Chia Kuei in the opera *The Famen Temple* who, when asked to take a seat, refuses to do so, giving the excuse that he is used to standing in attendance. Here we need to bestir ourselves, enhance our national confidence and encourage the spirit typified by 'Scorn US imperialism', which was fostered during the movement to resist US aggression and aid Korea.

Second, our revolution came late. Although the 1911 Revolution which overthrew the Ching emperor preceded the Russian revolution, there was no Communist Party at that time and the revolution failed. The victory of the people's revolution came in 1949, more than thirty years after the October Revolution. On this account too, we are not in a position to feel conceited. The Soviet Union differs from our country in that, firstly, tsarist Russia was an imperialist power and, secondly, it had the October Revolution. As a result, many people in the Soviet Union are conceited and very arrogant.

Our two weaknesses are also strong points. As I have said elsewhere, we are first 'poor' and second 'blank'. By 'poor' I mean we do not have much industry and our agriculture is underdeveloped. By 'blank' I mean we are like a blank sheet of paper and our cultural and scientific level is not high. From the standpoint of potentiality, this is not bad. The poor want revolution whereas it is difficult for the rich to want revolution. Countries with a high scientific and technological level are overblown with arrogance. We are like a blank sheet of paper, which is good for writing on.

Being 'poor' and 'blank' is therefore all to our good. Even when one day our country becomes strong and prosperous, we must still adhere to the revolutionary stand, remain modest and prudent, learn from other countries and not allow ourselves to become swollen with conceit. We must not only learn from other countries during the period of our First Five Year Plan, but must go on doing so after the completion of scores of five year plans. We must be ready to learn even ten thousand years from now. Is there anything bad about that?

I have taken up ten topics altogether. These ten relationships are all contradictions. The world consists of contradictions. Without contradictions the world would cease to exist. Our task is to handle these contradictions correctly. As to whether or not these contradictions can in practice be resolved entirely to our satisfaction, we must be prepared for either possibility; furthermore, in the course of resolving these contradictions we are bound to come up against new ones, new problems. But as we have often said, while the road ahead is tortuous, the future is bright. We must do our best to mobilize all positive factors, both inside and outside the Party, both at home and abroad, both direct and indirect, and build China into a powerful socialist country.

Chinese Measures and Western Equivalents

Area
1 *mou*   = 0.067 hectare or 670 square metres or 0.1647 acre
1 *mou*   = 10 *fen*
14.93 *mou*   = 1 hectare
6.07 *mou*   = 1 acre

Length
1 *li*   = 0.5 kilometre
1 *chih*   = 0.33 metre or 13.123 inches

Weight
1 *chin*   = 0.501 kilogram or 1.1023 pounds
1 *catty*   = 0.6 kilogram or 1.3 pounds
100 catties   = 1 *picul*
1 *tan*   = 100 *chin*
1 *tan*   = 50 kilograms or 0.05 metric tons or 110.23 pounds

Yield
To convert *chin* per *mou* to kilograms per hectare multiply by 7.48 (or by 0.00748 to obtain metric tons per hectare).

How to Find Out About and Keep Up With Economic Developments in China

Sources published in China for foreign readers
Despatches from China's official news agency, New China News Agency, provide an official English language record of developments in China. The Agency often reproduces extensive articles from the Chinese press that contain a great deal of economic material, much of which reappears in other English language materials. Three magazines with excellent economic articles and news items are: *Peking Review* (weekly), *China Reconstructs* (monthly with beautiful pictures), *China's Foreign Trade* (monthly).

In Japan the Chinese distribute a monthly, *Jinmin Chūgoku (People's China)*, which sometimes contains more detailed and interesting articles than any that appear in the English language publications.

Monitored broadcasts
There are two major series of monitored Chinese broadcasts, the *Foreign Broadcast Information Service* (American) and the *Survey of World Broadcasts* (British). China's radio is also monitored in Taiwan and the Taiwanese periodically make these records available. Monitored broadcasts are a valuable source of information about local affairs and provide relatively uncensored insights into Chinese life and economic happenings.

The daily press
In Britain, *The Financial Times* provides the most reliable, regular flow of information about China in both news items and analyses. The best American coverage is in the *International Herald Tribune* and the *New York Times*. The Hong Kong *South China Morning Post* is very good value for those working in Hong Kong. This paper has a regular page devoted to mainland affairs, providing many pieces of small information on shipping, trade and other matters that cannot be found elsewhere, and frequently reports items that have appeared in the Chinese language Hong Kong press. The *Post* also obtains interviews with people immediately after they have left China. In Japan the coverage of China is particularly good in the *Mainichi* newspapers—both the Japanese and English language editions.

Magazines and journals
The China Quarterly publishes many articles on economic matters and from its
regular *Chronicle and Documentation* section one can follow the major
economic and political trends in China. For members, the Sino-British Trade
Council publishes a monthly *Newsletter*. In the United States, the most useful
magazine is the *US-China Business Review* published by the National Council
for US-China Trade. *The Problems of Communism* (United States
Information Service) and *Asian Survey* (University of Berkeley, California)
are also helpful.

Many sources are published in Hong Kong. *Current Scene* (monthly)
prepared by the United States Information Service is exceptionally valuable. It
includes regular surveys of trade and economic matters (mainly in the
autumn), and a chronicle of comings and goings and important events in
China. Also published in Hong Kong are the *Far East Economic Review* and
the *China Trade Report*, both of which contain excellent economic material.
(All the above are available worldwide.) The United States Consulate in Hong
Kong prepares and distributes to many libraries (see below) important series of
translated Chinese press and periodical materials such as the *Survey of the
China Mainland Press*, *Current Background*, and *Extracts from China
Mainland Magazines*.

In Japan, the Japan External Trade Organization publish the JETRO *China
Newsletter* and the more detailed *Chūgoku Keizai Kenkyū Geppō (China
Economic Research Monthly)*. There are many other magazines with China
materials, and particularly reliable are the *Ajia Kuotari* (Asian Quarterly) and
the monthly *Ajia Jihō* (Asian Review) published by the Asian Affairs Research
Council (see below).

A number of sources are based in Taiwan. For example, the bi-weekly
handout *What's happening on the Chinese Mainland* is a publication which,
when one has managed to read between the lines, is full of insights and
unusual information.

More detailed materials from the Taiwan viewpoint are published in *Issues
and Studies*, a monthly publication of the Institute of International Relations.

Libraries and organizations
In Britain, the library of the School of Oriental and African Studies,
University of London, is the best and most accessible collection of materials
on the contemporary Chinese economy (Malet Street, London WC1E 7HP).
Other organizations capable of providing economic information include the
Sino-British Trade Council (25 Queen Anne's Gate, London SW1), the offices
of the Contemporary China Institute and *The China Quarterly* (School of
Oriental and African Studies, Malet Street, London WC1E 7HP), and The
Royal Institute of International Affairs (Chatham House, 10 St James's
Square, London SW1Y 4LE).

Elsewhere in Europe there are major organizations connected with trade
matters. Also in Germany the Institut für Asienkunde in Hamburg (32
Rothenbaumchaussee, Hamburg 2) holds a major collection of current
materials and has numerous experts on its staff.

In America, collections of Chinese economic materials are available at major university centres such as those at Harvard, Columbia, Ann Arbor, Berkeley, and Stanford. The most informed and accessible organization for information on trade and economic matters is the National Council for United States-China Trade (1050 Seventeenth Street, NW, Washington, DC 20036). Also in Washington, the Library of Congress keeps a great deal of Chinese material and access is possible to the very many specialists working in United States Government Departments. The US Government Bookshop and the store in the basement of the US Department of Agriculture are places where many publications with trade and economic materials may be obtained.

In Japan, the Japan External Trade Organization (JETRO) (2 Akasaka Aoi Cho, Minato-ku, Tokyo) deals with Sino-Japanese trade and economic affairs and publishes numerous materials of interest. The Asian Affairs Research Council (Ajia Chōsa Kai) (Nihon Building, 2-6-2 Ohtemachi, Chiyoda-ku, Tokyo, Japan) can provide advice on many aspects of Chinese affairs. Important specialist organizations responsible for promoting Sino-Japanese trade are the Nihon Kokusai Bōeki Sokushin Kyōkai (Nihon Building, Ohtemachi, Chiyoda-ku, Tokyo) and the Nichū Keizai Kyōkai (Aoyama Building, Kitaaoyama Minato-ku, Tokyo).

In Hong Kong both local universities maintain centres for the study of China, and the Universities Service Centre (155 Argyle Street, Kowloon) is a point of contact for visitors and enquirers. The Union Research Institute (9 College Road, Kowloon) houses a huge collection of classified press clippings and has published a number of books including some exclusively concerned with economic topics. Consulates in Hong Kong nearly all have economic specialists with China expertise on their staffs. Outstanding are the American and Australian Consulates.

The main academic centre for China in Australia is at the Australian National University, Canberra. The main expertise in China's economy and trade is in the Department of Overseas Trade, which publishes *Overseas Trading*, a journal that occasionally carries articles on the China trade.

Notes

Reading Note

Citation of Chinese titles in the original is avoided throughout these Notes. Where the source is in the Chinese language, this is indicated by (Ch.) after the title.

1 J. K. Galbraith, *A China Passage* (London, 1973), Mrs Javits, quoted in *Encounter*, December 1976, p.76. Denis Healey, in *The Sunday Times*, January 14, 1973. Joan Robinson, *Economic Management in China* (London, 1975), p.14.

2 For example, Robert L. Heilbronner, *An Enquiry into the Human Prospect* (New York, 1975). A contrary, sociologist's view is Peter L. Berger, *Pyramids of Sacrifice: Political Ethics and Social Change* (New York, 1976).

3 There have now been three of these compilations: Joint Economic Committee, *An Economic Profile of Mainland China* (Washington, 1967), two volumes and one volume of hearings; Joint Economic Committee, *People's Republic of China: An Economic Assessment* (Washington, 1972); Joint Economic Committee, *China, A Reassessment of the Economy* (Washington, 1975). These are referred to throughout as, JEC (1967), JEC (1972), and JEC (1975).

4 Two statistical compilations of particular interest are, *Ten Great Years* (Peking, 1960); and N. R. Chen, *Chinese Economic Statistics* (Edinburgh, 1966). Both of these contain unprocessed Chinese data whose interpretation therefore frequently requires skill and background information.

5 The problem is not just the *total* output, but the estimates for the different *parts* of grain output, for sown area, and for yields. To be credible, all these figures must be consistent. The CIA data for grain and many other economic series have been published in the JEC volumes and in the CIA *Research Aid* reports (Washington, various years). The US Department of Agriculture estimates appear mainly in USDA Economic Research Service Reports—particularly the *Review and Outlook* surveys for China and other Communist Asian countries.

6 Population and manpower estimates by J. S. Aird and J. P. Emerson are included in JEC volumes and are incorporated in the publications of other American Government organizations. Major studies appear as *International Population Reports* and are published by the US Department of Commerce.

Reading Note

To supplement this chapter the reader can learn more of the historical context (pre- and post-1949) in Dwight H. Perkins (ed.), *China's Modern Economy in Historical Perspective* (Stanford, 1975); and Christopher Howe and Kenneth R. Walker, 'Mao the Economist' in Dick Wilson (ed.), *Mao Tse-tung in the Scales of History* (Cambridge, 1977).

The reader with some background knowledge of China who seeks a broad economic perspective should consult Simon Kuznets, *Modern Economic Growth* (New Haven, 1967).

All readers should obtain some sense of the physical reality of China by reading a geography of China. One of the very best is still George Babcock Cressey, *China's Geographic Foundations: a survey of the land and its people* (New York, 1934). A later version is *Land of the 500 million: a geography of China* (New York, 1955).

Concise English language publications from China that are of use for general background are Cheng Shih, *A Glance at China's Economy* (Peking, 1974); *China—A Geographical Sketch* (Peking, 1974); and *New China's First Quarter-Century* (Peking, 1975).

1 According to Liu and Yeh, the share of gross domestic expenditure allocated to gross domestic investment in 1933 was 5 per cent. It probably declined between 1933 and 1949 due to disruption in agriculture; see T. C. Liu and K. C. Yeh, *The Economy of the Chinese Mainland: 1933-59* (Princeton, 1965), pp.77-78, and Y. L. Wu, *An Economic Survey of Communist China* (New York, 1956), pp.30-32.

2 Dwight H. Perkins, *Agricultural Development in China, 1368-1968* (Chicago, 1969.

3 John K. Chang, *Industrial Development in Pre-Communist China: A quantitative analysis* (Chicago, 1969).

4 *First Five Year Plan for Development of the National Economy of the People's Republic of China in 1953-1957* (Peking, 1956).

5 Wei I, 'On the problem of agricultural investment in China's First Five Year Plan', *People's Daily* (Ch.), August 19, 1955.

6 A full account of Mao's economic thinking and policies is in the article by Howe and Walker, cited in the Reading Note at the beginning of this chapter.

7 Kenneth R. Walker, 'Collectivization in retrospect: the "Socialist High Tide" of autumn 1955-spring 1956', *The China Quarterly*, No. 26 (1966), pp. 1-43.

8 Useful accounts of some of these developments are: Alexander Eckstein, 'Economic development strategies in China', and by the same author, *China's Economic Development* (Ann Arbor, 1975), pp. 259-75; Carl Riskin, 'Small industry and the Chinese model of development', *The China Quarterly*, No. 46 (1971), pp. 245-73; Nicholas R. Lardy, 'Centralization and decentralization in China's fiscal management', *The China Quarterly*, No. 61 (1975), pp. 49-56.

9 The best historical account of the Communes in the Leap is Gargi Dutt, *Rural Communes of China* (London, 1967), chapters 1-2.

10 'Chairman Mao comes to Hsühui', *People's Daily* (Ch.), August 11, 1958.

11 Claims and plans in various articles, for example, *Red Flag* (Ch.), 1959, No. 1.

12 Quoted in *Survey of World Broadcasts*, FE/2603/13/7, January 20, 1967.

13 The Chinese text was obtained by the Nationalist Chinese State Security Bureau, and translated and made available by the East Asian Institute of the University of Columbia, New York.

14 The *Seventy Articles* became available in the West by the same route as the *Sixty Articles* cited above.

15 This quotation from Mao (made in January 1961) is taken from Joint Publications Research Service, *Miscellany of Mao Tse-tung Thought* (Springfield, Virginia, 1974), p. 239.

16 The best account of these years is Richard Baum, *Prelude to Revolution* (New York, 1975). The quotations cited were attributed to Liu Chien-hsün (Party Secretary in Honan Province) and Li Ching-ch'üan (Party Secretary in Szechuan Province).

17 The most outspoken attack on trade was Fang Hai, 'Criticize the philosophy of being slaves to foreign things', *Red Flag* (Ch.), 1976, No. 4, pp. 21-26.

18 'Study theory well and implement policy', *People's Daily* (Ch.), June 11, 1975.

19 *Study and Criticism* (Ch.), 1976, No. 4, particularly p. 25. This issue contains the

fullest accounts of Teng's views we have.

20   Quoted in a particularly interesting exposé of the Gang by the Mass Criticism Group of the State Capital Construction Commission, 'Exposing Wang Hung-wen's scheme to throw China into disorder', *Peking Review,* 1977, No. 6, p. 10.

21   Many materials are now available on this, for example, 'How the Gang of Four undermined socialist economic construction', *New China News Agency,* January 6, 1977.

22   *Peking Review,* 1977, No. 21, pp. 13-14.

23   *Peking Review,* 1975, No. 38, p. 3.

24   *Peking Review,* 1977, No. 2, p. 14.

25   This comment is quoted in *Peking Review,* 1977, No. 1, p. 40.

26   'Family planning', *Peking Review,* 1977, No. 13, p. 29.

27   '300,000 ton Ethylene project', *Peking Review,* 1977, No. 5, p. 31.

1.   POPULATION AND HUMAN RESOURCES

Reading Note

The best writings on China's population and population policies are those of J.S. Aird. In JEC (1967) Aird provides a great deal of information about recent Chinese population materials together with his own interpretation and estimates. In JEC (1972) Aird analyses the history of population policy. In JEC (1975) Leo Orleans offers an alternative population estimate to that of Aird. Aird's latest estimates (without supporting argument) are in CIA, *Handbook of Economic Indicators* (1976). The history of China's population is best described in Ping-ti Ho, *Studies on the Population of China, 1368-1953* (Cambridge, Mass., 1959).

Employment problems, policies and estimates are discussed in Christopher Howe, *Employment and Economic Growth in Urban China, 1949-1957* (Cambridge, 1971), and in J.P. Emerson's writings, most conveniently in JEC (1967). The best account of the skilled manpower situation is J.P. Emerson, *Administrative and Technical Manpower in the People's Republic of China,* US Department of Commerce (Washington, 1973).

Chinese statements about population and employment are very scarce and lack detail when they appear. A typical statement of the present official view was reported in *New China News Agency,* April 30, 1976, and similar comments may be found in Cheng Shih, *A Glance at China's Economy,* Ch. 6.

There is no good account of China's educational system that analyses the reforms of the Cultural Revolution and the retreat from those reforms that has continued jerkily since 1971. There is a chapter on education in *New China's First Quarter-Century*, and many interesting articles in official English language publications from China. Since educational establishments have been well visited in recent years, many reports have been made of the situation in schools and universities, some of which have been published, for example in *The China Quarterly*.

1   *The Selected Works of Mao Tse-tung* (Ch.) (Peking, 1964), p. 1515. Li's statement is reported in *Foreign Broadcast Information* Service No. 230, November 30, 1971. Mao's support for population control is cited many times in the mid-1970s in Chinese books on Health Policy, for example, *Planned Birth* (Ch.) (Peking, 1975).

2   J.S. Aird, JEC (1967), and J.S. Aird, 'Population growth', in Alexander Eckstein, Walter Galenson and Ta-chung Liu, *Economic Trends in Communist China* (Edinburgh, 1968), p. 244.

3   A file of published reports of population data, and of data given to visitors, is maintained by the US Department of Commerce. The most recent account of

these is 'Provincial population figures', *Current Scene*, 1976, No. 11, pp. 16-19.

4 See note 1 above.

5 A number of Western articles have described the campaign of the 1970s and its results. In particular, Chen Pi-chao, 'Population policy; policy evolution and action programs', in Myron E. Wegman, Tsung-yi Lin and Elizabeth F. Purcell (eds), *Public Health in the People's Republic of China* (New York, 1973), pp. 236-41; Carl Djerassi, 'Fertility limitation through contraceptive steroids in the People's Republic of China', *Studies in Family Planning*, 1974, No. 1, pp. 13-30; Janet W. Salaff, 'Institutional motivation for fertility limitation in China', *Population Studies*, 1972, No. 2, pp. 233-62.

6 'At the same time as settling a fixed five year policy for grain purchase and supply tasks the Brigade fixed a five year plan for deferred marriage and births', quoted in *The People's Communes Leap Forward* (Ch.) (Shanghai, 1974), p. 224.

7 Reported by visitors to villages in South China. The old rule was that a one- or two-person household was allocated two *fen* of land (each *fen* equals 0.0165 of an acre) and that thereafter each additional household member had an entitlement of an additional *fen*. The new rule makes five *fen* the maximum holding, i.e. typically for two adults and three children—the norm of current population policy.

8 According to projections in Table 4, China will succeed in reducing the natural rate of growth to below 1½ per cent per annum—the target mentioned by Chou En-lai to President Echeverria of Mexico in 1973 and reported in *The Times*, April 24, 1973.

9 The most comprehensive published collection of urban population data is Morris B. Ullman, *Cities of Mainland China: 1953 and 1958*, US Department of Commerce (Washington, 1961). An example of a UN series of population data that show, without comment, urban population growth reflecting expansion of urban boundaries is UN *Trends and Prospects in the Population of Urban Agglomerations, 1950-2000, as assessed in 1973-1975* (New York, 1975), p. 42.

10 Anna Louise Strong, 'Interview with Pol-po on economic adjustment', *Impartial Daily* (Ch. pub. in Hong Kong), January 15, 1964, trans. in *Survey of the China Mainland Press*, No. 3152, 1964. 'Twelve Million School Graduates Settle in the Countryside', *Peking Review*, 1976, No. 2, p. 11.

11 *The Selected Works of Mao Tse-tung*, p. 1079.

12 *Miscellany of Mao Tse-tung Thought*, p. 276.

13 Shih T'ien, 'Research into the problem of the scale of urban development', *Planned Economy* (Ch.), 1958, No. 1, pp. 25-27.

14 Official policy towards fertility control distinguishes between dense and lightly populated areas; it encourages birth *limitation* in the densely settled and birth *increases* in the scarcely populated. *Peking Review*, 1976, No. 13, pp. 29-30.

15 Discussed in Howe and Emerson's work referred to in the Reading Note.

16 *New China News Agency*, July 25, 1957.

17 *Workers Daily* (Ch.), January 4, 1958.

18 For example Shanghai, a large city, claims 53 per cent of the population employed. Shashin, a small city, claims 48 per cent. *New China News Agency*, April 30, 1976, and May 3, 1972 respectively.

19 *Survey of World Broadcasts*, January 11, 1974, FE/4497/B11/25, and the same October 28, 1972, FE/4130/B11/9.

20 This discussion and these illustrations are taken from J.P. Emerson's writings cited in the Reading Note. Informants reported that among the lowest strata of non-agricultural labour, the *min kung* (people's worker), at least one third were illiterate in the late 1960s. This indicates an urban illiteracy rate of about 10 per cent—an improvement on the 1950s.

21   'He [Teng] alleged that "the quality of education is low" and "that scientific research has lagged behind" and these "have hampered the four modernizations" . . . and that "not reading books" and "not having culture" are "the greatest danger" and "the greatest crisis" today.' *Peking Review*, 1976, No. 17, p. 17.

22   Chou En-lai, quoted in J.P. Emerson, *Administrative and Technical Manpower in the People's Republic of China*, p. 73.

23   *Survey of World Broadcasts*, November 15, 1972, FE/4145/B11/13.

2.   PLANNING AND ORGANIZATION

Reading Note

There are very few comprehensive accounts of the planning system in either English or Chinese. In JEC (1975) there are useful articles by: Nicholas R. Lardy (the fiscal system); Thomas G. Rawski (the industrial system); and Frederick W. Crook (the Commune system). Rawski and Lardy have also recently published short summaries: 'Chinese economic planning', *Current Scene*, 1976, No. 4 pp. 1-15 and, 'Economic Planning and Income Distribution in China', *Current Scene*, 1976, No. 11 pp. 1-12. English language materials from China and Chinese language materials tend to deal with relatively specific subjects, i.e. the budgeting system, the operation of individual Communes and factories etc. The best of these are referred to as appropriate in the notes.

Note on research methods   Three difficult problems for any writer attempting to reduce our current information on Chinese planning into a concise narrative are: (a) identifying the *differences* between the system described in Chinese materials and the system as it works in practice. For the 1950s abundant formal materials (e.g. legal handbooks), and equally abundant informal materials (e.g. locally published newspapers), make it possible to sort this out. For the 1970s we are short of everything. This leads to problem (b) identifying *similarities* between the 1950s and 1970s. Fortunately there is evidence that these are numerous. This evidence comes in many forms, one of the most interesting of which is the testimony of international lawyers specializing in Chinese commercial cases. These lawyers deal with areas of Chinese activity that cannot be concealed, and they confirm that much of the legal material published in the 1950s is still valid—indeed has been more applicable between 1972 and 1977 than between 1966 and 1972. Finally, (c) is the problem of interpreting visitors' reports. There are dozens of these and since, together with local broadcasts, they are a major source of 'informal' information, they are important. Unfortunately they frequently contradict both each other and the evidence from documents. Also, recipients tend to place too much faith in the authenticity and importance of what they are told. Let me illustrate. Mrs Joan Robinson, the well known Cambridge (England) economist, has visited China many times and has written several important pamphlets and articles. In 1972 Mrs Robinson visited China and produced a pamphlet, *Economic Management in China*. On her first page, Mrs Robinson stated that 'as far as the state sector is concerned, that is to say the whole of regular industry and commerce, a clean sweep has been made of all individual payment by results.' This was completely untrue—as the author admitted, and philosophized about, in a later edition. Going to another extreme, valuable briefings on planning were given to members of a delegation to China of the National Committee on US-China Relations that visited China in December 1972/January 1973. This party contained distinguished scholars, some of whom had lived in China and spent a lifetime studying the Chinese scene. Nonetheless, some of the information given to them on planning, which they believed to have been completely unknown before their visit, only confirmed that rules in the late 1950s still applied at the time of their visit.

Faced with this bewildering variety of evidence, all one can do is to compare and evaluate it minutely, point by point, and indicate the relative probability that one's conclusions are correct whenever this is possible.

1   The only detailed study of China's private agricultural sector is Kenneth R. Walker, *Planning in Chinese Agriculture: Socialization and the Private Sector 1956-1962* (London, 1965). There is no reason to think that private agriculture has declined significantly since the period of this study.

2   Data on organization and personnel has been collected from many sources. Particularly valuable is Malcolm Lamb, *Directory of Central Officials in the People's Republic of China, 1968-1975* (Canberra, 1976), and issues of *Current Scene*. See also sources for Appendix B.

3   Reports cited in *China News Analysis*, 1975, No. 1005.

4   An important 'note' by Mao approving this charter was published for the first time in *People's Daily* (Ch.), March 22, 1977. The purpose of this exercise seems to have been to emphasize the continuity between Mao and Hua in attitudes to industrial organization—a continuity that in some ways is more apparent than real.

5   This section is based on Chinese industrial accountancy handbooks for the 1950s, 1960s, and 1970s, combined with information from visitors and informants. Particularly important recent Chinese sources are *Industrial Accounting* (Ch.) (Shanghai, 1975) and *Methods for Calculating the Costs of Industrial Products* (Ch.) (Peking, 1975).

6   Information obtained by the author in China in 1974.

7   This section is based on the sources cited in the Reading Note above, on trip reports, and on a large number of Chinese books and pamphlets published in the 1970s. Particularly interesting among these are Su Hsiung, *Our Country's Socialist Road* (Ch.) (Peking, 1976); *The People's Communes are Good* (Ch.) (Peking, 1973); *The People's Communes Leap Forward* (Ch.) (Shanghai, 1974). Particularly useful official English language materials on Communes include 'In the Communes—ownership on three levels', *China Reconstructs*, 1974, No. 1, pp. 35-38, and Chu Li and Tien Chieh-yun, *Inside a People's Commune* (Peking, 1974). The role of the Team and other aspects of Commune organization are specified in the Constitution, *Peking Review*, 1975, No. 4. Accounting handbooks published in the 1970s confirm that the basic regulations for Communes are the 'Sixty Articles' circulated in successive drafts between 1960 and 1962.

8   During the 1970s, rural accountancy handbooks have appeared from many Provinces. The author has consulted examples published in Tientsin, Peking, Kwangtung, Liaoning, and Kansu. An English language account of Commune income distribution is 'How Chiaoli Production Team distributes its income', *Some Basic Facts about China* (Peking, 1974).

9   The piece work system described here is one of the two major rural payments systems. The other system is known as the Tachai system. Introduced in the mid-1960s, the Tachai system evaluates the peasants in advance, i.e. a peasant will be rated an '8 point worker' and will earn 8 points per day irrespective of actual work done. This system has the advantage of not requiring daily checking of work done and, in practice, produces a more equal distribution of income. Its drawbacks are that 'evaluation meetings' (monthly to six monthly in frequency) tend to be strained and unpleasant, and that once evaluated, peasants do not work as hard as under continuous piece work. Both systems, and variants, have been reported in operation in the 1970s. It is also interesting to note that accounting handbooks emphasize that construction organized at the Team level is to be very restricted.

For example, one source makes the following extreme ruling: 'Capital construction for agricultural production should be carried out only when it is necessary and feasible and when it can have beneficial effects *in the current year* without adversely altering the members' livelihood for that year.' *Accounting in the Production Team of the Rural People's Commune* (Ch.) (Kwangtung, 1974), translated in *Chinese Economic Studies*, Fall-Winter, 1976-77, p. 110.

10 *Peking Review*, 1974, No. 39, p. 12.

11 This speech is summarized in *Peking Review*, 1975, No. 4, pp. 21-25.

12 For example by Chen Yung-kuei in his keynote speech on agricultural policy in 1977 reported in *Peking Review*, 1977, No. 2, p. 14. An account of the *Twelve Year Programme* by T'an Chen-lin is available in *Second Session of the Eighth National Congress of the Communist Party of China* (Peking, 1958) pp. 80-94.

13 *First Five Year Plan for Development of the National Economy of the People's Republic of China in 1953-1957* (Peking, 1955); *Proposals for the Second Five Year Plan* (Peking, 1956), reprinted in *Communist China 1955-1959; Policy Documents with Analysis*, with a Foreword by Robert R. Bowie and John K. Fairbank (Cambridge, Mass., 1962), pp. 204-16.

14 Translated in Jerome Ch'en (ed.), *Mao Papers: Anthology and Bibliography* (London, 1970), pp. 57-76.

15 An official report contained the estimate that there were 40,000 rural markets accounting for 25 per cent of all rural trade. *Red Flag* (Ch.), 1961, No. 18, p. 16. See also note below.

16 Speech to the Central Committee in 1959 quoted in Union Research Institute, *The Case of Peng Te-huai, 1959-1968* (Hong Kong, 1968), p. 25.

17 This section is based on Lardy (see Reading Note) and many Chinese materials. The Chinese frequently write about fiscal matters; particularly informative are: Wei Min, 'Chinese Tax Policy', *Peking Review*, 1975, No. 37, pp. 23-25, and a recent pamphlet, *Why China has no Inflation* (Peking, 1976).

18 The share of the value of agricultural output (i.e. all types of output) taken in tax fell from 12 per cent to 5 per cent between 1952 and 1975. See Wei Min cited above. The policy of drawing out revenue through taking taxes and profits on manufactured consumer goods involves very high profits in light industry. So much so that light industry profits in the one year of 1970 were reported to have been adequate to pay for *all* of the investment in this sector undertaken between 1950 and 1970. Chou Ching, 'Light industry develops apace', *Peking Review*, 1972, No. 41, p. 11.

19 Nicholas R. Lardy, 'Centralization and decentralization in China's fiscal management', *The China Quarterly*, No. 61, 1975, pp. 25-60.

20 *Why China has no Inflation*, p. 1.

21 The only full account of Chinese banking in English is Katharine Huang-hsiao, *Money and Monetary Policy in Communist China* (New York, 1971). Also valuable is Pierre Henri Cassou, 'The Chinese monetary system', *The China Quarterly*, No. 59 (1974), pp. 559-66. Scholarly research on banking is based on specialized journals, handbooks of financial regulations, and the handbook for accounting work in branches of the People's Bank.

22 This account is based on a fascinating account of the topic, Michel Oksenberg, 'Methods of communication within the Chinese bureaucracy', *The China Quarterly*, No. 57 (1974), pp. 1-39.

23 Wang Kuang-mei's investigations are described in detail in Richard Baum, *Prelude to Revolution*, Chapter 4.

24 *Survey of World Broadcasts*, March 19, 1974, FE/4554/B11/9.

25 *Survey of World Broadcasts*, January 3, 1974, FE/4490/B11/11.

26 Richard Baum, *Prelude to Revolution*, pp. 109-10.

27 Mao's attitude to coercion was that in excess it was counterproductive. Nonetheless, Mao favoured killing on occasion. For example, in his struggles in the Great Leap, Mao compared himself to one of China's tyrannical Emperors (Ch'in Shih-huang) with the comment, 'What did he amount to? He only buried 460 scholars, while we buried 46,000.' Later, in 1964, in his fight against 'capitalism and revisionism' Mao said, 'it is impossible for us not to kill, but we must not kill too many. Kill a few to shock them. Why should we be afraid of shocking them?' *Miscellany of Mao Tse-tung Thought*, Vol. 1, p. 98 and Vol. II, p. 426.

28 *Miscellany of Mao Tse-tung Thought*, Vol. II, p. 285.

29 Chu Li and Tien Chieh-yun, *Inside a People's Commune*, Ch. VI; 'A vast rural market', *Peking Review*, 1976, N.32-33, pp. 24-29.

30 *The Journal of Chungshan University* (Ch.) (Canton) 1975, No. 4, p. 23.

31 A medical informant has reported that when summoned for assignment to another city, his local ration card was taken away and he was given a temporary card to cover food requirements on the journey. A new ration card was issued on reporting for duty in his new post.

32 *Miscellany of Mao Tse-tung Thought*, Vol. II, p. 387.

33 Li Ching-ch'üan of Szechuan concealed statistics, and T'ao Chu of Kwangtung wanted a local Foreign Trade Office. (Later, localization of trade did occur, see Chapter 5.)

3. AGRICULTURE

Reading Note

In addition to material in JEC (1967, 1972, 1975), two exceptionally useful books are T.H. Shen, *Agricultural Resources of China* (Cornell, 1951); Chao Kang, *Agricultural Production in Communist China 1949-1965 (Madison, 1970)*. Annual data and evaluations of China's agriculture and agricultural trade now appear in US Department of Agriculture's *Foreign Agricultural Economic Report* series.

1 Quoted in a speech to the World Population Conference, *Peking Review*, 1974, No. 35, pp. 6-9.

2 Kaoliang is interplanted with wheat as described by the Chinese proverb, 'When the heads of wheat are cut off, the kaoliang will hide a cow' (i.e. it is tall enough to do so).

3 In the three Northern Provinces of Heilungkiang, Kirin and Liaoning, there were reported to be 670 hectares of vegetables protected by plastic sheeting. Similar measures are widespread in the horticultural Communes surrounding Peking and other large cities in North China. Further south in Kiangsu and Hunan Provinces, for example, yields over more than 100 tons per hectare are frequently reported in the press and to visitors. See 'New achievements in scientific vegetable farming', *Peking Review*, 1975, No. 21, p. 30; *New China News Agency* report on Peking, March 21, 1976; *An Outline of Shanghai's Geography* (Ch.), (Shanghai, 1974), p. 107.

4 *New York Times*, August 3, 1976.

5 Kiangsu's achievements described in *New China News Agency*, January 2 and 17, 1974; plan fulfilment reported in *Foreign Broadcast Information Service*, June 30, 1976.

6 Illustrative discussion and data in note 3. It must be remembered that yields of 70-120 tons per hectare quoted in climatically favourable urban suburbs will be far above those obtained elsewhere. In the late 1950s official Chinese data quoted average yields in the range of 35-40 tons per hectare. Thus even 50 tons per hectare represents very considerable growth. Data on 1950s yields is quoted in K.R.

Walker, *Planning in Chinese Agriculture,* p. 30.

7   *Miscellany of Mao Tse-tung Thought,* Vol. I, p. 355.

8   Feeding the cities was observed to be a special problem in the 1930s. This is discussed in T.H. Shen, *Agricultural Resources of China.*

9   This section is based on Simon Kuznets, *Population, Capital, and Economic Growth* (London, 1974) and numerous publications of the Food and Agricultural Organization and of the US Department of Agriculture. Particularly valuable studies are *The World Food Situation and Prospects to 1985* (Washington, 1974); and the papers and proceedings of the United Nations World Food Conference, 1974.

10 This is supported by estimates made in trade sources and those available in published form, for example, Kang Chao, 'The production and application of chemical fertilizers in China', *The China Quarterly,* No. 64 (1975), pp. 712-729; CIA, *People's Republic of China: Chemical Fertilizer Supplies 1949-1974* (Washington, 1975).

11 These data are from a study by Kang Chao, *Capital Formation in Mainland China 1952-1965* (Berkeley, 1974), Ch.7.

12 These data are taken from R.M. Field, *Real Capital Formation in the People's Republic of China: 1952-1973* (private circulation, 1976).

13 *New China News Agency,* November 14, 1975.

14 Discussed in Kang Chao, *Agricultural Production in Communist China 1949-1965.*

15 The policy of special assistance was explained to me by a senior official of the Ministry of Agriculture and Forestry in 1974. The policy of helping the backward Teams is widely reported in the press and was confirmed in details by a cadre responsible for agricultural planning in Kwangtung Province.

16 The study that puts this point in a detailed and incisive way is Shigeru Ishikawa, *Economic Development in Asian Perspective* (Tokyo, 1967). Recent research in the Philippines confirms water control as the major contributor to increasing rice yields.

17 Water problems are discussed by Chao in the work cited in the Reading Note. A Chinese account of some of the problems is *China Tames Her Rivers* (Peking, 1972).

18 'Reconstructing the Big Sanmen Gorge dam', *Peking Review,* 1975, No. 5, pp. 13-14.

19 US Department of Agriculture, *The Agricultural Situation in the People's Republic of China and other Communist Asian Countries 1975/1976,* pp. 26-27; Chou Chin, 'Mechanization: Fundamental way out for Agriculture', *Peking Review,* 1977, No. 9, p. 15.

20 *Miscellany of Mao Tse-tung Thought,* Vol. I, p. 171.

21 *New China News Agency,* October 10, 1975.

22 In addition to the very large factory in Loyang, tractor factories have been reported in Anshan, Tientsin, Hangchow, Canton, Wuhan, Shenyang, Shihchiachuang and Nanning.

23 The most famous pre-war account of Asian agriculture in which fertilization is extensively discussed is F.H. King, *Farmers of Forty Centuries* (London, 1926).

24 Some of these developments are described in Alexander Wrightman, 'Sino-Japanese cooperation agreements', *US-China Business Review,* March-April, 1974, pp. 3-6.

4. INDUSTRY

Reading Note

There are no general studies of China's industrial growth in English although there are a number of very valuable analyses of individual sectors which are referred to in the notes relating to each industry below. Analyses of industrial *output* are available in all the JEC series. The classic study of industry in Chinese is *China's Iron and Steel, Electric Power, Coal, Machine Building, Textile, and Paper Industries* (Ch.) (Peking, 1958).

1   *People's Daily*, December 16, 1953.
2   Based on the sources cited in Chapter 3, notes 11-12; and on the document of the First Five Year Plan cited in Chapter 2, note 13.
3   T.C. Liu and K.C. Yeh, JEC (1967), p. 65; Nicholas R. Lardy, *Current Scene*, 1976, No. 11, p. 3.
4   This section is based mainly on trade data cited in Chapter 5 and Peter D. Weintraub, 'China's minerals and metals', *US-China Business Review*, November-December, 1974, pp. 39-53; K.P. Wang, JEC (1967) and *The People's Republic of China: A New Industrial Power with a Strong Mineral Base* (Washington, 1975); CIA, *China's Minerals and Metals Position in the World Market* (Washington, 1976).
5   John Ashton, 'The development of electric energy resources in Communist China', JEC (1967), pp. 297-315; Yuan-li Wu, *Economic Development and the Use of Energy Resources in Communist China* (New York, 1963); V. Smil, 'Energy in China', *The China Quarterly*, No. 65 (1976), pp. 54-81. International data have mainly been obtained from publications and papers prepared by OECD and from International Energy Agency, *World Energy Consumption and Supply* (Paris, 1976).
6   Ho Pai-sha, 'Stir up local activism, greatly develop local coal mines', *Planned Economy* (Ch.), 1958, No. 2, pp. 12-17; Ch'in Kuei-cheng, 'In building new coal mines attention must be paid to the regional balance of production', *Planned Economy* (Ch.), 1958, No. 6, pp. 10-11.
7   Ch'in Kuei-cheng, cited above.
8   During 1977, attacks on the Gang of Four described one of their crimes as encouraging premature switching to oil and thereby causing an oil shortage.
9   *Peking Review*, 1975, No. 46, p. 3.
10 This section is based on references cited for energy, and on two reports, *China's Petroleum Industry*, special report No. 10, The National Council for US-China Trade (Washington, 1976); *Notes on China's Oil Industry*, prepared for the Sino-British Trade Council (London, 1975). These reports cite many supplementary sources. I have also used a report, *The Situation with Regard to China's Oil Output* (in Japanese) (Tokyo, 1976), prepared by the Research Department of the Japan Petroleum Development Corporation.
11 'Petroleum and coal mining achievements', *Peking Review*, 1977, No. 3, p. 7.
12 R.M. Field, JEC (1972), p. 75, and JEC (1975), p. 166 and the article by John Ashton cited above.
13 The most accessible sources for this section are Yuan-li Wu, *The Steel Industry in Communist China* (New York, 1965); M. Gardener Clark, *The Development of China's Steel Industry and Soviet Technical Aid* (Ithaca, 1973); Alfred H. Usack, Jr, and James D. Egan, 'China's iron and steel industry', JEC (1975), pp. 264-88; William W. Clarke, 'China's steel: the key link', *US-China Business Review*, July-August, 1975, pp. 27-40. Occasionally trade journals such as *American Metal Market* and *Metal Bulletin* carry interesting material on China.

14 The only comprehensive book on this industry is Chu-yuan Cheng, *The Machine Building Industry in Communist China* (New York, 1971). R.M. Field has also been responsible for very important work on this topic including CIA, *Production of Machinery and Equipment in the People's Republic of China* (Washington, 1975). On the vehicle industry the Sino-British Trade Council produced a useful paper, *A Survey of the Chinese Motor Vehicle Industry* (London, 1974). An unusual insight into the industry is found in David Scott, 'China opens doors for rare view of auto production', *Automotive Engineering,* August, 1974, pp. 30-33. Information on the electronics industry (including control applications) is in Bohdan O. Szuprowicz, 'Electronics in China', *US-China Business Review*, May-June, 1976, pp. 21-42.

15 This is discussed in Chu-yuan Cheng and further data are in CIA, *People's Republic of China: Estimated Yuan Value of Foreign Trade in Machinery and Equipment 1951-1973* (Washington, 1976).

16 *Current Scene*, 1976, No. 10, p. 20.

17 This is based on data in Philip W. Vetterling and James J. Wagg, 'The transportation sector, 1950-1971', JEC (1972), pp. 169-77; and Hans Heymann Jr, *China's Approach to Technology Acquisition: Part I—The Aircraft Industry* (The Rand Corporation), Santa Monica, 1975.

18 This section is based on the materials cited for Table 46 together with materials from trade sources.

19 Exceptionally useful supplementary material on this topic is included in, Sy Yuan, 'China's Chemicals', *US-China Business Review*, November-December, 1975, pp. 37-53.

20 Data on the number of rural and small-scale enterprises are scattered and difficult to interpret. In 1960 it was reported that after the consolidation and reorganization that followed the Great Leap there were 60,000 units controlled by Counties, and 200,000 controlled by Communes. In 1975 it was reported that 90 per cent of Communes and 60 per cent of Brigades had some industrial units, totalling 800,000 units in all. This figure implies that, if we add say 100,000 units controlled at County level (i.e. 45 units per County compared to 27 per County in 1960), the total number of units must be about 900,000.

   Data on the number of enterprises in *Economic Research* (Ch.), 1960, No. 6, p. 47; *Peking Review*, 1977, No. 2, p. 15.

21 An exceptionally interesting account of small-scale industry to be published in 1977 is the report of an American delegation that went to China under the leadership of Professor Dwight Perkins. The historical development of small-scale industry is analysed by Carl Riskin in 'Small industry and the Chinese model of development', *The China Quarterly*, No. 46 (1971), pp. 245-73.

22 Data on manpower, *Red Flag* (Ch.), 1961, No. 8, p. 25; and a figure reported to a visitor; see Sigurdson, cited in Table 47.

23 Mao's early point of view is emphasized in 'Develop local industry, more, faster, better, and more economically', *Red Flag* (Ch.), 1970, No. 6, pp. 82-88.

5. FOREIGN TRADE

Reading Note

In addition to material in JEC (1967, 1972, 1975), there are two good books on China's foreign trade: Alexander Eckstein, *Communist China's Economic Growth and Foreign Trade* (New York, 1966); Feng-hwa Mah, *The Foreign Trade of Mainland China* (Edinburgh, 1972). An outstandlingly useful periodical is *US-China Business Review,* published by the National Council for US-China Trade. I have also used both the

Japan External Trade Organization, *JETRO China Newsletter,* and publications of the Sino-British Trade Council. A great deal of information on China's trade appears in the press and I have drawn heavily on *The Financial Times* (London); the *New York Times* and the *International Herald Tribune; The South China Morning Post* (Hong Kong); *The Mainichi Daily News,* and *The Japan Times* (Tokyo). Among periodicals, *The Far Eastern Economic Review* and the *China Trade Report* (Hong Kong) carry a great deal of information unavailable elsewhere. The main source for China's view is *China's Foreign Trade,* which is published in many languages.

A great deal of information can also be obtained from participants in China's trade, some of whom have exceptionally interesting observations to make off the record.

1   This subject is excellently dealt with in Alexander Eckstein, *Communist China's Economic Growth and Foreign Trade*, Chapter 5. Supplementary material is available in the article by Robert L. Price, 'International trade of Communist China, 1950-1965', JEC (1967), pp. 579-608.
2   Cited in, Feng-hwa Mah, *The Foreign Trade of Mainland China,* p. 2.
3   Li Po-fang, 'Actively strengthen the organisation of export supplies', *Planned Economy* (Ch.), 1958, No. 2, pp. 28-31.
4   Cited by Feng-hwa Mah, p. 2.
5   For example, *English, Chinese, Russian Language compendium of Common Terms used in Trade and Foreign exchange* (Ch.) (Peking, 1963).
6   JETRO, *China Newsletter*, 1976, No. 10, p. 9.
7   There are no official data on China's overall balance of payments. Various conjectures have been made of the size of items such as China's earnings from businesses in Hong Kong and remittances from overseas Chinese. Guesses have also been made of the extent of China's gold and foreign exchange reserves. According to some, the latter peaked at $1.02 billion in 1973 (of which the gold component valued at $35 per ounce was $610 million). Data on reserves are quoted in JETRO, *China Newsletter*, 1976, No. 12, p. 10.
       An estimate of China's balance of payments for 1950-65 is in Appendix A, JEC (1967), pp. 622-59.
8   Fang Hai, 'Criticise the philosophy of being slaves to foreign things', *Red Flag* (Ch.), 1976, No. 4, pp. 21-26; Kao Lu and Chang Ko, 'Comments on Teng Hsiao-p'ing's economic ideas of the comprador bourgeoisie', *Peking Review,* 1976, No. 35, p. 9.
9   *Enlightenment Daily* (Ch.), April 21, 1976. In English, Li Hsin, 'Self reliance is a question of the line', *Peking Review*, 1975, No. 32, pp. 14-15. Li wrote, 'We can advance unswervingly along the road of self-reliance only by breaking down blind faith, emancipating the mind, and displaying enormous drive.'
10 For example, 'Advance on own strength; use foreign things for China', *Enlightenment Daily* (Ch.), November 22, 1976.
11 Wang Yao-t'ing, 'China's foreign trade,' *Peking Review*, 1974, No. 41, pp. 18-20.
12 Useful accounts of the system are in Eugene A. Theroux, 'Legal and practical problems in the China trade', JEC (1975), pp. 535-99; Feng-hwa Mah, *The Foreign Trade of Mainland China,* Ch. 1; Gene T. Hsiao, 'The organisation of China's foreign trade,' *US-China Business Review*, May-June, 1974, p. 9. The system is in constant flux and current trends can be followed only by reading periodical literature and talking to traders.
13 The Bank has attracted considerable foreign comment; some of this is speculative, but some is based on analysis of the Bank's annual balance sheet. Dick Wilson, 'Another good year for the Bank of China', *US-China Business Review*, May-June, 1976, pp. 8-9; Barry Kramer, 'People's Banker', *The Asian Wall Street Journal*, December 2, 1976.

14   Source cited in note 3.
15   A selection of examples on local trade reform is quoted in Leo Goodstadt, 'The shape of trade to come', *China Trade Report,* February, 1976, pp. 8-9. Issues of *US-China Business Review* also contain a great deal on this, notably that of July-August 1974.
16   The Fair is fully reported in *Current Scene* and the international financial press. See also Daniel Tretiak, 'The Canton Fair: an academic perspective', *The China Quarterly*, No. 56 (1973) pp. 740-48; 'Canton with a difference', *China Trade Report*, October, 1976.
17   Some useful information on this is included in Alistair Wrightman, 'How Japan finances trade with China', *US-China Business Review*, March-April, 1975. pp. 30-34.
18   James B. Stepanek, 'How are China's exchange rates set?', *US-China Business Review*, January-February, 1976, pp. 11-15.
19   An article that analyses the interplay between trade and agriculture very succinctly is Dwight H. Perkins, 'Forecasting China's trade over the long term', *Current Scene*, 1975, No. 9, pp. 10-19.
20   Provisional estimates by R.M. Field, *Real Capital Formation in the People's Republic of China: 1952-1973.*
21   Sy Yuan, 'China's chemicals', *US-China Business Review*, November-December, 1975, pp. 37-53.
22   Hans Heymann Jr, 'Acquisition and diffusion of technology in China', JEC (1975), pp. 678-779. This is one of several important articles by Dr Heymann. Appendixes list China's major plant imports. More recent plant imports are listed in CIA, *People's Republic of China: International Trade Handbook* (1976), pp. 21-23.
23   A revealing account of Sino-Japanese technical exchange is Satoshi Imai, 'Technology exchange and exhibitions in China', JETRO, *China Newsletter*, 1976, No. 11, pp. 1-10.
24   The Chinese report the Japanese economy as being 'in chaos', 'at a standstill' and argue that it is suffering from the effects of high speed growth and 'overproduction'. *New China News Agency*, February 24, April 13, 1974.
25   Detailed data on Sino-American trade are made available by the National Council for US-China Trade, both in their *Review* and in a separate publication, *Sino-US Trade Statistics.*
26   Quoted in Feng-hwa Mah, *The Foreign Trade of Mainland China*, p. 3.

6.   INCOMES, PRICES, AND THE STANDARD OF LIVING

Reading Note

The best short introduction to the problem of measuring China's National Income is Dwight H. Perkins, 'Growth and changing structure of China's twentieth century economy' in Perkins (ed.), *China's Modern Economy in Historical Perspective*, pp. 115-65. Another major source for this subject is T.C. Liu and K.C. Yeh, *The Economy of the Chinese Mainland* (Princeton, 1965). Information on more concrete aspects of living standards, i.e. consumption of grain, cotton, housing, etc. is scarce. Data on the wage system may be found in Christopher Howe, *Wage Patterns and Wage Policy in Modern China 1919-1972* (Cambridge, 1973). Chinese books and articles in English contain many illustrative facts about living standards, but these rarely give an overall picture of the situation.

1   Western measures of Gross National/Domestic Product usually include a wider range of economic activities than socialist ones. Measures of China's product are

in practice based heavily on estimates of the output of industry, agriculture, and on construction activities. Little research has been done on services. Perkins and Field in their estimates of Gross Product divide services into two groups, (a) transport, trade and finance, which are estimated to grow at the same rate as *physical output*, and (b) government administration, personal and other services, which are estimated to grow at the same rate as *population*. See sources cited in Reading Note.

2 Bruce Reynolds, *Observations on the Chinese Economy* (mimeo) (New Haven, 1973).

3 These rates may be too high. One reason for this is that I think the assumptions made about services are rather optimistic, another is that the index of industrial production—which accounts for a great deal of the growth—may also have been overestimated.

4 The Chinese distinguish three states of grain: (1) *unhusked*, ('raw' or 'natural'), (2) *husked* ('commercial grain'), (3) *fine*, i.e. processed grain. At each stage the weight of grain is reduced. For example, husking involves a cost of about one-fifth of the original weight. This must be borne in mind when measuring consumption per head. Note also that 'fine' grain may refer to the type of grain, i.e. wheat and rice as distinct from 'coarse' grains such as maize, kaoliang, etc. K.R. Walker, *Provincial Grain Output in China 1952-1957: a Statistical Compilation*, p. 3.

5 The rural 'basic' grain ration is reported to be 11.5 kg of unhusked rice per month. (Urban rations are usually, but not invariably, quoted in husked grain.) In interpreting rural rations in different agricultural regions it is essential to bear in mind that the lost weight from husking will vary according to the composition of grain consumed, e.g. there are no husking losses from potatoes, but substantial losses for wheat and rice. I have used a husking coefficient of 0.9 to reduce rural rations to unhusked form—reflecting the fact that peasants consume disproportionate quantities of coarse grains that have small husking losses. According to Soviet sources, Chen Yung-kuei in his secret briefings to local leaders in 1974 (see Chapter 2) reported that official policy was to raise the basic ration by a third, i.e. from 0.75 Chinese *chin* per day to 1 *chin* per day. Because different grains have different calorie values, to estimate the calorie value of output one has to know, or make estimates of, the shares of the different grains that make up the total grain supply (see Chapter 3).

6 The degree of inequality before and after interprovincial grain transfers is indicated by Professor Walker's estimate that grain *production* in Hopei Province in the late 1950s was about 235 kg per head, compared to 529 kg per head in Heilungkiang, while *availability* (after transfer of grain to other Provinces) was 252 kg and 417 kg respectively. According to the remarks of a Chinese official in 1974, transfer of grain *within* and *between* Provinces begins when the supply falls to 183 kg per head (i.e. some transfer occurs if supply in an area falls below 70 per cent of the national average).

7 An analysis of the situation in Shanghai up to 1965 is Christopher Howe, 'The supply and administration of urban housing in mainland China: the case of Shanghai', *The China Quarterly*, No. 33 (1968), pp. 73-97. Recent data on Shanghai housing is quoted in *New China News Agency*, June 12, 1972. In Foshan, according to data supplied in 1974 and published materials, the trend rate of growth of population since 1952 has been exceeding the rate of growth of new housing by about 1 per cent per annum.

8 Housing is often still privately owned in China and may be transmitted to heirs. Control of housing—public and private—is exercised by local Housing Management and Housing Construction Bureaux. These allocate housing, fix rents, and control all building work through minute control of housing materials. A private

house owner cannot get even a small pane of glass without permission. This sanction is sometimes used to make householders give their houses to the state—such properties usually then being rented back to them for life.

9 Most of this is described in my work cited in the Reading Note above. The terminology used to describe special payments changes, but evidence for the mid-1970s shows that many still exist. The official view of the evolution of these payments is contained in *Lectures on Political Economy* (Ch.) (Peking, 1976), pp. 206-7.

10 A useful published collection of these is Carl Riskin, 'Workers' incentives in Chinese industry', JEC (1975), pp. 199-224.

11 *Planned Economy* (Ch.), 1958, No. 4, p. 27.

12 Two remarkably detailed articles on rationing in Canton were published in Hong Kong in 1976 by a former resident: Ting Shan, 'A discussion of Canton ration cards', *North to South* (Ch. published in Hong Kong) Nos. 70-71 (1974), pp. 18-20.

13 We know in detail the labour laws and regulations made in the 1950s. See Christopher Howe, *Employment and Economic Growth in Urban China*. Visitors' reports of current rules show that these have remained virtually unchanged down to the mid-1970s and see also 'Labour Insurance and benefits to the workers', *China Reconstructs*, 1974, No. 5, p. 35.

14 Reported in 'Statistical materials on the improved situation of workers and staff standard of living', *Statistical Work* (Ch.), 1957, No. 14, pp. 13-14.

15 'A grass roots trade union organization', *Peking Review*, 1975, No. 39, p. 31.

16 'On the problem of the standard of living of workers and peasants', *Statistical Work* (Ch.), 1957, No. 13, pp. 4-5. A large number of articles on this topic appeared in the national and local press in 1957. Many of these are collected in the files of the Union Research Institute, Hong Kong.

17 According to official sources, the rural share of health, education, and welfare expenditure rose from about one-third to two-thirds between the pre-1966 period and the mid-1970s. *New China News Agency*, June 25, 1976. The estimate of the 10-15 per cent rise is based on work by Professor Peter Schran communicated to me by Professor Nicholas Lardy.

18 'A preliminary survey into the agricultural industrial income differential in Kiangsu Province', *Labour* (Ch.), 1957, No. 21, pp. 18-21.

19 *Shensi Daily* (Ch.), July 18, 1957.

20 'We must fight on', *Study and Criticism* (Ch.), 1975, No. 7, p. 6.

21 This is largely based on the sources cited in Christopher Howe, *Wage Patterns and Wage Policy in Modern China 1919-1972*, together with examination of the material in *Miscellany of Mao Tse-tung Thought*, Parts 1 and 2.

Index